Andrew Bisset

The History of the Struggle for parliamentary Government in England

Vol. I

Andrew Bisset

The History of the Struggle for parliamentary Government in England
Vol. I

ISBN/EAN: 9783337151546

Printed in Europe, USA, Canada, Australia, Japan

Cover: Foto ©ninafisch / pixelio.de

More available books at **www.hansebooks.com**

THE HISTORY OF THE STRUGGLE FOR PARLIAMENTARY GOVERNMENT IN ENGLAND.

BY

ANDREW BISSET.

IN TWO VOLUMES.

VOL. I.

HENRY S. KING & CO., LONDON.
1877.

PREFACE.

In saying that Plato, "seeing clearly the necessity of identifying the interests of the guardians with the interests of the guarded, bent the whole force of his penetrating mind to discover the means of effecting such identification; but being ignorant, as all the ancients were, of the divine principle of representation, found himself obliged to have recourse to extraordinary methods,"[1] James Mill makes perhaps the best defence that could be made for the "extraordinary methods," proposed by Plato in his "Republic" for producing good government and happiness for states. But suppose that Plato succeeded in making philosophers of the guardians of his Republic, where is the proof of what he lays down as a "universal truth," that their rule would have secured the happiness of those they guarded and governed? Plato himself did not at Syracuse exhibit to the world a successful example of philosopher turned ruler.

[1] James Mill's Fragment on Mackintosh, p. 289.

Xenophon was more successful as a leader in the retreat of the Ten Thousand, and his case is made the most of by Bacon. And indeed Xenophon, though essentially a man of action and not a theorist, might, inasmuch as he extracted philosophy from experience of the variable temper of armies and the difficulties and dangers he had encountered in his adventurous life, be styled a philosopher more justly than Plato who undervalued him, if philosophy implied a love of and search after truth. For Xenophon did not, like Plato, introduce his master Sokrates as the utterer of theories or opinions which the real Sokrates would have repudiated as no progeny of his. Neither did he in the "Hieron," like Plato in the "Gorgias," soar into a region of sublime paradox where abundant eloquence covers faulty dialectic; but, following his master, applied to human life the measure of a rational common sense.[1] Nevertheless, when Xenophon attempted the solution of the political problem which perplexed him as well as Plato—the attainment, namely, of what he calls "that good, not human but divine, command over willing men"[2]—having no facts that could serve his purpose, he could only, like Plato, have recourse to fiction. He composed a philosophical romance, which, whatever other merits it might possess, can hardly be said to have afforded any more help than

---

[1] See Grote's Plato, and the other Companions of Sokrates, iii. 577.
[2] Τὸ ἐθελόντων ἄρχειν.—Xen. Œcon., xxi. 10-12.

Preface. vii

Plato's philosophical romance afforded towards the solution of the problem that was solved by the discovery of the principle of representative government. But however inferior Xenophon might be to Plato as a thinker, he possessed qualities of which Plato gave no sign—practical sagacity and the ability to command and lead armies under very difficult circumstances, and to obtain willing obedience when he was elected one of the generals of the Ten Thousand; a body of Greeks from different cities, most of them unknown to him personally, but putting themselves under his command because they were in extreme peril, and had observed in him qualities that inspired confidence.

This does not advance us much towards the reception of the "universal truth," that there can be no happiness for states until either philosophers are the rulers, or the rulers philosophers. For Xenophon's romance only proposes to set forth the advantages of a good despotism. Now, a good despotism has been shown to be "an altogether false ideal, which practically becomes the most senseless and dangerous of chimeras. Evil for evil, a good despotism, in a country at all advanced in civilisation, is more noxious than a bad one; for it is far more relaxing and enervating to the thoughts, feelings, and energies of the people."[1]

[1] Considerations on Representative Government, by John Stuart Mill, p. 53. London, 1861.

Moreover, when Bacon[1] and James Mill cited Plato's opinion as given in his "Republic," respecting the government of states by philosophers, they would seem to have overlooked the change that took place in Plato's opinion on this matter, a change expressed in a very marked manner in his Dialogue entitled "Leges—De Legibus." What Plato had laid down as a "universal truth" in his "Republic," had become no truth at all when he wrote his "Laws;" for, like other men called philosophers who "unsay in one passage what they say in another,"[2] he unsays in one Dialogue what he says in another. Plato founded what he called philosophy, not, like Newton, on observed facts, but on fictions of his own invention; fictions quite as mischievous as those of the poets whom he reprobated; or as the hypotheses on which so many men build systems of various kinds.

More than a thousand years after the time when Plato wrote down his dreams about the best means

---

[1] Bacon does not, like James Mill, announce it as a "universal truth," but says, "For although he might be thought partial to his own profession, that said, 'Then should people and estates be happy, when either kings were philosophers, or philosophers kings;' yet so much is verified by experience, that under learned princes and governors there have been seen the best times" (Bacon's Works, Montague's edition, vol. ii. p. 64)—an assertion not verified but most thoroughly falsified by the experience of England under the learned James I. and his most learned Chancellor Francis Bacon.

[2] See Grote's Aristotle, vol. ii. p. 269. Mr. Grote in his "Plato" gives the following account of the change that took place in Plato's opinions as to the government of states by philosophers between the writing of his "Republic" and the writing of his "Laws:" "Considering the numerous enemies which philosophy has had at all times, we may be sure that such enemies would be furnished with abundant materials for invidious remark—by the entire failure of Plato himself at Syracuse—as well as by the disgraceful proceedings, first of

of governing mankind, Simon de Montfort, as appears to be generally admitted, first reduced to practice, if he did not first devise, that which has been designated the grand discovery of modern times—the principle of representation; and thus a warlike baron, in a rude and dark age, hit upon that which those who are held up as the greatest philosophers of antiquity missed in all their political speculations; and for want of which all the attempts at good government made by the most free and enlightened nations of antiquity had proved such utter failures. What the great discovery of Newton was to Plato's fantastic speculations on astronomy, this discovery of Simon de Montfort was to Plato's speculations on government.

This invaluable discovery, however, of representative government, which had now worked in England for some four hundred years, not, it seems, finding favour in the sight of Charles I., was in danger of being lost not only to England, but, as a consequence of such loss, to France, to America,

Dion, next of his assassin Kallippus: both of them pupils, and the former a favourite pupil, of Plato in the Academy. The prospect which accident had opened of exalting philosophy into active influence over mankind, had been closed in a way no less mournful than dishonourable. Plato must have felt this keenly enough, even apart from the taunts of opponents. We might naturally expect that his latest written compositions would be coloured by such a temper of mind: that he would contract, if not an alienation from philosophy, at least a comparative mistrust of any practical good to come from it: and that if he still continued to throw out any schemes of social construction, they would be made to rest upon other foundations, eliminating or reducing to a minimum that ascendency of the philosophical mind, which he had once held to be omnipotent and indispensable."—Grote's Plato, iii. 302-304.

and to every other nation which might seek to advance in the career of freedom and civilisation. If Charles I. had succeeded in his designs of enslaving England, the world would have seen the strange phenomenon of an institution, the result of a political discovery by a very great man, crushed by a very small man. How this very small man came to possess so much power in England may be briefly shown. At the commencement of the wars of the Roses, the power of the English kings was limited by the swords of the barons and their vassals more effectually than by the Great Charter. At the end of those wars the power of the barons was gone, while that of the kings remained without check. "The force," says Raleigh, "by which our kings in former times were troubled, is vanished away."[1] The power, therefore, of Charles I. did not arise from his own strength, but from the weakness of those who should have opposed him—a weakness so great that it needed something like a miracle to raise up a man possessed of genius and courage sufficient to oppose him successfully in his nefarious designs against the English nation.

If "in the grand discovery of modern times, the system of representation," the only securities for good government are to be found,[2] it follows that the two most important events in English history

---

[1] Raleigh's Prerogative of Parliaments. Birch's edition of Raleigh's Works, i. 206.

[2] James Mill's Essay on Government, section vi.

are the wars of the Barons under Simon de Montfort against the tyranny of the Plantagenets, and the wars of the Commons under Oliver Cromwell against the tyranny of the Stuarts; for the fate of Sir John Eliot sufficiently proves that Parliamentary government was not to be obtained by Parliamentary harangues and resolutions. The result of the first was the creation of the House of Commons. The result of the second was the rendering the House of Commons the supreme power in England. For a complete history of the great work accomplished by Simon de Montfort the materials do not exist. For a history of the work done by Oliver Cromwell the materials are abundant. The following pages contain the results of an examination and study of those materials continued for many years.

While the materials for the history of the work done by Cromwell may be said to be abundant, the materials constituting evidence as to the character of the Government which preceded the Commonwealth in England are not likely to be found in the English archives. No papers will be found in the English archives—except a few fragments preserved by some accident defeating the intention of their destruction—which will either let out anything against the Government, or throw any light on the true characters of the persons who occupied the throne. In all the darkest questions " precisely those papers which constitute the most important evidence are missing."[1] In all State trials down to the time of the Commonwealth, examinations were taken in secret, and often wrung from the prisoners by torture. Such parts of these examinations as suited the purpose in view were read before a judge removable at the will of the Crown, and a jury packed for the occasion, who gave their verdict under the terror of fine and imprisonment. The Government then published such accounts as suited their purpose; in which accounts truth and falsehood are mixed up together with all the art which the subtlety of a Crown lawyer can employ in his work.[2] In regard to the destruction of historical materials bearing on the character of the English Government before the Commonwealth, I will cite another writer who brought to the examination of documentary evidence great acuteness and more than ordinary knowledge and industry, and who says: "Sir F. Bacon, in the speech which he prepared for delivery in case the Countess of Somerset had pleaded not guilty, mentions two examinations of Franklin, one taken on the 16th and another on the 17th of November, and it has been seen that in the MS. report of the Earl's trial a third examination of Franklin is mentioned, bearing date the 12th of November. But no such documents are now to be found in the State Paper Office, in the British Museum, or other public

---

[1] Jardine's Criminal Trials, vol. ii., Preface, p. x. See also Amos, Trial of the Earl of Somerset, p. 338.
[2] See Jardine's Criminal Trials, ii. 4, 5.

repositories which have been searched for the purpose." This writer then repeats in substance the remark of Mr. Jardine, that while evidence of minor importance is to be found in abundance, those papers which constitute the most important evidence are missing; and adds, "The original confession of Lord Cobham upon which Sir Walter Raleigh was convicted; and the Duke of Norfolk's confession, which was much relied upon at his trial in the reign of Elizabeth, baffled the researches of Mr. Jardine."[1]

The period of English history here treated has been the subject of so many publications that novelty in regard to the mere facts is hardly to be expected. But the interpretation of the facts so as to bring out the meaning of them admits of novelty. For instance, although Mr. Jardine has published some most important facts proving the habitual use of torture in England under the Tudors and Stuarts by royal warrant—he has printed fifty-five of these warrants from the Council books—the conclusion he thence draws, that the use of the rack and other kinds of torture was anciently a lawful exertion of royal prerogative, can be proved to be

---

[1] The Trial of the Earl of Somerset, by Andrew Amos, Esq., late Member of the Supreme Council of India, p. 338. London, 1846. Mr. Amos, who I believe succeeded Lord Macaulay as the Legal Member of the Supreme Council of India, was also a Fellow of the same college, Trinity College, Cambridge, of which Lord Macaulay had been a Fellow. Mr. Amos had also received a legal education, had studied minutely the subject of judicial evidence and as a legal writer had shown that he possessed an acute and disciplined legal intellect. I mention these facts because, in examining and weighing historical evidence, it may perhaps be admitted to be some advantage to a man to have received a careful legal education.

erroneous. And what is, as far as I know, a new view of English history presented in the following pages is the conclusion legitimately drawn from the proceedings of the last Plantagenets, at least of Edward IV., and of the Tudors and the Stuarts, that their deliberate purpose being to destroy utterly the English Constitution as it had existed from the establishment of the House of Commons by Simon de Montfort, and such purpose having become an overt act by the habitual use of torture and the abolition of the ancient rule of evidence, that the accuser and accused should be brought face to face, it was the right and the duty of any resolute body of Englishmen, as soon as they had the power, to make an example of the first of those tyrants, whether bearing the name of Plantagenet, Tudor, or Stuart, who should fall into their hands—such example being the only way of saving from destruction the system of representation, without which both reason and experience have proved that good government is impossible. The conclusion is inevitable, that the execution of Charles I. was a political necessity.

Instead of "good government" I should have said "government not intolerably bad," for absolutely good government, as far as we know at present, is impossible; and though Parliamentary government is the nearest approach to good government as yet discovered, nevertheless it has, to borrow the words of Lord Macaulay in one of his latest and best writings, "like every other contrivance of man, its advantages and its disadvantages. On the advantages there is no need to dilate. The history of England during the hundred and seventy years which have elapsed since the House of Commons became the most powerful body in the State—her immense and still growing prosperity, her freedom, her tranquillity, her greatness in arts, in sciences, and in arms, her maritime ascendency, the marvels of her public credit, her American, her African, her Australian, her Asiatic empires—sufficiently prove the excellence of her institutions. But those institutions, though excellent, are assuredly not perfect. Parliamentary government is government by speaking. In such a government the power of speaking is the most highly prized of all the qualities which a politician can possess; and that power may exist, in the highest degree, without judgment, without fortitude, without skill in reading the characters of men or the signs of the times, without any knowledge of the principles of legislation or of political economy, and without any skill in diplomacy or in the administration of war. Nay, it may well happen that those very intellectual qualities, which give a peculiar charm to the speeches of a public man, may be incompatible with the qualities which would fit him to meet a pressing emergency with promptitude and firmness. It was thus with Charles Townshend. It was thus with Windham. It was a privilege to listen to those accomplished and ingenious orators. But in a perilous crisis they would have been found far inferior in all the qualities of rulers to such a man as Oliver Cromwell, who talked nonsense, or as William the Silent, who did not talk at all. When Parliamentary government is established, a Charles Townshend or a Windham will almost always exercise much greater influence than such men as the great Protector of England, or as the founder of the Batavian Commonwealth. . . . On these grounds, some persons, incapable of seeing more than one side of a question, have pronounced Parliamentary government a positive evil, and have maintained that the administration would be greatly improved if the power, now exercised by a large assembly, were transferred to a single person. Men of sense will probably think the remedy very much worse than the disease, and will be of opinion that there would be small gain in exchanging Charles Townshend and Windham for the Prince of the Peace, or the poor slave and dog Steenie."[1]

This description of Parliamentary government, or government by speaking, is the more valuable as coming from one who was himself one of the most

---

[1] Lord Macaulay's Essay on William Pitt, contributed to the "Encyclopædia Britannica." The expression here used by Lord Macaulay to describe the Duke of Buckingham is taken from his own letters to King James, which commence with the words "Dear dad and gossip," and end with the words "Your Majesty's most humble slave and dog, Steenie." Several of these letters will be found in the publication entitled "Memorials and Letters relating to the History of Britain in the Reign of James I.," edited from the original MSS. in the Advocates' Library at Edinburgh by Sir David Dalrymple (Lord Hailes). Glasgow, 1762.

effective speakers that ever spoke in that place, which may be termed the birthplace of Parliamentary government—the English House of Commons. On several occasions his speech absolutely determined the division, which was considered certain of producing a large majority the other way before Macaulay rose to speak. One of these occasions was the copyright question. Another was Lord Hotham's measure, the chief object of which was to exclude the Master of the Rolls from the House of Commons. Mr. Trevelyan gives an interesting account of Macaulay's speech on this occasion, June 1, 1853—of the rush from the committee-rooms on hearing the words "Macaulay is up"—of the great orator's torrent of words—of the "great applause," as he said himself in his diary, "and, better than applause, the complete success."[1] More than twenty years before that time, I have myself witnessed the rush of members from the library and committee-rooms into the House when Macaulay rose to speak. In regard to the comparison sometimes made between Macaulay and Burke, it is to be remembered that Burke's speaking emptied the House, whereas Macaulay's filled it. Macaulay's power as an orator is incontestable. His power as a debater would probaby have been so too if he had not chosen to sacrifice politics to literature.

[1] Trevelyan's Life and Letters of Lord Macaulay, ii. 334-337. London: Longmans & Co. 1876.

CONTENTS.

CHAPTER I.

A SUMMARY OF THE SYSTEMATIC ATTEMPTS OF THE ENGLISH KINGS OF THE FAMILIES OF PLANTAGENET, TUDOR, AND STUART, TO REDUCE THE ENGLISH PEOPLE TO SLAVERY . . . 1

CHAPTER II.

THE FIRST THREE PARLIAMENTS OF CHARLES I. . . 37

CHAPTER III.

THE ADMINISTRATION OF LAUD AND STRAFFORD . 71

CHAPTER IV.

SHIP-MONEY RESISTED BY JOHN HAMPDEN—PICTURE OF THE ENGLISH COURT 117

CHAPTER V.

THE STRUGGLE OF LAUD WITH THE SCOTTISH PRESBYTERIANS—THE FOURTH PARLIAMENT OF CHARLES I.—THE LAST CASE OF TORTURE IN ENGLAND 140

CHAPTER VI.

MEETING AND FIRST PROCEEDINGS OF THE LONG PARLIAMENT . 167

CHAPTER VII.

TRIAL AND EXECUTION OF STRAFFORD 190

CHAPTER VIII.

THE IRISH MASSACRE — THE GRAND REMONSTRANCE — IMPEACHMENT OF LORD KIMBOLTON AND THE FIVE MEMBERS OF THE HOUSE OF COMMONS 222

CHAPTER IX.

PREPARATIONS FOR WAR BETWEEN THE KING AND PARLIAMENT 250

CHAPTER X.

COMMENCEMENT OF THE WAR — BATTLE OF EDGEHILL — KING'S ATTACK ON BRENTFORD 264

CHAPTER XI.

SIEGE OF READING—WALLER'S PLOT—BATTLES OF STRATTON—LANSDOWN—ROUNDWAY DOWN—DEATH OF SIR BEVILL GRENVILLE—OF SIDNEY GODOLPHIN—OF HAMPDEN—TIME AT WHICH THE AFFAIRS OF THE PARLIAMENT WERE AT THE LOWEST—FIRST BATTLE OF NEWBURY—DEATH OF LORD FALKLAND—SOLEMN LEAGUE AND COVENANT—DEATH OF PYM—CHARACTER OF THE YOUNGER HOTHAM 291

HISTORY OF THE STRUGGLE FOR PARLIAMENTARY GOVERNMENT IN ENGLAND.

CHAPTER I.

A SUMMARY OF THE SYSTEMATIC ATTEMPTS OF THE ENGLISH KINGS OF THE FAMILIES OF PLANTAGENET, TUDOR, AND STUART, TO REDUCE THE ENGLISH PEOPLE TO SLAVERY.

THE struggle for parliamentary government in England may be said to have lasted for some four hundred years. But to trace it through all its various stages and fluctuations for that long tract of time would be uninstructive and useless. The crisis came on in the seventeenth century. The portion, therefore, of the long contest between the English people and their kings which began and ended in the second quarter of the seventeenth century is the subject of the following pages. Of the earlier parts of that long struggle, and of the means adopted by the kings to defeat those who sought, by parliamentary government, to emancipate themselves from monarchical tyranny, I will give a summary in this chapter.

The first relief which the oppressed English obtained

from the tyranny of their Norman oppressors came from the violent dissensions between the Norman kings and their barons, and the consequent necessity the Norman barons found themselves under of seeking the aid of the English against the fresh bands of military foreigners whom their kings were constantly bringing in to coerce or destroy them and seize their baronies. Charles I. attempted to play the same game, but he found in the English Independents an enemy more formidable than John, or Henry III., or Richard II. had met with in the Anglo-Norman barons.

When it is said that the principle of representation had, when Charles I. succeeded to the English throne, worked in England for four hundred years, it is not meant that parliamentary government had been established. Though the struggle had been going on for that time, that struggle had not yet terminated in the establishment of parliamentary government. It is unnecessary to go further than Mr. Forster's "Life of Sir John Eliot," compiled from original MSS., many of them in Eliot's own handwriting, to see that government in England, from the accession of Charles I. to the death of Buckingham, was not parliamentary government, but government by Buckingham, "the poor slave and dog Steenie;" and after the death of Buckingham to the meeting of the Long Parliament, was government by King Charles and Archbishop Laud.

When Simon de Montfort in 1265, or rather 1264—the date of the writs being the 12th of December 1264—after the battle of Lewes, in calling a Parliament, issued writs requiring the several Sheriffs to return, besides two knights for each shire, two citizens for each city, and two burgesses for each borough, it is not likely that he foresaw all the consequences of his general summoning;

Attempts to Reduce the People to Slavery. 3

for to him seems to be attributable the first general summoning—there may have been partial or occasional summoning before of representative citizens and burgesses to Parliament.[1] Neither is it probable that either Simon de Montfort or Edward I., in calling together so large a number of representatives from towns, foresaw that they were calling into existence a power which, though at its origin it seemed by no means formidable, was in time to become the destroyer of the pretensions of feudalism. It is vain to inquire what were the precise views with which Simon de Montfort issued his writs of summons to the cities and boroughs to send representatives to Parliament. De Montfort's views may have been of larger scope than taxation merely; but it may be affirmed that Edward I., in following the example of De Montfort in issuing writs of summons to the cities and boroughs, did it simply for the purpose of taxing them with greater facility and uniformity. But the King soon found that the citizens and burgesses, in their representatives, were apt to get

---

[1] If the authority of Sir Robert Cotton be accepted for the authenticity of the Roll of Parliament from which Sir John Eliot read in the second Parliament of Charles I. a precedent of 16th Henry III. for the Commons refusing a supply to the King, though the first *general* summoning of representative citizens and burgesses to Parliament seems to be attributable to Simon de Montfort in the year 1265, while Henry III. was a prisoner in De Montfort's power after the battle of Lewes, there must have been before that date *occasional and partial* summoning of citizens and burgesses to Parliament for the purpose of being called upon to supply the King with money. And this will explain the precedent in 16th Henry III., when, in the words of Sir John Eliot, "the Commons being required to make a supply unto the King, excused themselves, because, says the record, they saw all things disordered by those that were about him." See the rest of this precedent quoted in Chapter II. of this History. This precedent, furnished to Sir John Eliot by Sir Robert Cotton, and published by Mr. Forster from the MSS. at Port Eliot, will help to explain the reason why no writer of the time notices the summoning of the citizens and burgesses by De Montfort as an innovation, nor are the writs so framed as to lead us to suppose that the practice was then introduced for the first time.

notions into their heads that they came to Parliament for some other purposes besides that of paying money to the King. Then began a struggle between the English people and their kings, which went on with various results for some four centuries, and in which the kings employed various means to attain their object—the subjection of the people to a state of absolute slavery.

An account of the systematic attempts of the English kings to crush liberty in England necessarily includes some notice of the arts they employed to render the system of parliamentary representation a delusion. The attempts I have alluded to divide themselves into two kinds —fraud and force. The attempt to render parliamentary representation a delusion, and to alter the laws of evidence in state trials, comes under the head of fraud. To the head of force, accompanied by the most inhuman cruelty, belongs the use of torture introduced into England in the fifteenth century. I will first say a few words as to the fraudulent attempts to corrupt or pervert the representative system; and then proceed to the subject of force and inhuman cruelty, exhibited both in illegal imprisonment, in the use of the rack, and in the mode of execution for what was called high treason.

The writ addressed to the Sheriff specified no particular city or borough, but required him "to cause to be elected two citizens for each city, and two burgesses for each borough, in your bailiwick." This original frame of the parliamentary writs established the principle that, through the Sheriff, every city and borough was to be summoned. At the same time, as appears from the returns made by the Sheriffs, a sort of discretionary power was supposed to rest with them of determining what cities or boroughs were qualified to send representatives. Nevertheless, although inability to pay the parliamentary wages of representatives was admitted as a valid plea of exemption from electing in the case of individual boroughs, the principle of the right of every municipal town to be summoned was long the admitted doctrine. In this state of things, the interference of the crown was limited to influencing, through the Sheriffs, the return of individual members. Thus the statute of the 7th Henry IV. (1406), passed "on the grievous complaints of the Commons against undue elections from the partiality of Sheriffs," imposes heavy penalties upon Sheriffs who proceeded irregularly in elections, or made illegal returns.

But in time the interference of the crown, which at first was confined to employing the Sheriffs to make illegal returns of individual members, was extended further. Nor is this a matter to create surprise when it is remembered that the crown is one and the people are many; that the crown has always large means of purchasing for its service the astuteness and learning of lawyers, and the powers of speech and writing, not only of legal, but of political practitioners. Accordingly, the crown proceeded in a more wholesale way in its encroachments upon the constitution of Parliament. To omit any of the towns which had a prescriptive right to return members was too open an attack on the freedom of Parliament; but restoring the right in boroughs wherein it had long lain dormant, or granting the right to boroughs that had never had it, answered the purpose of the crown equally well. Thus in the reigns of Edward VI., Mary, and Elizabeth, 17 boroughs were restored to the power of sending members, and 46 first began to send members, making an addition to the former representation of 63 places, returning 123 members. At the same time the crown assumed the right of remoulding, by governing charters, the municipal constitution of these new or revived parliamentary boroughs. Those charters were so framed as to vest the election of the parliamentary representatives in small councils, originally nominated by the crown, and to be afterwards self-elected. The judges were made use of to promote this object, and in the 12th of James I. declared that the King could, by his charter, incorporate the people of a town in the form of select classes and commonalty; and while vesting in the whole corporation the right of sending representatives to Parliament, restrict the exercise of that right to the select classes. According to this form, James I. created four parliamentary boroughs; and under James I. and Charles I., seventeen parliamentary boroughs were revived.

But the proceedings above indicated on the part of the English kings of the families of Plantagenet, Tudor, and Stuart, present but a faint and imperfect image of their doings to the end and intent of establishing a pure despotism in England. The other measures they resorted to for that purpose were the introduction of torture into England, and the subversion of the old English rule of evidence, which required that the accuser and the accused should be brought face to face. What cruelties they perpetrated in the course of their long war against English liberty I will now attempt to relate.

It is far easier for us of the present day to contemplate death as preferable to life, under the tyranny of Plantagenet, Tudor, and Stuart, than it was for the men who had the misfortune to live under the government of the rack. We must remember that during the period of nearly two centuries, namely, from the time when Edward

IV., by the destruction of the warlike nobility in the sanguinary Wars of the Roses, was free to give the reins to his evil passions, resistance to tyranny in England did not merely involve a simple and sudden though violent death, and "there an end;" for tyrants had invented slow and exquisite tortures, which, to borrow the words of a writer of that time, might make men "wish and kneel in vain to die."

I have sometimes been inclined to think that civilisation in Europe for several centuries, even after the twelfth century, did not advance at all; that instead of advancing it retrograded. The common law of England, which neither admitted of torture nor of any penal infliction not warranted by a judicial sentence, was set aside for nearly two centuries; and the English kings, whose power had been limited by the swords of the great barons, were, by the sanguinary conflict of one civil war, transformed into Asiatic sultans, so thoroughly that it required a second civil war, still greater than the former, to retransform them into English kings. Edward IV. was the first of these tyrants[1] freed from all salutary constitutional control; and as the last case of torture occurred in the year 1640, in the reign of Charles I., the first occurred in 1468, in the reign of Edward IV., when one Hawkins was convicted of treason by his own confession on the rack, and executed. From that time till 1640 the use of torture was frequent and uninterrupted, the cases being recorded in the Council books, and the torture-warrants in many cases being still in existence. Judicial torture

---

[1] Shakespeare has made Richard III. say to Sir William Catesby, "*Slave*, I have set my life upon a cast;" and in other instances he has made his kings apply the word "slave" to a subject. In this Shakespeare merely uses the language which in his time described the idea the English kings had of their subjects.

formed a part of all the European legal systems which adopted the Roman law; and as England did not adopt the Roman law, in England torture was not, as in the countries which had adopted the Roman law, subject to specific rules and restrictions, but there were no rules, no restrictions, no law, but the will of the King. "The rack," says Selden, "is nowhere used as in England. In other countries it is used in judicature where there is *semiplena probatio*, a half-proof against a man; then, to see if they can make it full, they rack him if he will not confess. But here in England they take a man and rack him—I don't know why nor when—not in time of judicature, but when somebody bids."[1] Consequently, a tyranny existed in England for nearly two hundred years, supported by the use of torture, in direct violation of the laws of England, and not even subject to the rules and restrictions under which torture was applied in those countries which had adopted the Roman law. A terrible necessity was thus forced upon the English people of delivering themselves for ever from such a tyranny as this, or of perishing as a free people from the face of the earth.

There is but one case, as far as I have been able to discover, of torture under the Plantagenets—that of Hawkins in 1468. This was the first instance of torture in England, according to Mr. Jardine's elaborate investigation of the subject; but from that time to the time of the Commonwealth, the practice was frequent and uninterrupted. The instruments of torture are so numerous and various,[2] as to give the rulers who made use of them, in defiance of the ancient and unrepealed law of

---

[1] Table-Talk, "Trial."
[2] See an account of them in Jardine's Criminal Trials, i. 22, 23.

England, a title to be ranked as cruel and sanguinary tyrants with Nabis and Phalaris, and furnish irrefragable arguments for making a memorable example of the first of those tyrants who should fall into the hands of, not the people of England—for the bulk of them might be, as the Presbyterian Lady Fairfax said, weak enough not to see the necessity of such a proceeding—but of such a resolute and intelligent body of Englishmen as that army, created and led by Cromwell. It was not likely that such men were to be turned from their purpose either by Queen Henrietta and her priests, or by Lady Fairfax and her ministers; and whatever else those men did, whether good in the opinion of some or evil in that of others, there will hardly be any now found to murmur disapproval, when it is said that they abolished torture in England, and also restored the practice of bringing the state prisoner and the accuser, or the accusing witness, face to face.

Mr. Jardine, in his very learned and ingenious "Reading"[1] on the use of torture in England, has proved, by a series of royal warrants for the application of torture extracted from the Council books, and extending from the beginning of the reign of Edward VI. to the commencement of the civil war, that the use of torture had, under the Tudors, become a uniform practice, which, under the name of prerogative, overrode and trampled down both the common and statute law of England. He has printed fifty-five of these warrants, including several issued by each of the five rulers who reigned in the period gone

[1] "A Reading on the Use of Torture in England previously to the Commonwealth." Delivered at New Inn Hall in Michaelmas Term 1836, by appointment of the Honourable Society of the Middle Temple. By David Jardine, Esq., of the Middle Temple, Barrister-at-Law. 8vo. London, 1837.

over,—Edward VI., Mary, Elizabeth, James I., and Charles I.

It is to be carefully noted, that though, as Coke said in the House of Commons in the debates on the Petition of Right, "prerogative is part of the law," yet "sovereign power is no parliamentary word;" and that, though the power of sending ambassadors and the power of creating peers may be parts of the royal prerogative recognised by the law of England, it does not by any means follow that, though a line of English kings and queens for several generations had done certain acts by royal warrant, these acts should have been thereby rendered legal. The inference which Mr. Jardine draws from the uniform practice of torture by royal warrant, that though *not* lawful either by the common law or by Magna Charta, or any other statute, it *was* lawful as an act of prerogative, appears to me strangely illogical; indeed, every argument by which Mr. Jardine attempts to show that the use of the rack or other torture was anciently a *lawful* exertion of royal prerogative, may, as Lord Macaulay has observed,[1] "be urged with equal force, nay, with far greater force, to prove the lawfulness of benevolences, of ship-money, of Mompesson's patent, of Eliot's imprisonment, of every abuse, without exception, which is condemned by the Petition of Right and the Declaration of Right." The logical inference appears rather that the English kings and queens who had acted thus in torturing the people of England had forfeited their title by a breach of the laws of England, and had furnished most cogent arguments to the first body of Englishmen who should be placed in the position occupied by the victors of Marston Moor and Naseby for

[1] Note to his Essay on Lord Bacon.

taking most ample securities against the renewal of the torturing process by their native oppressors, whether called kings, queens, or protectors.

"I would know," says Sir John Hawles, who was Solicitor-General under William III., in his pamphlet relating to the trial of Lord Russell, "by what law is the deposition of a person who might be brought face to face to the prisoner read as evidence; I would know by what law it is forbidden that the accuser should be brought face to face with the accused?" And the answer might be, By no law, but by prerogative, which, under the Tudors and Stuarts, overrode law in England. Moreover, the continuance for so long a time of the use of torture, which is declared illegal by Fortescue and Coke, and all other English lawyers, furnishes conclusive evidence of the existence of a power above the law, subverting *the law of the land*, and setting up in its place *the King's law*, that is, law made according to the King's convenience and the King's will and pleasure. Under that system of government, everything that power, assisted by the servile subtlety of the crown lawyers, could do, was done, first to murder the prisoner under the form of law, and then to blacken his memory by carefully striking out of the report of the trial put forth by the Government—and no other report was allowed to be put forth—everything that might be favourable to his character. Thus in the original, in the State Paper Office, it is stated that the Earl of Essex "in his usual talk was wont to say that he liked not that any man should be troubled for his religion." These words are omitted by Bacon in his published report. They are also marked for omission by Sir E. Coke, and were therefore not read at the trial, in accordance with the prevalent usage of omitting whatever was favourable to a prisoner.

There is also in the State Paper Office a paper entitled "Directions to the Preachers," for the purpose of employing the pulpits in the business of blackening the Earl of Essex's memory. This is an example of "tuning the pulpits"—an expression attributed to Elizabeth or her Minister. That indeed was the time when the English monarchs might be said to make religion as well as law; or, to use the words of Elizabeth's successor, to "make what liked them law and gospel."

Under the Tudor and Stuart kings, down to the time of the Commonwealth, the proceedings against persons accused of state crimes, though they bore the name of trials, were in fact only employed by the Government for the purpose of destroying those persons with sufficient pomp and display to awe the multitude. The result was so certain, that, as Mr. Hargrave says, "to be accused of a crime against the state and to be convicted were almost the same thing." The one was so certain a consequence of the other, that Lord Dacre's case, in Henry VIII.'s reign, and Sir Nicholas Throckmorton's, in his daughter Mary's, are almost the only examples to the contrary. In Throckmorton's case, the jury having, in accordance with the evidence, but in opposition to the will of the court, brought in a verdict of not guilty, were committed to prison. Four of them afterwards made their submission, and were discharged. Of the other eight, five were discharged after having lain eight months in prison, from the 17th of April till the 12th of December, on the payment of fines of £220 apiece, and the remaining three, having set forth in a petition that their estates did not amount to the sum they were required to pay, were discharged, December 21, on the payment of threescore pounds apiece. Of the abject condition of the people at that time in England, the words of the foreman of the jury present a striking picture. "*Foreman*—I pray you, my lords, be good unto us, and let us not be molested for the faithful discharge of our consciences. We are poor merchant-men, and have great charge in our hands, and our livelihood depends upon our travails. We beseech the court to appoint a certain day for our appearance, because perhaps else some of us may be in foreign parts about our business."[1]

That the law of the land had been altered and overridden by what was called prerogative is evident from such passages as this in the trial of the Duke of Norfolk in the reign of Queen Elizabeth. The Duke says —"I pray you let the witnesses be brought face to face to me; I have often required it, and the law, I trust, is so." To which he is answered—"The law was so for a time, in some cases of treason; but since, the law hath been found too hard and dangerous for the Prince, and it hath been repealed."[2] This shows how the laws of England had been altered by the Tudors to suit their tyranny, though it had not, as the crown lawyer here asserts, been "repealed;" for even then the crown had not the power either to make or repeal a law. And Sir Walter Raleigh, upon Lord Cobham's examination being read, which was the principal evidence adduced against him, said—"I beseech you, my lords, let Cobham be sent for; charge him on his soul, on his allegiance to the King; if he affirm it, I am guilty."

Sir W. Raleigh—" Good, my lords, let my accuser come face to face. Were the case but a small copyhold, you would have witnesses or good proof to lead the jury to a verdict; and I am here for my life."

Popham, C.J.—" There must not such a gap be opened

[1] Jardine's Criminal Trials, i. 109.   [2] Ibid., pp. 167, 168.

for the destruction of the King as would be if we should grant this; you plead hard for yourself, but the laws plead as hard for the King."[1]

These words of Popham, "the laws plead as hard for the King," suggest what the tyrants whom Popham then represented had done for the laws of England. Under the Tudors and the two first Stuarts, the law was, even in the technical language of the judges, considered as completely in the King's power, so that the law was no longer the law of the land but the King's law, to do what he liked with. In the articles which the Lords of the Council presented to Henry VIII. against Cardinal Wolsey, the laws of England are styled your Grace's laws, and your laws of this your realm, though the articles are signed by Sir Thomas More, Chancellor, and the two Chief Justices. And James II.'s judges declared, "That the laws were the King's laws; that the King might dispense with his laws in case of necessity; and that the King was judge of that necessity."[2] The doctrine had, it seems, survived the great shock it had received from the armies of the Long Parliament; but it did not survive long.

The tyranny and cruelty of those times when torture was in use are remarkably manifested in the case of Peacham—a case which shows that any Englishman might in those times be imprisoned and put to the torture on the mere suspicion or caprice of the Government. It is a case exemplifying strikingly the truth of Selden's remark, quoted above—" Here in England they take a man and rack him—I do not know why nor when—not in time of judicature, but when somebody bids."

In 1614 Peacham, an aged clergyman, was accused of

[1] Jardine's Criminal Trials, i. 427.
[2] Ibid., p. 383.

high treason for certain passages in a sermon written by him and found in his study, but never preached or published. This accusation of high treason, got up in such a manner, shows that the Government was a complete tyranny, employing spies to worm themselves into the confidence of individuals. How otherwise could a man's private papers be made known to a government? Peacham was examined upon interrogatories "before torture, in torture, between torture, and after torture," by a commission of which Bacon was an active member, and whose correspondence with King James on that and similar subjects is very characteristic, both as regards Bacon and Bacon's master. When any person in that age was charged with treason—and how wide the meaning of that word was then may be inferred from the case of Peacham—the practice was to arrest that person, and to keep him in strict imprisonment till it suited the purposes of the crown to try him. When he was brought to trial, he came with his body and mind weakened by confinement, and hearing the charge against him for the first time when the indictment was read on his arraignment, and being compelled to plead instantly to it, he was, as the Duke of Norfolk said, "brought to fight without a weapon." "I have had short warning, and no books, neither book of statutes, nor so much as a breviate of the statutes. I am brought," said the Duke, "to fight without a weapon. I was told, before I came here, that I was indicted upon the statute of the 25th Edward III., and now I do not hear the same statute recited, but am put at once to the whole herd of laws, not knowing unto which particularly I am to answer." The Duke then asked for counsel, to which request Dyer,

C.J., replied—"All our books forbid allowing of counsel in the point of treason."[1]

During the time of his imprisonment, which was quite without limit in practice, however illegal according to old laws, which though not repealed were practically dead, there being instances of imprisonment for many years without trial, the condition of the prisoner was very similar to the condition of prisoners when the Roman imperial tyranny was at its height. Persons were sometimes introduced into the society of the prisoner to draw confessions from him under the show of sympathy, which might be made a ground for prosecution for criminal charges involving his life. Thus Sir Thomas Wilson, a man of learning and polished manners, qualified for such an employment by inhumanity, meanness, and cunning, was shut up in the Tower with Sir Walter Raleigh for upwards of a month, for the purpose of drawing from him materials for a criminal accusation. Sir Thomas Wilson was at that time Keeper of the State Papers, and his own original minutes of the conversation and conduct of Sir Walter Raleigh during the time he was with him in the Tower are preserved in the office over which he presided. His instructions were to take exclusive charge of Raleigh in the Tower, "to keep him safe, and to suffer no persons to come at him but such as were necessary for his diet, &c.;" and he was directed to draw from him such information, either with respect to his communication with the French ambassador, or his Guiana expedition in general, as might promote the object of the Government, namely, his destruction. Raleigh's own servant was immediately dismissed, and a man appointed by Wilson took his place. Lady

[1] Jardine's Criminal Trials, i. 146.

Raleigh and her son were excluded from the Tower, but she was permitted to correspond with her husband, and the notes which she sent, as well as Raleigh's answers, were intercepted by Wilson's man, and sent to the King and Council for their perusal before they were delivered. Wilson never left his prisoner from the time he opened his door in the morning till he locked him up for the night. Wilson, of course, uses such language respecting Raleigh as he thinks would be agreeable to the King, such as "hypocrite," "arch impostor," a man "*tam ingeniose nequam*," as he never before dealt with. He removed Raleigh into apartments of greater security than those in which he had been placed by Sir Allan Apsley, and then wrote to Sir Robert Naunton, one of the Secretaries of State, "I have removed this man into a safer and higher lodging, which, though it seemeth nearer heaven, yet there is there no means to escape but into hell." Again, in a letter to the King, he says, "I hope by such means as I shall use to work out more than I have yet done; if not, I know no other means but a rack or a halter." Although it might be thought that Raleigh had seen too much of courts to be easily imposed upon by his simulation of candour and sympathy, in a note to Lady Raleigh, preserved in the State Paper Office, Raleigh calls him "this honest gentleman."

The proceedings of "this honest gentleman" furnish an instructive illustration of the manner in which "suspiria subscribebantur," in which a prisoner's very sighs were registered for his destruction under the Roman imperial tyranny and the tyranny of the Tudors and Stuarts in England. Raleigh, at this time in his sixty-seventh year, was suffering from an intermittent fever and ague; his body was covered with painful imposthumes, and he had a swelling on his left side which caused perpetual uneasiness, in addition to which he was affected by a hernia. In the note to his wife above referred to, Raleigh says, "My swollen side keeps me in perpetual pain and unrest;" and at his execution, the Sheriff having offered to bring him down off the scaffold to warm him by a fire, he said, "No, good Mr. Sheriff, let us despatch, for within this quarter of an hour mine ague will come upon me, and if I be not dead before then, mine enemies will say that I quake for fear." Nevertheless, Wilson represented his complaints as being either wholly counterfeited or greatly exaggerated; and the proof he alleges is that Raleigh, with whom he pretended to sympathise, occasionally forgot his sufferings when his powerful mind was led to look back on the actions of his adventurous life.

Raleigh's sentence, at his trial at Winchester, was due to the verdict of condemnation given by the jury, whose conduct was universally reprobated by contemporaries. It is stated by the author of "Observations on Sanderson's History of the Reign of James I.," that in the first instance another jury had been nominated, consisting principally of near servants of the late Queen Elizabeth, but that these, being suspected, were changed over-night, and others who could be depended upon substituted for them. One more remark I will make on this subject. After the reading of Lord Cobham's letter to the Lords at the trial at Winchester, Sir Edward Coke, the Attorney-General, thus delivered himself:—" O damnable atheist! He counsels not to confess to preachers, as the Earl of Essex did. That noble Earl died indeed for his offence, but he died the child of God, and God honoured him at his death. Thou wast by when he died. *Et lupus et turpes instant morientibus ursi.*"[1] These last words are very apt, and may be justly applied to Coke himself, as he thus insulted over Raleigh, who was brought to fight for his life, as the Duke of Norfolk said, without a weapon. And indeed the whole pack of courtiers and court or crown lawyers of the Tudors and Stuarts were a pack of wolves in the human form.

It appears, then, that under the Tudors and the first two[2] Stuarts, any man in England might be seized, imprisoned, tortured, brought to a trial which was a mere mockery, and condemned to death, by witnesses who were not brought face to face to him, but were examined in secret, always threatened with and often subjected to torture, and of whose depositions thus obtained just as much was produced in court by the crown lawyers as suited their purposes. And all this was contrary to the laws of England, and was therefore done illegally by the tyrants who, from the fifteenth to the seventeenth century, had got hold of the English government. The men who tried Charles I. did not use torture to witnesses, as the Tudors and Stuarts did, yet Charles I. considered himself extremely ill-used because the men who had now gotten him in their

---

[1] Jardine's Criminal Trials, i. 446. The last word has been printed "ursæ" in the trial quoted and elsewhere. Ovid's lines are :—

> "Quo quis enim major, magis est placabilis iræ;
> Et faciles motus mens generosa capit.
> Corpora magnanimo satis est prostrasse leoni :
> Pugna suum finem, cum jacet hostis, habet.
> At lupus, et turpes instant morientibus ursi;
> Et quæcunque minor nobilitate fera est."
> Ovid. Trist., Lib. III., Eleg. 5, vv. 31-36.

[2] This is not strictly accurate, as appears from a passage which, says Mr. Amos, "has escaped the notice of writers on the subject in Tongue's trial, 14 Car. II., 6 Howell's St. Tr., wherein Tongue says, 'I confess I did confess it in the Tower, being *threatened* with the rack.'"—Amos's Trial of the Earl of Somerset, p. 309, note.

gripe gave him at least as fair a trial as had been given to the Duke of Norfolk, the Earl of Essex, and Sir Walter Raleigh. I desire particularly to have it understood that I make no affirmation either as to the guilt or innocence of these persons. I only affirm that none of them had a fair trial, or anything approaching to a fair trial; and I use the word "tyrants" advisedly—not rhetorically—for Bracton expressly says that the name "tyrannus," and not "rex," belongs to the person set up as king "when his pleasure and not the law prevails;"[1] and Fleta declares that a king becomes a tyrant when he violates his true function.[2] Can there be any doubt, then, that these English tyrants, having been for some two hundred years oppressing the people of England contrary to the laws of England, without having the pretext of a new conquest and a totally new code or system of laws, had rendered themselves responsible to the first body of Englishmen who should have gotten the power of punishment?

But this is not all. By the accession of the Scottish King to the throne of England on the death of Elizabeth, England had received a fresh blessing in addition to those which she already enjoyed through her native oppressors of the Plantagenet and Tudor line, which have been shortly shown in the preceding pages of this chapter. For England had received the gift from her last tyrant, Elizabeth, of a tyrant who went beyond the Tudors. There was one device of tyranny introduced in modern Europe during the sixteenth century which England had hitherto escaped, though it is a wonder that Henry VIII. or his daughter had not introduced it into England, but which the native

[1] Bracton, Lib. I. c. 8, § 5, and Lib. III. c. 9, § 3.
[2] Fleta, Lib. I. c. 17, § 3. Sir Thomas Smith, though writing under the Tudor tyranny, draws the same distinction between king and tyrant. Commonwealth of England, Book I., chap. 7, ed. 1621.

country of the Scottish king who succeeded Elizabeth in England enjoyed in perfection. In 1540 the practice (borrowed from the Roman law) of producing in court the dead bodies of persons accused of high treason, in order, by going through the mockery of a trial, to obtain a forfeiture of their estates to the Crown, was introduced into Scotland. Even under Tiberius and Nero the Roman law was not so; if the person accused died before judgment, his property descended to his heirs. So that it was only in its later stages, when tyranny had advanced far towards perfection, that the Roman law authorised this practice, which in its worst form was copied by many of the modern European tyrants.[1] The reader of Tacitus need not be reminded of the numerous examples, in those times of which Tacitus writes, of persons preventing judgment by a voluntary death, in order that their children or heirs might not be deprived of their property; and in that case the Emperor had to pay his bloodhounds who had hunted the victim to death out of his privy purse, *fiscus*, as opposed to *ærarium*, the public treasury.[2] And this marks the measure by which the condition of Scotland under this Stuart King James VI., afterwards James I. of England, was worse than

---

[1] See Julii Pacii Analysis Instit., Lib. iv. tit. 18, § 3. Though the English kings were precluded by the English law from this mode of acquisition, it has been thought by some English lawyers that it was probably with a view to such forfeitures that the punishment of the *peine forte et dure* was made so excruciating (Amos, Trial of the Earl of Somerset, p. 374 note). In the same note Mr. Amos mentions the case of a man who suffered himself to be pressed to death in order to preserve his estate for his child, which would have been forfeited had he pleaded and been convicted. The same case is given in Christian's note to 4 Bl. Com. 325: in which note it is also stated that "in the legal history of England there are numerous instances of persons who have had resolution and patience to undergo so terrible a death in order to benefit their heirs by preventing a forfeiture of their estates, which would have been the consequence of a conviction by a verdict."

[2] See Tacit. Ann., iv. 30.

the condition of Rome under Tiberius and Nero. For in accordance with this law, the form of a trial was gone through before the Scottish Parliament with regard to the Earl of Gowrie and his brother, Alexander Ruthven, who had been murdered in their own house by King James VI.'s[1] orders, under circumstances of unparalleled infamy. The dead bodies of the two brothers were produced before the Parliament that met at Edinburgh on 1st November 1600. An indictment for high treason was preferred against them. The depositions of witnesses were produced. If the witnesses themselves had been produced, they could only have been brought face to face with their dead bodies, instead of being, as the old English law required, brought face to face with the accused. The result of this mockery of a trial was, that by the sentence or "Doom of Parliament," as it was called, the punishment of traitors was inflicted on the dead bodies of the murdered Earl of Gowrie and his brother, and the large and valuable estates of the Gowrie family were declared forfeited to the King. The whole history of this case exhibits a picture of unprincipled tyranny on the part of the King and of unprincipled servility on the part of the Parliament of Scotland to which ancient and modern times will scarcely furnish a parallel. It was, indeed, according to all human foresight, a black day for England when this King of Scotland succeeded to the throne of Elizabeth. And if he had fallen upon the days of the stern Puritans, who, twenty

---

[1] I have examined the whole of the evidence that exists in the affair which King James called the Gowrie Conspiracy, and have shown that the assertion of the existence of the alleged conspiracy on the part of the two murdered boys, the Earl of Gowrie and his brother, Alexander Ruthven, is based only on a fabric of circumstantial falsehood, propped up by perjury, torture, forgery, and murder. See "Essays on Historical Truth," pp. 190-302. London: Longmans & Co. 1871.

years after his death won the right, by so many hard-fought battles, of punishing the crimes of kings as well as those of nobles, his public execution as a tyrant and murderer would have been a righteous manifestation of justice. If Charles I. had repudiated the principles and the deeds of James I., exception might be taken to the introduction of his name and character here; but Charles I. not only never evinced any disapprobation of the character, deeds, and principles of James I., but adopted one of the worst of James I.'s minions as his own minister. It therefore is not irrelevant to our subject to say something of James I. in this place, when his representative, Charles I., was to be made accountable to *man* for his deeds as well as to God. Indeed, the character of James I. and his court had so much to do with calling up the spirit that produced the great Puritan rebellion of the succeeding reign, that the true nature of that great insurrection cannot be thoroughly understood without at least some knowledge of the character of King James and his court.

I have mentioned the care taken for the destruction of all evidence throwing light on the true character of the English Government before the Commonwealth. So successful had the result been in establishing a false character, very different from the true one, that Mr. Pitcairn, the laborious editor of the "Criminal Trials" of Scotland, printed from the Scottish records, in reference to one of these cases, which only forms "one of a series of sanguinary and barbarously vindictive acts of King James, which unquestionably must leave an indelible stain on his memory and character as a despotic and cruel tyrant,"[1] says, "Had mention been made of this fact in any private correspondence of the

[1] Pitcairn's Criminal Trials in Scotland, iii. 445. 3 vols. 4to. Edinburgh, 1833.

period, or in contemporary memoirs or annals, it would have been at once discredited by all as an unprincipled libel on the character of our British Solomon."[1] One of Mr. Pitcairn's series of cases gives a curious picture of this British Solomon, and shows how far those are correct who say that he confined his despotism to theory and to talk.

Thomas Ross, a Scotchman who had been reduced from affluence to extreme poverty, had affixed a lampoon on the Scotch to the door of one of the Colleges at Oxford. Being challenged as the author, Ross, who seems to have written the pasquil during a temporary derangement of mind, brought on by the privations to which he had been subjected, thought he was called on to defend his thesis, avowed what he had done, and stated with much simplicity, as the cause which induced him to write it, that he thought it might, as a specimen of his talents, be the means of bringing him into notice, and so providing him with bread. King James knew that by the laws of England he could not get this man hanged. He therefore wrote a letter to his Privy Council of Scotland, informing them of the inconvenient restriction placed on his kingly power in his new kingdom, offering the honour of trying Ross to the more accommodating laws of his native country, and hinting that the last punishment of the law would be an acceptable service, if it could possibly be administered.

The Privy Council of Scotland entered at once into the views of their master. Some of the expressions of their letter throw a curious light upon their notions of a legal

[1] Pitcairn, iii. 359. It appears from the evidence produced in great abundance in Pitcairn's Criminal Trials, that when King James was able to work out his purpose, as he was in Scotland, he never failed to hunt his victim to death—a strange specimen of a saint for the worship of mankind. Yet Archbishop Laud informs us that "his rest is, without question, in Abraham's bosom."

trial. They inform their royal master that they have given directions to the magistrates of Edinburgh, as soon as Ross shall arrive, to commit him close prisoner in their "Irne House" [iron room or cage, in which desperate criminals were confined before their execution], and to lay him in irons. Their letter then has the following remarkable declaration—" We shall conveene and examine him; and accordinglie we shall give directioun for his tryall and *convictioun*, and shall superceid the pronouncing of doome, till we understand your Majestie's further pleasure anent the forme of his punishment. Oure opinion is that he shall be hanged at the Market Cross of Edinburghe, and his head affixt on ane of the Postis [city gates]. But in this we submitt our selffis to your Majestie's discretioun; quhairunto we shall conforme ourselffis."[1]

Ross underwent his sentence, which was—first his right hand to be stricken off, and then his head.[2]

At the same time that the Privy Council of Scotland wrote this letter (July 30, 1616), Thomas Hamilton, Lord Binning, a member of the Council, wrote a private letter to the King, in which he says—" It is a foolish[3] presumption in subjects to think that the Kings whom God has chosen as His Lieutenants to reign over so great nations should have hearts of no greater excellence than the vulgar sort. If God had not prepared the heart of Solomon in his youth to command the houris child to be divided betwixt her and her neighbour, who claimed the living bairne, what judge in the world could certainly have determined to which of the two the living child did belong?"[4]

---

[1] Pitcairn, iii. 585. [2] Ibid., iii. 454.
[3] I have modernised the spelling of this extract, with the exception of one word, which he writes "houris," the meaning of which will be obvious to the English reader. [4] Pitcairn, iii. 161.

When we look at the character of the king who succeeded Elizabeth Tudor, we are apt, without a competent knowledge of contemporary royal personages, to be struck with incredulity. But when we look somewhat closely at the contemporary kings, queens, princes, and princesses, who, like James, were in the enjoyment of the divine-right privileges, our incredulity at once vanishes, and we perceive that there was nothing particularly anomalous or out of the royal road in James's conduct—that in some of his qualities he only resembled Philip II., and in others the sons of Catherine de' Medici. There were some curious points of resemblance between Philip II. and James. In the first place, both were cowards. Philip, indeed, by the immense extent of dominion which he inherited, was able, with perfect security as regarded his own person, to carry on wars and to attempt foreign conquests; while in the case of James, the truthful historian must be content with the recital of murders instead of battles. Both, however, were, in point of fact, neither statesmen nor generals, but only plotters and assassins. Both were, among other murders, charged with the murders of their sons. There were other points of resemblance between Philip and James. Both were men of feeble bodies and of inordinate pride—the pride of birth and of the divinity of kingship. Both were as deficient in manly energy as in masculine understanding. Both were great scribblers, though in different ways. Philip wrote notes in a schoolboy's hand on the margin of letters written by high functionaries, which couriers were waiting to carry off to all the four quarters of the globe, freighted with the doom of millions of human beings. James wrote defences of the divine right of kings and counterblasts against tobacco; and the labours of his Secretaries of State comprehended the subject of the King's hounds, hawks, and cormorants.[1] There were also strong points of contrast between Philip and James. For James only scribbled by fits and starts, while Philip sat every day seven or eight hours at his writing-table covered with piles of despatches. Philip only occasionally followed field sports, when urged by his physicians to try the effect of the chase as a change from his sedentary habits. The chase was the occupation of James's life. The manner in which James followed the chase has been often described, and was quite in accordance with the timidity of his character.

The character of James I., about which there was, and perhaps is still, a difference of opinion, was by no means so easy to be deciphered as some writers have assumed, when they assume him to be simply a fool and pedant. For there is a certain amount of truth in the eulogy of D'Israeli, "James was no more a pedant than the ablest of his contemporaries; nor abhorred the taste of tobacco, nor feared witches more than they did: he was a great wit, a most acute disputant."[2] All this, says Gifford, "is simple truth; and it is mere dotage to re-echo at this day, the senseless and savage yell of the Nonconformists of James's time."[3] King James, if not "a most acute disputant," was really a wit, even by the admission of Sir Anthony Weldon, who assuredly did not write to eulogise him; and in the grave manner in which, according to Weldon, he delivered his witty jests, at which he would not smile him-

[1] Sir Francis Wortley to Secretary Conway, July 29, 1623, about a cormorant—MS. State Paper Office. Secretary Conway, September 29, 1623, to John Wood, Keeper of the Cormorants, to seek after a cormorant purloined, and to seize and bring it back with whomsoever it be found—MS. State Paper Office. The quantity of papers in the State Paper Office relating to the hounds, hawks, cormorants, kitchen, cellar, and similar subjects, afford some measure of the proportion which this King's personal pleasures and amusements bore to his performance of his duties as a king.

[2] Calamities of Authors, ii. 245.   [3] Gifford's edition of Ben Jonson, i. cxi.

self, evinced that characteristic which has been observed in Swift and others, of moving laughter without joining in it. But though King James did not talk like a wise man, when he made speeches to his Parliament, yet in that important quality of wisdom which enables a man to accomplish his ends, James was a match for the ablest men of his time. In fact, what seems on a superficial view ridiculous—the comparison sometimes made of James to Tiberius—is on a closer examination a very apt comparison. In power and penetration of mind, indeed, James cannot be compared to Tiberius; but in the success with which he involved his vices in darkness—a darkness such that some writers even to this day affirm that he had no vices—James was not much inferior to Tiberius. On the envelope of his letters to Sir George More, Lieutenant of the Tower when Carr, Earl of Somerset, was a prisoner there, the character of King James is thus expressed in the handwriting of the early part of the seventeenth century, "He was the wisest to work his own ends that ever was before him,"—those ends being to envelope in darkness the secrets of his palace. There are touches in the portrait which Tacitus has drawn of Tiberius bearing a strong resemblance to certain features in the portrait which Count Tillières, the French ambassador at the English court, has drawn of James. Plato has said in his description of the mind of the despot, that the best parts of the despot's mind are under subjection to the worst; that the rational mind is trampled down by the appetitive mind with its insane cravings; and that he is tormented with incessant perturbation, anxiety, and fear.[1] Tacitus quotes a few words of a letter of Tiberius to the Senate, from which he infers that the description of Plato is applicable

[1] Plato, Republic, ix. 577–580.

to Tiberius.[1] I do not think it likely that Count Tillières had read the "Republic" of Plato, but there is a passage in one of the despatches of Tillières, written within two years of King James's death, that appears to render Plato's description remarkably applicable to the mind of King James, when advancing age had rendered his appetites more and more eccentric; and when he became conscious of failing strength, and conscious too, notwithstanding the flattery of courtiers, that he was the object, not of the love and honour, but of the hatred of mankind. "The King," Tillières writes under date March 25, 1623, "will have no man about him of condition, intellect, or judgment; but little people, who defer to him in everything, who praise his vices as others praise virtues, and who calumniate all men of honour and virtue. He hates such mortally, thinking that they defame and despise him; he would fain avoid the sight of them, because he thinks their countenances reproach him for his abominable and scandalous life."[2] Tillières, in other despatches, enters into particulars into which I will not follow him further than to say that Tillières compares James's life at Newmarket to the life led by Tiberius at Caprea;[3] though just before he had used still stronger language, saying that at Newmarket

[1] Tacit. Ann., vi. 6.
[2] Tillières, in Raumer's "History of the Sixteenth and Seventeenth Centuries," English Translation, London, 1835, vol. ii. p. 278. Tillières, in reference to the orgies of James at the house of the Duke of Buckingham, says:—"I have too much modesty to describe, in the terms of strict truth, things which one would rather suppress than commit to writing in ambassadorial despatches destined for the perusal of exalted persons."—Ibid., ii. 260, 261. And yet the English translator has considered himself compelled to omit one passage at least, which is at page 317 of vol. ii. of Von Raumer's original German work, "Letters from Paris illustrating the History of the Sixteenth and Seventeenth Centuries," and which Von Raumer has not translated into German, but has left in the original French of the French ambassador's despatch as it remains in the archives of France. [3] Ibid., ii. 265, 266.

"he leads a life to which past and present times present no parallel."[1]

When, some three hundred years before the time of James I., Edward II. displayed eccentricities somewhat similar to those of James I., the representatives of the English nation at that time deemed it their duty to depose him and hang his favourites; and the representatives of the English nation at the beginning of the seventeenth century would have deemed it their duty to depose James I. and hang his favourites, if they had not at that time fallen into a state of weakness so great that the ambassadors from foreign states resident in England repeatedly express their astonishment at it, calling it cowardice.[2] The assertion of Hume and others that King James had no vices, and only too much good nature, cannot be true, unless it be proved that the despatches of the French ambassador Tillières in the French archives published by Von Raumer, and the original letters in the Advocates' Library published by Lord Hailes, are forgeries.

[1] Raumer, ii. 264. The statements of Tillières are fully borne out by the letters published from the original MSS. in the Advocates' Library by Lord Hailes, in a small volume entitled, "Memorials and Letters relating to the History of Britain in the Reign of James I." Glasgow, 1762.

[2] "Everybody is indignant at this Government; everybody hates and despises the King in an incredible manner, but their courage is so sunk, and the country so little favourable to revolt, that nothing but the uttermost climax of the evil can wake them from a lethargy."—Tillières (May 22, 1622) in Raumer, ii. 270, 271. In another despatch (January 6, 1622) Tillières writes of what he terms "the spirit of cowardice which a long peace has brought upon this country, but," he adds, "we cannot but believe that in some way or other this spirit will come to an end, and then be converted into fury."—Ibid., ii. 263-265. In the same despatch Tillières says—"The King has no other view than that of depriving the Parliament of its rights, and thinks he has attained his end when he has scolded it. This design was put into his head during the lifetime of the treasurer, Cecil [Earl of Salisbury], who, on account of his mal-administration, was afraid of such an overseer as the Parliament."

"To be honoured," says the "Hieron" of Xenophon, "is the greatest of earthly blessings, when a man obtains honour from the spontaneous voice of freemen. But a despot enjoys no such satisfaction. He lives like a criminal under sentence of death by every one. He can neither endure his present condition nor escape from it. The best thing he can do is to hang himself."[1]

That the Tudors and the Stuarts did not obtain honour from the spontaneous voice of freemen is abundantly manifested by their use of the rack. No writer of their time could say so, indeed, except under the garb of fiction; and the words which were put by Shakespeare into the mouth of Macbeth were really applicable to the tyrants under whom Shakespeare lived—for tyrants who used the rack must not look to have honour, love, obedience; but only mouth-honour, which the people they oppressed would refuse if they dared.

If Plato had written his "Republic" and Xenophon his "Hieron" under the reign of the rack, which lasted in England for some two hundred years, even though they had not published those works, they would have been first racked and then executed for high treason. Haywarde; but for Bacon's turning aside the Queen's anger by a jest, would have been put to the rack by Elizabeth for what Hume calls a most innocent performance.[2] And Peacham, as

---

[1] Grote's "Plato and the other Companions of Sokrates," iii. 573-575. The words of Xenophon which Mr. Grote has condensed into the sentence, "The best thing he can do is to hang himself," are,—'Ἀλλ' εἴπερ τῳ ἄλλῳ λυσιτελεῖ ἀπάγξασθαι, ἴσθι ὅτι τυράννῳ ἔγωγε εὑρίσκω μάλιστα τοῦτο λυσιτελοῦν ποιῆσαι.—Xen. Hier., vii. 513. The "Hieron" describes a supposed conversation between the poet Simonides and Hieron the despot of Syracuse, who had personally known both the life of a private citizen and that of a despot.

[2] "The Queen's manner," says Hume, "of trying and punishing Haywarde for treason could easily have been executed, let his book have been ever so innocent. While so many terrors hung over the people, no jury durst have

before mentioned, was put to the rack by James for a sermon neither preached nor published, and which assuredly contained no picture so dark and revolting of the minds of tyrants as that drawn by Plato and Xenophon. Imagine the fury of a Tudor or a Stuart if a writer had introduced Henry VIII. or James I. describing his condition as Xenophon has made "Hieron" describe *his* condition, with its climax—"The best thing he can do is to hang himself." The description given by the French ambassador Tillières of the patience with which England submitted to the misgovernment and tyranny of James I., might almost lead to the conclusion that the long reign of the rack had done its work so effectually as to change the character of Englishmen, and give them the servile disposition of Asiatics.[1] But such a conclusion would have been false; for the spirit of Englishmen was not dead, though it might seem to be so. It only slept, and

acquitted a man when the court was resolved to have him condemned. The practice, also, of not confronting witnesses with the prisoner gave the crown lawyers all imaginable advantage over him."—Appendix III. "The jails were full of prisoners; and these unhappy victims of *public* jealousy were thrown into dungeons and treated in the most cruel manner without their being able to obtain any remedy from law."—Ibid. It is very remarkable that a man of such acuteness, and even originality as a thinker, as Hume, should have cheated himself with words, as Hume often did. It will be observed that, in the sentence last quoted, he calls those victims of the tyranny of the individual who happened to be on the throne at the time the "victims of *public* jealousy." Hume says in his autobiography, "It is ridiculous to consider the English constitution before the Revolution of 1688 as a regular plan of liberty." Observe the reasoning; because the English constitution under the Plantagenets was not a *regular plan of liberty*, the two first Stuarts were to be backed up in their attempt to make it a *regular plan of slavery*. Hume admits, *and seems to regret*, that it was *very nearly* a regular plan of slavery under the Tudors, and yet he defends the Stuarts for attempting to make it *altogether* a regular plan of slavery.

[1] A few days before Buckingham was stabbed by Felton, some of his friends advised him to wear some secret defensive armour. "It needs not," said Buckingham; "there are no Roman spirits left."—D'Ewes's *Autobiography*, i. 381.

was to have, before many years passed over, a terrible awakening. And even before that awakening came, the hatred, rising to fury, of the populace of London towards the Duke of Buckingham, and their behaviour on his murder by Felton, showed that they viewed a tyrannicide very much as the Greeks of Xenophon's time did.[1]

It appears, then, that the English kings employed torture, subversion of the English law of evidence, and fraudulent proceedings in the election of the English representative body, in order to establish an absolute despotism in England. All these acts of fraud, and force, and inhuman cruelty were unable to break the spirit of the English people, who finally, after defeating in many battles the man who had persisted in attempting to enslave them, executed him, not as Edward II. and Richard II. had been slain, in darkness and mystery, as if the deed were a deed of darkness, but in front of his own palace in open day.

It has been said that the personal tastes and appetites of rulers have been insisted upon more than their historical importance warrants. To this it may be answered, that to the personal tastes and appetites of King John England is indebted for Magna Charta; to those of Henry III. for the rise of the English House of Commons; to those of James I. and Charles I. for what measure of civil and religious liberty the English people at present enjoy. But further, it is a not unimportant inquiry, What are the effects produced by placing human beings in such a position as that in which the Plantagenets, Tudors, and Stuarts were placed, upon those

---

[1] Mr. Forster shows that both King James and Buckingham viewed with approbation assassination for political purposes. Forster's Life of Sir John Eliot, ii. 349, 375. Second edition. London, John Murray, 1865.

human beings themselves? When we look at some of those effects, we are driven to the conclusion that it is unjust to place any human being in a position where the temptations to commit crime are so great as to be irresistible; and when we see men murdering their nearest relations for the sake of a crown, as King John and King Richard III. are admitted, and others are said, to have done, we may conclude that such persons would not scruple to murder hundreds or thousands of those, not their relations, who stood in the way to the objects of their ambition. Lord Macaulay has pronounced James II. to be the worst of the Stuarts. Who was the worst of the Tudors? might be a curious question. And when we turn our attention to the question, Who was the worst of the Plantagenets? we find ourselves embarrassed by the number of claims to that pre-eminence. There is John, who murdered his nephew; there is Richard III., who murdered his two nephews, his brother, and several cousins; there is Elizabeth, the daughter of Edward IV., who, instead of aversion, showed the utmost impatience for the proposed marriage with her uncle Richard III., the murderer of her two brothers. The family of Plantagenet has produced a considerable number—few families have produced an equal number—of men of courage and ability; and among those who think that there is no excess of wickedness for which courage and ability do not atone, even he who obtained the crown of England by a long series of murders, including the murder of his two nephews, may have admirers. Nevertheless, taking military success as the basis of our estimate, let us compare the results of the wars conducted by kings, some of them, Edward I., Edward III., and Henry V., men of military talent, and of the wars conducted by men who were not

Attempts to Reduce the People to Slavery. 35

kings. If all the achievements in war of all the Plantagenets, and all the Tudors, and all the Stuarts, were put into one scale of a balance, and the achievements in war of Fairfax, Cromwell, and Blake into the other, the latter would probably be found to outweigh the former.

When the army of the Long Parliament of England had beaten and broken in pieces all the armies which the King had brought against it, they sent up a Remonstrance to the Parliament demanding justice upon the King. In that Remonstrance they refer to those "Court maxims concerning the absolute impunity of kings, their accountableness to none on earth, and that they cannot do wrong," even though, as has been shown, they may murder their own nephews and cousins, "which principles were, the Remonstrance says, begot by the blasphemous arrogance of tyrants upon servile parasites, and remain in our law-books as heir-looms only of the conquest." They then declare, that if the English kings claim by right of conquest, God hath set aside that claim, and hath delivered the English people from that bondage which had oppressed them for six hundred years. And that army of the Parliament of England might truly say that they had delivered the people of England from a possibility of the kings of England ever again acting "as if," to borrow the words of the Remonstrance, "the whole people were made only for them and to serve their lusts."[1] For the army that sent this Remonstrance was not an army of mercenaries, but an army of Englishmen of the industrious classes, who knew what they fought for, and knew also what their enemies, whom they defeated, fought for. Some of the soldiers of that army might, like Milton, find themselves in their old age "fallen on evil days," and

[1] Parl. Hist., iii. 1111.

might almost feel that they had fought in vain. Nevertheless they had done deeds which were imperishable; and one effect of them was that that exercise of tyranny which has formed the subject of a considerable portion of this chapter, the use of torture, was never more ventured upon in England. They had given a warning which the son of the last divine-right King of England did not venture to disregard entirely, though he "was not a man whom any common warning would have restrained from the grossest violations of law. But it was no common warning that he had received. All around him were the recent signs of the vengeance of an oppressed nation; the fields on which the noblest blood of the island had been poured forth, the castles shattered by the cannon of the Parliamentary armies, the hall where sat the stern tribunal to whose bar had been led, through lowering ranks of pikemen, the captive heir of a hundred kings, the stately pilasters before which the great execution had been so fearlessly done in the face of heaven and earth."[1] These were the things that moved tyrants, who were unmoved by the wail and curses of millions, and who laughed at Parliamentary harangues and resolutions.

[1] Lord Macaulay's Essay on Sir William Temple.

CHAPTER II.

THE FIRST THREE PARLIAMENTS OF CHARLES I.

IN the sixteenth century the great fight for liberty, civil and religious, had been chiefly maintained by Holland and the Netherlands against Spain and Rome. But though the Hollanders, after a long and severe struggle, had in some measure attained their object, the fight was not over. Tyrants and bigots had not yet abandoned their grand scheme of enslaving mankind, and the seventeenth century was to witness a renewal of the great conflict. This time, a wider space, a greener field, was to be given for the deadly combat than the swamps and dykes of Holland and the Netherlands, and the combatants were to be more equally matched than when the peasants and burghers of the Netherlands were opposed, at tremendous disadvantage, to the disciplined valour and native ferocity of the Spanish infantry, directed by the strategic genius of Alva and of Farnese. Moreover, a most important result was to be obtained. In the Netherlands struggle it might seem to have been demonstrated that weavers, brewers, and the like, could never be a match as soldiers for princes, nobles, and gentlemen. In the English struggle a brewer or gentleman-farmer—no matter whether he was a brewer or not, he was certainly a gentleman-farmer—proved himself a soldier and a commander, beside whose exploits the deeds of Alva and Farnese look like those of a butcher killing sheep; and, out of a collection of "mean tradesmen, brewers, tailors, goldsmiths, shoemakers, and the like,"[1] this Englishman made an army to which, even by the admission of its mortal enemies whom it had defeated and broken in pieces, "victory was entailed, and which, humanly speaking, could hardly fail of conquest whithersoever it should be led; an army whose order and discipline, whose sobriety and manners, whose courage and success, made it famous and terrible over the world."[2]

James I. died on the 27th of March 1625, and was succeeded by Charles I. Although historical truth can now be put forth to a far greater extent than it could half a century ago, the question of paternity raised by the statement of Sir Edward Peyton[3] respecting two of the sons of Anne of Denmark, even if capable of solution, which it is not, could only be useful as throwing light on the state of morals of the European courts of that age; and we have evidence of an unexceptionable kind without using any which is of an inferior value. Besides the unequivocal language in many of the letters of Count Tillières, the French ambassador, we have the authority of Mrs. Hutchinson,[4] whose words forcibly describe the character of the court of James I. and the influence of that court in setting the fashion in morals to the English nobility and gentry. Now the influence of a court in setting fashions, either in dress, manners, or morals, being so great, we may form at least a faint and imperfect idea of the elements in which moved the characters that appeared

---

[1] Denzil Holles's Memoirs, p. 149. London, 1699.

[2] From the Lord Chancellor Hyde's speech to the Houses at the adjournment, Sept. 13, 1660.—Parl. Hist., iv. 123, 124.

[3] See Sir Edward Peyton's "Divine Catastrophe of the House of Stuart," in a work in two vols. 8vo, published in Edinburgh in 1811, entitled "Secret History of the Court of James I.," with notes and introductory remarks by the editor, known to be Sir Walter Scott, though the publication is anonymous.

[4] Memoirs of Colonel Hutchinson. Bohn's edition, London, 1854.

The First Three Parliaments of Charles I. 39

upon the scene in the great English Rebellion of the seventeenth century. For it must be borne in mind that Charles I., though sometimes held up as a contrast to James I., did in reality evince no disapprobation, but rather the reverse, of the morals of James I.'s court, as shown by the fact of his adopting as his favourite and all-powerful minister James I.'s minion, the Duke of Buckingham. While the courtiers and Royalists moved in the moral atmosphere above indicated, the Puritans, who were opposed to them, moved in an atmosphere which, whether it was so or not, received the name of pure, though the name was given in derision, as contrasted with the other, which might be described, with no small degree of truth, as foul and polluted.

Those who say that insincerity or faithlessness was the chief fault of Charles I., and the chief cause of his disasters, as well as those who vindicate him from the charge of insincerity, appear to forget what were the principles of government which prevailed among the ruling families of Europe during the sixteenth and seventeenth centuries. According to those principles, sincerity was regarded as vice or folly or weakness ; insincerity as wisdom or virtue. This is strikingly exhibited in the enumeration given by Machiavelli of the cherished familiars of the "glorious Alexander,"[1] as he designates Pope Alexander VI. (Borgia). Machiavelli only mentions as the favourite vices of Borgia, "sensuality, simony, and cruelty," but not faithlessness.

[1] The first "Decennale" of Machiavelli thus alludes satirically to the death of Alexander VI. :—
> "Maló Valenza ; e per aver riposo
> Portato fù frà l'anime beate
> Lo spirto d Alessandro glorioso
> Del qual seguirno le sante pedate
> Tré sue familiari e care ancelle,
> Lussuria, simonia, e crudeltade."

As an Italian of that age, he might view faithlessness not as a vice, but as a virtue. But it is only fair to him to let him give his own account of the matter. In the 18th chapter of his " Principe," Machiavelli begins by observing that everybody knows how laudable it is for a prince not to commit breaches of faith; but yet, he adds, "we have seen in our own times that those princes who have cared little about faith and have known how to deceive mankind have effected great things." He thence concludes that, though if all men were good a different course might be followed, as they were bad, and would not keep faith with you, you must not keep faith with them, but must rule both by force and fraud, and adopt the ways both of the lion and the fox. He then cites the example of Pope Alexander VI., who did nothing else but deceive men, and never thought of any other means, alway confirming his promises with the most solemn oaths, and always succeeding in deceiving those with whom he dealt. It is reported of this Pope's son, Cæsar Borgia, that notwithstanding his often proved perfidy, he had a joviality and apparent simplicity of manner which amused men and put them off their guard, thus throwing them more readily into his trap. King James I.'s "Kingcraft" was by no means so dim, faint, and feeble a copy of Borgianism, as has been generally supposed. The man who could render some of his actions the "darkest puzzles in history," as the affair called the Gowrie Conspiracy and the murder of Sir Thomas Overbury have been termed, must be allowed to have possessed some genius for plots. King Charles I. was very far from showing the genius for plots evinced by James, though some writers attribute to the former abilities very superior to those of the latter. But though Charles's plots were all or almost all utter failures, he showed himself, quite as much as any Borgia or Valois, a disciple of Machiavelli, inasmuch as he was unboundedly liberal of promises, because he never intended to be bound by any, and thus far at least transacted business with "a princely intelligence such as private persons cannot imitate."[1]

Not long before the accession of Charles to the throne

[1] This is a phrase of Queen Elizabeth's. "Princes," said her Majesty in her reply to the Netherland envoys, February 7, N.S. 1587, "transact business in a certain way, and with a princely intelligence such as private persons cannot imitate."—Hague Achives, MS., cited in Motley's "History of the United Netherlands," ii. 199. Her Majesty also said on the same occasion, "Among us princes we are not wont to make such long orations as you do, but you ought to be content with the few words that we bestow upon you."—Ibid., p. 200. In the year 1502 Machiavelli was sent by the Government of Florence to make professions of friendship to Cæsar Borgia, and to watch his movements. Machiavelli was three months in the court and camp of Borgia, which may be considered as the most perfect school of that policy which he developed in his treatise "Del Principe;" and which has been admired and imitated by so many tyrants since. Machiavelli's letters written during this mission are curious and interesting. Two of the greatest masters of the art of lying were pitted against each other. Borgia hated the Florentines as much as the Florentines hated Borgia. But they were both kept in check by the fear of France, and they made the most friendly professions towards each other. Borgia even assumed a confidential tone, and told Machiavelli of the treachery of his former friends, who began to be alarmed at the increasing ambition and cruelty of Borgia. While the negotiations were going on, Machiavelli witnessed some examples of the "princely intelligence" with which Borgia "transacted business," one of which was this : On the last day of December 1502, Borgia, followed by Machiavelli, marched with his troops to Sinigaglia, where the Orsini, Vitellozzo, and Oliverotto were waiting for him by appointment to have a conference. As soon as his troops entered the town, Borgia arrested those chiefs, strangled two of them that very night, but kept the Orsini in prison till he heard that his father, the Pope, had secured the person of their relative, Cardinal Orsini, at Rome, when he put them also to death. Borgia then sent for Machiavelli, and said he had done a great service to Florence in ridding the world of those men who were the sowers of discord. It may, I think, be inferred from the way in which Bacon tells the story in his "Apophthegms," that he and his master admired the "fine art" with which Borgia "transacted this business." In the agreement between Borgia and the lords of Romagna, Bacon says, "There was an article that he should not call them at any time all together in person. The meaning was, that knowing his dangerous nature, if he meant them treason, some one might be free to

of England, Cardinal Richelieu had commenced his memorable administration of the government of France—a man compared to whom, in all the qualities of mind which in that age were considered requisite for state affairs—at least for making a king absolute and his subjects slaves—in craft and resolution, in the bold and skilful management of falsehood, his contemporary enemies and oppressors of mankind were pigmies. The marriage of the Princess Henrietta of France with King Charles had been promoted by Richelieu as a means of securing the neutrality of England in a war against the Huguenots. When Charles married the Princess Henrietta by proxy, the Duke of Buckingham was sent to conduct the Queen to England. In consequence of intrigues at the French court, not political, respecting which it is not very easy and not very important to know the exact truth, Richelieu and Buckingham did not part on good terms. Whatever may have been Buckingham's feeling towards Richelieu, it may be supposed that contempt would be too largely mingled in that of Richelieu towards Buckingham to permit it to attain to the dignity of hatred.

All Richelieu's instructions to the French ambassadors display superiority of intellect, sagacity to perceive, and dexterity to hit the decisive point of a question. He is indifferent about trifles, and never looks for important re-

revenge the rest. Nevertheless, he did with such fine art and fair carriage win their confidence, that he brought them all together to council at Cinigagli, where he murdered them all. This act being related unto Pope Alexander, his father, by a cardinal, as a thing happy but very perfidious, the Pope said, " It was they that had broke their covenant first in coming all together." It is superfluous to talk about want of sincerity in a man brought up, whether in a court or in any place, where Borgia's or Elizabeth's or James's manner of "transacting business" was called "princely intelligence," and esteemed a fine thing, and where the first words heard were, " Qui nescit dissimulare nescit regnare," or "The science of reigning is the science of lying."

sults from insignificant things. Anne of Austria in this matter showed herself inferior to Elizabeth in good sense. When the Lord Treasurer, Lord Burleigh, in the latter part of his life, was much afflicted with gout, Queen Elizabeth always made him sit down in her presence, saying on such occasions, " My lord, we make use of you not for your bad legs, but for your good head." Anne of Austria little understood the importance of a good head if she preferred Buckingham and Mazarin to Richelieu. Richelieu's good head did not with her atone for his bandy legs. But, after all, the world is governed by heads and not by legs.

There could hardly be a stronger proof of the truth of the observation of Tillières, that "the extravagance of the minister's humour and the mental constitution of this weak King exceed all imagination,"[1] than that they should quarrel with such a minister as Richelieu, instead of cultivating to the utmost his friendship, and thereby obtaining some knowledge of the art, which Richelieu was then practising, of making a king absolute and his subjects slaves. Instead of this, Buckingham made this weak King declare war against France. And on what grounds, it may be asked? When he found that, if he executed his purpose of returning to Paris, he should, as Richelieu wrote to the French ambassador in England, meet with an ill reception, he flew into a passion, and swore "that he would see the Queen in spite of all the power of France;" and from that moment determined to engage England in a war with that kingdom.[2]

The first Parliament of Charles, which met on the 18th of June 1625, showed little disposition to supply the King with money for the prosecution of his wars either with

[1] Count Tillières to the King of France, August 28 and 31, 1625. Raumer, ii. 294.
[2] Clarendon, i. 38.

Spain or with France. Sir Edward Coke and Sir Robert Cotton, or rather Sir John Eliot, to whom Cotton, who had intended to speak, handed the precedents he had collected, urged without effect a return to the ancient constitutional course for supplying the wants of the Government without overburthening the subject with taxation. "The King's ordinary charge in Edward III.'s time," said Coke, "was borne by the King's ordinary revenues;"[1] and Sir Robert Cotton insisted much on "acts of resumption of the crown lands" as "the just and frequent way" to supply the wants of the Government, "for all," he said, "from Henry III. but one, till the 6th Henry VIII., have used it."[2] The Commons having proceeded to the consideration of grievances, and having postponed the supply, the King dissolved the Parliament. The Lord Keeper Williams exercised all his abilities to no purpose to prevent this measure—so characteristic of the King and his minister. In the course of his argument to the Duke of Buckingham, Williams used these remarkable words—"No man that is wise will show himself angry with the people of England."[3]

[1] Parl. Hist., ii. 11, 12. (ed. 1807).

[2] Ibid., ii. 14-17, (ed. 1807). "It was," says Mr. Forster, "Cotton's intention to speak in the debate, and with that view he had collected precedents. But he abandoned his original purpose, and handed over to Eliot the precedents he intended to have used. Eliot used them with decisive effect; and the speech in which he did so, now first printed as his, is not only reported by him in his memoir, but has been found by me among other papers at Port Eliot in his own handwriting. Strange to say, however, almost the whole substance and much of the expression of this speech have already been printed in the Parliamentary Histories as delivered by Cotton (Parl. Hist., vi. 367-372, ed. 1763; Parl. Hist., ii. 14-17, ed. 1807); a mistake probably originating in the circumstance that a draft of the speech, as originally to have been spoken by himself, with matter suggested by Eliot, had been found among his papers when Charles's seizure and closing of his library broke the old man's heart, and was published by Howell in his *Cottoni Posthuma*, two years after Charles's death."—Forster's Life of Sir John Eliot, i. 412, 413, 2d edition. London: John Murray, 1865.

[3] Hacket's Life of Williams, part ii. p. 16.

Since the days of Caligula and his horse, which he is said to have destined for the consulship,[1] no greater insult has been offered to a nation than that which this King put upon the English people by thrusting forward as he did "that weak, violent, and dissolute adventurer, with no talents or acquirements but those of a mere courtier,"[2] and "of every talent of a minister utterly destitute,"[3] to whom in a great crisis of foreign and domestic politics had been intrusted not only the post of Prime Minister, but the command of all the fleets and armies of England. Thucydides has not shrunk from narrating a great expedition unwisely undertaken and unskilfully conducted, which, though it ended in defeat and disaster, may serve as a lesson and a warning to men. But it would be an insult to Nikias to compare him with Buckingham, and an insult to the Athenian democracy to compare it with the Stuarts; and men can learn nothing from the enterprises of such things as Stephano, Trinculo, and Caliban. Any one might predict as safely of the enterprises of Charles and Buckingham that they would terminate in disaster and disgrace, as that those of Stephano, Trinculo, and Caliban would terminate in a horse-pond. Can there be a doubt but that, if the other inhabitants of England had been brained like Charles and his minister, England would long since have disappeared from the catalogue of nations? Moreover, when we reflect to what circumstances this Buckingham owed his power over the mind of this King, his career, even if he had been an able instead of a very weak man, would have been about the most repulsive subject in the whole range of English history—a subject, in

---

[1] "Consulatum quoque traditur destinasse." Suet. Calig., cap. 55.
[2] Lord Macaulay's Essay on Lord Nugent's Memorials of Hampden.
[3] Hume's Hist., ch. xlix.

fact (to borrow the apt words of Lord Macaulay), "from which History averts her eyes, and which even Satire blushes to name."[1]

But it is fit that we should consider some of the incidents and consequences of those disgraceful expeditions. The fleet sent against Cadiz in the beginning of October 1625 consisted of eighty sail (with the addition of twenty Dutch), carrying 10,038 land forces. On the return of the fleet, the forces that returned from Cadiz were kept on foot and dispersed into several parts of the kingdom.[2] To the imposition of a general forced loan was added the outrage of billeting these soldiers in private houses.[3] "The companies," says Rushworth, "were scattered here and there in the bowels of the kingdom, and governed by martial law. The King gave commissions to the Lords-Lieutenants and their deputies in case of felonies, to proceed as in time of war; and some were executed by these commissions. Nevertheless the soldiers brake out in great disorders; they mastered the people, disturbed the peace of families, and the civil government of the land; there were frequent robberies, burglaries, rapes, rapines, murthers, and barbarous cruelties; unto some places they were sent as a punishment, and wherever they came there was a general outcry. The highways were dangerous, and the markets unfrequented; they were a terror to all, an undoing to many."[4]

Denzil Holles, writing from Dorchester to his brother-in-law, Sir Thomas Wentworth, afterwards the celebrated Earl of Strafford, under date August 9, 1627, gives a picture of the state of England under the government of this King Charles, which resembles that of a country

[1] Essay on Frederic the Great.
[3] Rushworth, i. 417, 418.
[2] Rushworth, i. 196, 197.
[4] Ibid., i. 419, 420.

overrun by a victorious enemy. "Since these wars," he says, "all trading is dead, our wools lie upon our hands, our men are not set on work, our ships lie in our ports unoccupied, to be sold as cheap as firewood; land, sheep, cattle, nothing will yield money, not to speak of other petty inconveniences we have found by the soldiers' ravishing men's wives and daughters, killing and carrying away beefs and sheep off the ground (stealing of poultry was not worth the speaking of), killing and robbing men upon the highway, nay, in fairs and towns (for to meet a poor man coming from the market with a pair of new shoes, or a basket of eggs or apples, and take them from him, was but sport and merriment), and a thousand such other petty pranks; come a dozen of them to a Justice of Peace and Deputy-Lieutenant's house, and make my lady give them five or six pieces to be gone."[1]

These accounts of the manner in which Charles and Buckingham governed England are fully borne out by the MS. evidence in the State Paper Office. Thus on March 1, 1628, Captain John Watts and four other officers of the regiment of Sir Thomas Fryer, stationed in the county of Dorset, write to Sir Thomas Fryer that divers officers of his regiment met the Commissioners at Blandford to complain of their soldiers being turned out of their billets by violence, the billeters alleging that they would not provide any billets, but that the soldiers must shift for themselves. "The soldiers are thus reduced either to steal or starve. The gentry contemn the Deputy-Lieutenants' warrants for billeting, and are ill precedents to the commonalty. If some speedy course be not taken, the greatest part of the men will run from their colours."[2]

---
[1] Strafford's Letters and Dispatches, i. 40.
[2] 1628, March 1. MS., State Paper Office.

The billeting of soldiers in private houses was a proceeding which even Hume does not defend. "The soldiers," he says, "were billeted upon private houses, contrary to custom, which required that in all ordinary cases they should be quartered in inns and public-houses. Those who had refused or delayed the loan were sure to be loaded with a great number of these dangerous and disorderly guests."[1]

The second Parliament of Charles met on the 6th of February 1625-26.

It has been remarked that "nature, fertile in everything, does not reproduce the same physiognomies and does not repeat the same events."[2] Nevertheless, there is a considerable resemblance between some features of the times of Simon de Montfort and those of Oliver Cromwell. Henry III. and Charles I. were the sons of two of the worst kings and worst men that have ever appeared upon earth. Yet in the four centuries between Henry III. and Charles I., servility and falsehood had made such progress, that while Archbishop Laud and Williams speak of James as Virgil and Horace speak of Augustus, as if he were, what Bacon terms him, "a mortal god on earth," the earlier annalists say that John, when he ceased to pollute the earth, descended into hell to contaminate the fiends.[3] Henry and Charles, the sons, at least the heirs, of these two men, John and James, were both very weak men, and both very much under the influence of foreign wives. But Henry had a son of great energy and great military talent. A consequence of this was that at Evesham Simon de Montfort, not however

---

[1] Hume, Hist., chap. l.; Rushworth, i. 419.
[2] Frederick II. *Avant Propos* to his *Histoire de la Guerre de Sept Ans.*
[3] Sordida fœdatur, fœtente Johanne, gehenna.—Scriptores rerum Angliarum.

before he had done his work, "with all his peerage fell." Charles had no such son, and he had himself no military or any other kind of genius. John Churchill was not born till more than a year after the stern Puritans had cut off Charles's head; and if he had been born in the same year with Oliver Cromwell, it is very doubtful if even his military genius would have been able to overcome the forces, moral and intellectual as well as physical, which the genius of Oliver Cromwell brought into action.

Sir John Eliot, in a speech printed from the original MS. at Port Eliot in Mr. Forster's "Life of Sir John Eliot," cited two precedents with which he had been furnished by Sir Robert Cotton from his invaluable collection of ancient records; and those precedents gave such offence to King Charles, that this speech of Eliot was afterwards referred to as that in which the two precedents were quoted, or as the speech of the two precedents. The first precedent had reference to the misgovernment of Henry III., the second to that of Richard II. It is the first precedent quoted by Eliot that has a remarkable coincidence with what I have said in the preceding paragraph. "The first precedent," said Eliot, "was in 16th Henry III., when the Commons, being required to make a supply unto the King, excused themselves; because, says the record, they saw all things disordered by those that were about him. But when, upon their advice, he had resumed the lands of the crown that were unjustly and unnecessarily given away; when he had yielded his ministers up to question; when he had not spared that great officer of his court, Hubert de Burgh, a favourite never to be paralleled but now, having been the minion both to the King then living and to his father which was dead; when they had seen, as another author says, those sponges of the Commonwealth squeezed into the King's coffers; then, though they had formerly denied it, they did freely grant an aid."[1]

Next day, the King sent to request the Houses to attend him on the following morning at Whitehall, whither they went at nine o'clock on the 29th of March. After the Lord Keeper Coventry had made a long speech, telling the Commons that the condition they had appended to their vote of subsidies was a dishonour to his Majesty; that the conduct of their debates had been insufferable, in permitting his greatest servant to be traduced by men who neither by years nor education could attain to that depth; that they had allowed his Council, his government, and his servants to be paralleled with times of the worst exception; that this violation of royal rights under colour of Parliamentary liberty was not his view of the uses of a Parliament; that if they did not vote a sufficient and unconditional supply, they must expect to be dissolved; and that he should expect their final answer (that day being Wednesday) on Saturday next. "Remember," said the King, when Coventry had ended, "that Parliaments are altogether in my power for their calling, sitting, and dissolution; and therefore, as I find the fruits of them to be good or evil, they are to continue or not to be." Well might Mr. Forster say of this exhibition of King Charles's opinions respecting Parliament—"Sir Robert Cotton could have produced no precedent, in his record of eight hundred years, for such a pretension as that. The forms of the constitution all men knew; but that they could be applied to the entire abolition of Parliaments, no man had ever suspected."[2]

---

[1] Forster's Life of Sir John Elliot, i. 522, 2d edition. John Murray, London, 1865.

[2] Ibid., i. 527. In a note, p. 528, Mr. Forster quotes these words from

The principal business which occupied the Commons in this Parliament was the impeachment of the Duke of Buckingham. In the debates connected with this business, Sir John Eliot made those speeches against Buckingham which may be said to have been as fatal to himself as Cicero's speeches against Antony, particularly that (published though not spoken) known as the second *Philippic*, were to Cicero. Cicero's death, by the swords of Antony's soldiers, may be considered as preferable to the slow, lingering death of Eliot in his prison in the Tower. And this is the only case in English history that affords a parallel to the case of Cicero's eloquence costing him his life. Yet the eloquence of Eliot shows but faint and dim compared to that power of invective displayed in the second *Philippic;* and it would almost seem that if Cicero had hit no harder than Eliot has done, "Antoni gladios potuit contemnere." But the oratorical power of Cicero has set a brand upon Antony that will last as long as the world lasts, while the speeches of Eliot are comparatively little known. Cicero's second *Philippic* abounds with scandalous anecdotes of the life of Antony, which even if, as some critics have thought, exaggerated by the malice of the orator, give in a few strokes a vivid picture of the orgies of Antony—a very repulsive picture indeed of Roman manners at that time; yet not more repulsive than Eliot might have given of the orgies of James I., at which this King Charles and this Duke of Buckingham were present, and assisting. What a picture is given in these thirteen words, "Natabant pavimenta vino; made-

a letter of Mede to Stuteyile—"Sir Robert Cotton's books are threatened to be taken away, because he is accused to impart ancient precedents to the Lower House." Mr. Forster adds—"The threat was beyond doubt connected with the two precedents vouched by Eliot, which had so embittered the King's resentments."

bant parietes; ingenui pueri cum meritoriis, scorta inter matresfamilias versabantur."[1] And yet Tillières has given a dim outline of still darker orgies held at the house of this Buckingham when he feasted King James and Prince Charles; and the words of Milton intimate that he knew something of them as well as Tillières, for Milton's words of Charles are, "Quem cum Duce Bucchingamio *flagitiis omnibus* co-opertum novimus."[2] Cicero, moreover, makes one terrible charge[3] against Antony, the sting of which probably more than anything else in the invective cost Cicero his life. But this was a sting that went deep; deeper from Cicero's expressly stating that he spoke from personal knowledge; for even in that depraved age of Rome, men who shrunk from no vice shrunk from the brand of disgrace implied in such a charge. Now Eliot—if he had had the liberty of speech which Cicero had, or *thought* he had, for the penalty Cicero paid for it—his life—showed that he was on dangerous ground—might have brought such a charge against Buckingham with much more truth and force than Cicero brought it against Antony. And Buckingham had literally nothing to be weighed against it; even his most enthusiastic admirers, if he has any such, would hardly venture to assert that he was such a soldier and such an orator as Antony was. For it is admitted that Antony was a good soldier; and his speech over the body of Cæsar, of which Shakespeare has given so noble a version, proves that he was a most skilful mover of the passions of men. And though Antony might be a man stained with vices numerous and hideous enough to form a groundwork for the terrible picture which Cicero in the second *Philippic* has drawn of his life, he might, as compared with Buckingham, be termed a great man—a man pos-

[1] Cic. Phil., 2. 41.   [2] Pro Pop. Ang. Def., c. 4.   [3] Cic. Phil., 2. 18.

sessed of military and political talent sufficient to enable him to contest with the second Cæsar the empire of the world.[1]

But Buckingham and his master were too powerful for the Commons at that time. Such was Buckingham's insolent sense of impunity, that during the speech of Sir Dudley Digges at the bar of the Lords he sat jeering at his expressions. Sergeant Glanville was so provoked by his insolence, that, turning to the Duke, he exclaimed—"My Lord, do you jeer me? Are these things to be jeered at? My Lord, I can show you when a man of greater blood than your Lordship, as high in place and power, and as deep in the favour of the King as you, hath been hanged for as small a crime as the least of these articles contain."[2] There had indeed been in England a time when such a criminal as Buckingham would have been hanged. But it was not the year 1626, though the time was to return sooner than might have been expected, as the fate of Strafford in 1641 witnessed.

In one of his speeches Eliot compared Buckingham to Sejanus. The allusion to Sejanus appears to have given great offence to the King. "Implicitly," he exclaimed, "he must intend me for Tiberius."[3] And both Eliot and Digges were committed to the Tower for the freedom with which they had spoken. The Commons highly resented the imprisonment of their two members, and resolved "not

[1] It has been said that on the day before the battle of Actium, Antony had thirteen kings at his levee.
[2] Meade in Ellis's Original Letters, iii. 226, 2d edition. Mr. Forster says, "An obvious mistake is made by the letter-writer in substituting Glanville for Digges."—Life of Sir John Eliot, i. 535, note. London: Longmans & Co., 1864. The remark, however, seems more like what might be expected from Glanville, a learned constitutional lawyer, than from Digges.
[3] Harleian MSS., 383—Letter of Meade, dated May 11, 1626, cited in Forster's Life of Sir John Eliot, p. 45. London, 1836.

to do any more business till they were righted in their privileges."[1] Sir Dudley Carleton, Vice-Chamberlain of the King's household, observing a sullen silence, as he termed it, in the House, made a speech in which, after alluding to the King's threat to "use new counsels if his demands were not unconditionally granted," he thus proceeded: "Now, I pray you consider what these new counsels are and may be: I fear to declare those that I conceive. In all Christian kingdoms you know that Parliaments were in use antiently, by which their kingdoms were governed in a most flourishing manner, until the monarchs began to know their own strength, and seeing the turbulent spirit of their Parliaments, at length they, by little and little, began to stand upon their prerogatives, and at last overthrew the Parliaments throughout Christendom, except here only with us. And indeed you would count it a great misery if you knew the subjects in foreign countries as well as myself, to see them look, not like our nation, with store of flesh on their backs, but like so many ghosts, and not men, being nothing but skin and bones, with some thin cover to their nakedness, and wearing only wooden shoes on their feet; so that they cannot eat much, or wear good clothes, but they must pay and be taxed unto the King for it. This is a misery beyond expression, and that which yet we are free from."[2] This is a most important exposition, and coming from the quarter it came from, proves that Charles had cast his eyes on the existing state of the Continent with a view of assimilating his power to that of the Continental despots. And it also proves that Charles, true to his nature, was not deterred by the contemplation of the

[1] Parl. Hist., ii. 119.
[2] Rushworth, i. 359; Parl. Hist., ii. 120, 121.

grievous consequences of such a change to the English nation.

Of the sophistry to which, like Hobbes, Hume descends at times, though like Hobbes also so able to expose sophistry in others, the way in which he sums up his character of Buckingham is an example. "His faults and blemishes," says Hume, "were in many respects very great; but rapacity and avarice were vices with which he was entirely unacquainted."[1] The mode in which Hume in this sentence has connected rapacity and avarice might seem to convey the meaning that he who has not the miser's rage for hoarding or saving could not, or would not, be likely to have the robber's rapacity. But there is no fact better established than that where prodigality is boundless, rapacity is boundless too. It has been observed in all the ages of which man has a record, that the robber or pirate, by sea and land, in court, camp city, or parliament, the man who seeks to get by force or fraud the fruit of other men's labour, while he is "sui profusus," is "aliêni appetens"—if, indeed, that which he has thus acquired can ever justly be called his own, being the fruit not of industry or honest labour, but of rapine or fraud.

The object of Charles was to make himself an absolute king. To attain this end he required money; and if he had been a man of even average sagacity in adapting means to ends, he would have seen the necessity of exercising the utmost economy and frugality; whereas to allow Buckingham to waste or squander the public money as he did, argues on the part of Charles not merely the want of profound sagacity, but the possession of profound stupidity. If Buckingham had spent the money he got as Lord High-Admiral, not in fine clothes and jewels, houses and

[1] History of England, ch. 50.

furniture, and sumptuous banquets, but in rendering the English navy thoroughly efficient, it is possible that the struggle of the English nation against the English King, Charles I., might have been a much harder one than it was, and that its termination in favour of the nation might have been at least considerably postponed. Charles felt that he could lie as boldly as Borgia or Richelieu; but he did not seem to be aware that something else was needed for the attainment of his ends. It certainly does seem a high pitch of audacity and arrogance in a man of such a mental constitution to fancy that he could do what the ablest of the Plantagenets and the Tudors had failed in doing,—reduce the people of England to a condition of absolute slavery. Such a man seemed designed by Providence to serve as a warning example to all who might in after-ages be tempted to make war against the "indestructible prerogatives of mankind."

We have seen in the preceding chapter the use made of the pulpits by the Tudor Government, exemplified in a striking manner by the paper preserved in the State Paper Office, entitled, "Directions to the Preachers," and prepared for the purpose of blackening the memory of the Earl of Essex after the Tudor Queen had succeeded in depriving him of life. The pulpits were now resorted to for the purpose of inducing the people to give money to the King, under the name of a loan; and Laud was employed to draw up instructions to the clergy of the Church of England. In accordance with these instructions, Sibthorp, vicar of Brackley, in Northamptonshire, composed, preached, and published a sermon on the occasion, wherein he says, "If princes command anything which subjects may not perform, because it is against the laws of God or of nature, or impossible, yet subjects are bound to undergo the punishment without either resistance, or railing, or reviling, and so to yield a passive obedience where they cannot exhibit an active one. I know no other case, but one of these three, wherein a subject may excuse himself with passive obedience; but in all others he is bound to active obedience."[1] And Dr. Roger Manwaring, one of the King's chaplains, and vicar of St. Giles-in-the-Fields, preached two sermons before the King and court, in which he maintained that the King is not bound to observe the laws of the land; that his royal command in imposing loans and taxes, without the consent of Parliament, obliges the subjects' consciences upon the pain of eternal damnation; that the authority of Parliament is not necessary for the raising of aids and subsidies, which are due to kings by natural and original law and justice.[2] Manwaring, having expounded his political speculations, thus states his theological conclusions, from which it will be seen that, with him and his royal master, "*the utility of religion*" was a much more simple question than some philosophers seem to imagine, being summed up in the doctrine of giving all you possess, not to feed the poor, but to feed the King and his court. "Of all relations," says Manwaring, "the first and original is between the Creator and the creatures; the next between husband and wife; the third between parents and children; the fourth between lord and servants: from all which forenamed respects there did arise that most high, sacred, and transcendent relation between king and subject."[3] "A strange expression," observes Hacket, "which calls the last a transcendent relation, arising out of all the former, when the first is between the Creator and the

---

[1] Rushworth, i. 422; Whitelock, p. 8.   [2] Ibid.   [3] Rushworth, i. 423.

creature."¹ Hacket further observes, that "the venom of the new doctrine would have reduced the people to the state of Turkey."² This last comparison being in a different manner used by Hume in his third "Appendix," when he says that the English government under Elizabeth "bore some resemblance to that of Turkey," suggests the reflection that Hume is much more right than some of his opponents in his description of the government of Elizabeth. It is futile to cite Fortescue and other constitutional writers to prove the theoretical freedom of England, when it can be proved, as has been done in the preceding chapter, that the government was almost a pure despotism. But the wonder is that Hume, who saw this, should have set up as the advocate of Charles I., who laboured to make the government not merely almost, but altogether, a pure despotism. As Lord Macaulay has remarked, "Never, in our history, had there been an interval of eleven years without a Parliament. Only once had there been an interval of even half that length. This fact alone is sufficient to refute those who represent Charles as having merely trodden in the footsteps of the Plantaganets and Tudors."³ And a further wonder is that Hume should have here stood forward as the advocate of a man who certainly would have cut off his ears for his "Essay on Miracles." It would take an "Essay on Human Nature" more profound than Hume's to expound this paradox.

It is remarked by Fletcher of Saltoun that Charles made the mistake of attempting to seize the purse before he had made himself master of the sword. Charles, however, had sense enough to perceive that the drum ecclesiastic was not of itself quite sufficient for the accomplishment of his

---

¹ Hacket's Life of Williams, part ii. p. 74. ² Ibid., p. 76.
³ History of England, i. 42.

purpose, the complete command of his subjects' purses and consciences. Perceiving that, in order to assimilate his government to that of France, he required the assistance of a mercenary army, he secretly gave orders for providing arms and raising German troops to be brought into England, in addition to the force already kept up within the kingdom, in opposition to the constitutional laws of England. He accordingly remitted to the Continent a part of the money he had taken by various illegal means from his subjects, for the purpose of enabling him to gain a complete power over them and all they possessed.

Charles's third Parliament met on the 17th of March 1628.

In a debate in the House of Commons on the 2d of April 1628, Sir John Eliot having alluded to the unparalleled mismanagement and consequent disaster and disgrace in "those two great undertakings at Cadiz and Rhé," Sir Edward Coke delivered that remarkable speech in which he contrasted with her present condition the times when England under the Plantagenets successfully defended herself against far more numerous enemies than then threatened her. "When poor England stood alone," said Coke, " and had not the access of another kingdom, and yet had more and as potent enemies as now it hath, yet the King of England prevailed. In the Parliament Roll, 42d Edward III., the King and Parliament gave God thanks for the victory against the Kings of Scotland and France; he had them both in Windsor Castle as prisoners. What was the reason of that conquest? Four reasons were given :—1. The King was assisted by good counsel. 2. There were valiant men. 3. They were timely supplied. 4. Good employment. In 3d Richard II. the King was environed with Flemings, Scots, and French, and the King of England prevailed. In 17th Edward II. wars were in Ireland and Scotland, and yet the King of England prevailed, and thanks were given to God here."[1]

Well might Coke say, "When money is taken of our gift" under pretence of guarding the seas, "it may be diverted another way," when he recollected that England had then a Lord High Admiral who spent upon his own person and its incidents more than equipped and sent forth the fleet that destroyed the Spanish Armada. In his speech against the Duke of Buckingham, Sir John Eliot had said, "He intercepts, consumes, and exhausts the revenues of the crown, not only to satisfy his own lustful desires, but the luxury of others; and, by emptying the veins the blood should run in, he hath cast the body of the kingdom into a high consumption. Infinite sums of money, and mass of land exceeding the value of money, nay, even contributions in Parliament, have been heaped upon him; and how have they been employed? Upon costly furniture, sumptuous feasting, and magnificent building, the visible evidences of the express exhausting of the state."[2]

The third Parliament of Charles I. is memorable for having passed the Petition of Right, grounded on Magna Charta and other ancient statutes, particularly the numerous statutes confirming Magna Charta. Sir Edward Coke's words are, "Seven Acts of Parliament which indeed are thirty-seven, Magna Charta being confirmed thirty times."[3] "He might have said thirty-nine times, if Magna was confirmed thirty-two times, as he had said elsewhere."[4] It is important to observe that when Sir Edward Coke was fighting the Parliamentary fight against the crown in the

---

[1] Parl. Hist., ii. 255.
[2] Forster's Life of Sir John Eliot, pp. 43, 44. London, 1836.
[3] Parl. Hist., ii. 271.
[4] Coke, 2 Inst. proem.

House of Commons, all the precedents he cited are from the Plantagenet times. If any had existed to serve his purpose during the period the Tudors had occupied the English throne, Coke would certainly not have overlooked or neglected them. This fact furnishes tolerably conclusive evidence of the greatness of the change, almost amounting to a revolution, that had taken place in the English Government since the destruction in the Wars of the Roses of the ancient, warlike, and powerful nobility, and the inability of the Commons to be the check on the crown which the old nobility had been, had rendered the crown almost, though not altogether, absolute. Neither the later Plantagenets nor the Tudors had been able to change this "almost" into "altogether." And it was reserved for this King Charles, who will hardly be reckoned, even by his warmest admirers, as able a man as Edward IV., as Richard III., as Henry VII., or as Henry VIII., to rush upon ground where the boldest of those princes did not venture to tread.

The King had made a speech by the Lord Keeper desiring the Parliament to rely on the royal word for their liberties—a strange demand certainly when each confirmation of the great charter was a separate and distinct proof that the royal word was not to be relied on; for if the charter had not been broken it needed not to be confirmed. It thus appeared that the royal word was constantly liable to be broken. "Was it ever known," said Sir Edward Coke (May 4), "that general words were a sufficient satisfaction to particular grievances? Was ever a verbal declaration of the King *verbum regni* [a record of the kingdom]? When grievances be, the Parliament is to redress them. Did ever Parliament rely on messages? They put up petitions of their grievances, and the King ever answered them. The King's answer is very gracious, but what is the law of the realm? That is the question. I put no diffidence in his Majesty, but the King must speak by a record and in particulars, and not in general. Did you ever know the King's message come into a bill of subsidies? All succeeding kings will say, Ye must trust me as well as you did my predecessor, and trust my messages. But messages of love never came into a Parliament. Let us put up a PETITION OF RIGHT."[1] And at a conference with the Lords on the 8th of May, Coke said, "That the Commons had drawn up a Petition of Right, according to ancient precedents, and left space for the Lords to join therein with them. And that this manner of proceeding by petition was the ancient way until the unhappy divisions between the houses of York and Lancaster."[2]

After a great deal of discussion on the state of the country, the Commons passed certain resolutions declaratory of the rights of the people, and appointed a conference with the Lords in order that both Houses might concur in a petition to the throne, founded upon Magna Charta and other statutes, strengthened on the point of personal liberty by twelve direct and thirty-one indirect precedents. This petition received the name of the PETITION OF RIGHT, because it required nothing but the recognition of violated laws; and the object was to obtain the King's assent in Parliament, that it might have the force of a special enactment, and as such be enrolled among the statutes. This petition was prepared by some of the greatest lawyers that England ever saw, being drawn up by Sir Edward Coke himself, assisted by Selden.[3] The vast legal research and great ability dis-

[1] Rushworth, i. 564; Parl. Hist., ii. 348, 349.
[2] Parl. Hist., ii. 351.   [3] Rushworth, i. 565.

played by the popular leaders are very conspicuous in all these proceedings.

On the 17th of May, the Lords' Committee brought in an addition to the Petition of Right, which was read in these words: "We humbly present this petition to your Majesty, not only with a care of preserving our own liberties, but with due regard to leave entire that sovereign power wherewith your Majesty is trusted, for the protection, safety, and happiness of your people."[1] The debate which immediately followed on this addition, when the Commons returned to their House, is very remarkable, not only for the speech of Coke, but for the speeches of Wentworth and Noye, which contain the condemnation out of their own mouths of the subsequent conduct of those two men. Coke said in the course of his speech, "Take we heed what we yield unto. Magna Charta is such a fellow, that he will have no 'sovereign.' I wonder this 'sovereign' was not in Magna Charta, or in the confirmations of it. If we grant this, by implication we give a 'sovereign power' above all laws."[2]

On the 5th of June Sir Edward Coke, then in his seventy-ninth year, spoke for the last time in the House.[3] After his usual manner, he again gave the House a number of precedents, all taken from the Plantagenet reigns. "We have dealt," he said, "with that duty and moderation that never was the like after such a violation of the liberties of the subject; let us take this to heart. In the 30th Edward III., were they then in doubt in Parliament to name men that misled the King? They accused John de Gaunt, the King's son, the Lord Latimer, and Lord

---

[1] Parl. Hist., ii. 355.   [2] Rushworth, i. 568; Parl. Hist., ii. 357, 358.
[3] At least there is no report of any subsequent speech of his in the House, though we find his name occurring in important business afterwards.

Nevil, for misadvising the King, and they went to the Tower for it. Now, when there is such a downfall of the state, shall we hold our tongues? How shall we answer our duties to God and men? In the 7th and 11th of Henry IV., there the Council are complained of, and removed from the King, because they mewed him up, and dissuaded him from the common good: and why are we now to be tied from that way we were in? And why may we not name those that are the cause of all our evils? In the 4th Henry III., and the 27th Edward III., and in the 13th Richard II., the Parliament moderated the King's prerogative."[1]

These precedents cited by Coke place in a strong light the change produced in the English Government by the Wars of the Roses—a change which, as I have before said, transformed the English King into an Asiatic sultan. This is strikingly manifested by the fact mentioned by Coke, that the Parliament could send to the Tower those whom they accused of "misadvising the King"—one of them being John of Gaunt, the King's son, and that King being Edward III.; whereas now they cannot send to the Tower the new Piers Gaveston, the poor slave and dog Steenie, who misadvised the weak King who now occupied the throne once occupied by Edward III. But the revolution effected by the civil war of the fifteenth century had made that weak Stuart King more powerful than the strongest of the Plantagenets; and Coke's utterances of precedents were but so much wasted breath—powerless towards the determination of a question that could only be settled by the sword.

Coke then named the Duke of Buckingham as "the cause of all our miseries." "That man," he said, "is the

[1] Parl. Hist., ii. 403, 404.

grievance of grievances; let us set down the causes of all our disasters, and they will all reflect upon him. . . . It is not the King, but the Duke" [A great cry of "'Tis he, 'Tis he,"] "that saith, 'We require you not to meddle with state government, or the ministers thereof.'" Mr. Kinton said: "The Duke is not only admiral by sea, and hath undone all the shipping, but is also admiral by land, and hath ruined, by oppression and violence at home, and connivance abroad, the whole state of this kingdom; and his treachery, it is like, will overthrow His Majesty, being that he will not suffer the King to hear the truth; for he that speaks truth to His Majesty is ruined by the Duke." Many other members spoke to the like effect, among them Prynne and Selden."[1]

A member of the House, writing to a friend the day after, gives a description of the scene presented by the House on this occasion, which would seem to show that the men of that age in England were more addicted to shedding tears, in public at least, than the men of the nineteenth century in England. It follows that displays of this kind in such a man as Cromwell have not so much weight as peculiarities of character as have been supposed. The Letter-writer says: "Sir Robert Philips spoke and mingled his words with weeping; Sir Edward Coke, overcome with passion, seeing the desolation that was like to ensue, was forced to sit down when he began to speak, through the abundance of tears; yea, the Speaker in his speech could not refrain from weeping and shedding of tears; besides a great many, whose great griefs made them dumb and silent."[2]

In conclusion, the House agreed upon several heads concerning innovation in religion, the safety of the King and kingdom, misgovernment, the late misfortunes, with

[1] Parl. Hist., ii. 403-405.   [2] Rushworth, i. 609.

the causes of them; and whilst it was moving to be put to the question, That the Duke of Buckingham shall be instanced to be the chief and principal cause of all those evils, the Speaker, Sir John Finch, who, when he had leave to go out, went privately to the King, brought this message, "That His Majesty commands for the present they adjourn the House till to-morrow morning, and that all committees cease in the meantime." The House was accordingly adjourned.[1]

The King, after many attempts to evade giving his assent to the Petition of Right in the proper form, came on the 7th of June to the House of Lords, and the Commons with their Speaker attending, the Petition of Right was read, and then the Clerk read this answer, being the usual form in which the King gave his assent to Petitions of Right,[2]—"*Soit droit fait comme il est desiré.*"[3] There is a memorandum entered in the "Lords' Journal," "that at the end of the King's first speech, at the answer to the Petition, and on the conclusion of the whole, the Commons gave a great and joyful applause." Rushworth informs us that the Commons returned to their own House with unspeakable joy, and resolved so to proceed as to express their thankfulness. Accordingly, on the 12th of June, the Commons read a third time and passed the bill for granting five subsidies to the King, and ordered that it should be carried up to the Lords. Sir Edward Coke went with it, and almost the whole House accompanied him.[4] The Commons, however, were dealing with a man who considered himself as little bound by promises, supported by the most solemn oaths, as Pope Alexander VI., or his son Cæsar Borgia; and, as his subsequent acts fully proved,

[1] Parl. Hist., ii. 405. [2] See Selden's Observations, Parl. Hist., ii. 431.
[3] Parl. Hist., ii. 409. [4] Rushworth, i. 613.

had no thought of conforming his conduct to the provisions of the Petition of Right. But for the diseases of such minds as those of Borgia and of Stuart there is but one remedy—that of which Raleigh on the scaffold, as he poised the axe in his hand, and felt along the edge of it with his thumb to see if it was keen, said, smiling, "This is a sharp medicine, but it will cure all diseases."

We have seen Sir Edward Coke as the Attorney-General of James hunting Raleigh to death with the temper and heart of a bloodhound. But a change had come over him since those days. The treatment he had met with from the court when his subservience was found not to come up to the mark of such slaves as Bacon and Buckingham, his subsequent attempts to regain court favour, the humiliations he had made with that view, the bitter disgust and mortification when he found that those humiliations had been made in vain; all these things must have combined to determine Coke to pursue the course of an uncompromising opponent of the royal prerogative. But whatever were his motives, and whatever may have been the infirmities and the vices that left their stain on some portions of Sir Edward Coke's long career, the close of it presents a line of conduct to which is due the gratitude, if not the reverence, of after-ages. We behold the quaint but acute and tough old man in his seventy-ninth year battling with the fire and energy of youth, directed, not subdued, by the experience of age, against an unprincipled and faithless King, and his vile and profligate minister. When Coke again entered the House of Commons after his dismission from his office of Chief-Justice of the King's Bench, the struggle of the Commons against the crown was at exactly that point of its progress where the aid of such an adherent was calculated to be of very great and especial service. In the work of opposing law and precedent to the tyrannical pretensions of the two first Stuarts, Coke rendered inestimable service to his country. In the use of such weapons none could cope with him. Though Selden's black-letter learning might be as great, or even greater, Selden had not Coke's practised skill and weight as a speaker or debater. And such weapons as legal precedents in Coke's hands, backed by the authority of Coke's name, had more weight with such audiences as he had to deal with than any appeal to the understanding drawn from abstract principles would have had.

In regard to the debates in the House of Commons on the matters in dispute between the Puritans and Arminians, it is to be observed that the Arminian party comprehended Laud, Neile, Montague, and all the other churchmen and laymen who were favourable to absolute kingly and priestly power. Therefore whatever Arminianism might be in the abstract, Arminianism was at that time a doctrine which the English House of Commons had good reason both to hate and to fear. In the debates of the Commons at that time may be observed strong indications of that religious enthusiasm which a few years after was to animate the Parliamentary armies. And it is in these debates that Oliver Cromwell first emerges, complaining of one who, he was told, "preached flat Popery."[1] Nevertheless the demeanour of the Commons was at that time very different from what it became after Marston Moor and Naseby. This is remarkably exemplified by an expression used in a speech of Sir Henry Martyn at a conference with the Lords on the addition proposed by the Lords to the Petition of Right. The words also show the Commons were fully aware how far they had at that

[1] Parl. Hist., ii. 464.

time declined from the attitude of power and independence which they maintained before the civil wars of the fifteenth century had left them the slaves of their Kings. After alluding to the "discontents, pressures, and grievances under which themselves in great number, and the parts for which they serve, lamentably groaned when they first arrived here, and which was daily represented unto them by frequent packets and advertisements out of their several counties,"—"My Lords," he continued, "we are not ignorant in what language our predecessors were wont to express themselves upon much lighter provocation; and in what style they framed their petitions: no less amends would serve their turn than severe commissions to inquire upon the violation of their liberties; banishments of some, executions of other offenders; more liberties, new oaths of magistrates, judges, and officers; with many other provisions, written in blood; yet, from us, there hath been heard no angry words in this petition; no man's person is named; *we say no more than what a worm trodden upon would say (if he could speak)*, 'I pray, tread upon me no more.'"[1] These are, indeed, remarkable words, having in them, though eloquent too, a force, a weight, and a significance far greater than the power of what is vulgarly called eloquence. If words could produce such an effect, which they cannot, they might have led those whom they concerned to ponder on their import, and pause before they trod upon the humble worm, lest in so doing they should transform the creature which they now despised into an enemy whose sting was death.

On the 26th of June the King prorogued the Parliament. On the 23d of August 1628 the nation was delivered from the Duke of Buckingham, not by the hands of the hang-

[1] Parl. Hist., ii. 368, 369.

man, as he had been openly told in the House of Lords by the members of the House of Commons whom he was insulting it ought to be, but by the knife of John Felton. But in the place of Buckingham the English people were soon to see two tyrants in Laud and Wentworth, pursuing the same ends as the dead minion, and destined to a fate which that minion had more than merited.

By giving in return for five subsidies, after many delays and much equivocation, his full and solemn consent to the Act of Parliament known by the name of the Petition of Right, the King bound himself to raise no taxes without the consent of Parliament, to imprison no man except by legal process, to billet no more soldiers on the people, and to leave the trial of causes to the ordinary tribunals. But in direct violation of the Petition of Right, and in direct violation of his own word, he continued to raise taxes without the consent of Parliament, to billet soldiers upon the people, to imprison Englishmen without legal process. Among these were some of the most eminent members of this Parliament which had passed the Petition of Right, one of whom, Sir John Eliot, was kept four years in prison, when his death, caused by his close confinement, released him for ever from the power of the tyrant who thus sought to wreak his malice upon the man who had taken a prominent part in the impeachment of Buckingham. It was clear then that the five subsidies which had been given as the price of the national liberties had been given in vain, and that the Petition of Right was to be a dead letter for the present.

CHAPTER III.

THE ADMINISTRATION OF LAUD AND STRAFFORD.

THE great work of Simon de Montfort—to which the word immortal may be more fitly applied than to any of the works of man on which that much-abused word is lavished—was now doomed to destruction, if Charles Stuart had possessed the power to accomplish such a doom. For the last four years, England, Scotland, and Ireland had been governed not by parliamentary government, but by King Charles and the Duke of Buckingham; and those four years were perhaps the most inglorious and humiliating in the English annals. Of the eleven years between the dissolution of the third Parliament of Charles on the 10th of March 1628-29, and the meeting of the Long Parliament on the 3rd of November 1640,[1] the dull, dreary course without the noise of Parliament at home or of wars abroad, and broken but by the fitful cry of agony of some persecuted Puritan or some refractory member of the last Parliament, resembled the breathless preternatural silence that precedes an earthquake. Through those heavy and clouded years, the principal figures on the scene are William Laud and Thomas Wentworth.

The springs of Wentworth's conduct are now laid open to an extent that few men's have been by the publication of the two large folio volumes of his "Letters and De-

[1] The fourth Parliament of Charles, which met on the 13th of April 1640, sat only about twenty days.

spatches," one of the most valuable collections of state papers, both in a political and historical point of view, ever made public. In that collection, besides other indications that Wentworth meant from the first to sell himself to the court as soon as the state of the market met his views, in other words, enabled him to obtain the price he set on himself, there are two letters to Sir Richard Weston,[1] Chancellor of the Exchequer, containing very unequivocal overtures, the non-acceptance of which at that time would seem to have produced soon after in Parliament that indignant burst of patriotic eloquence which tended greatly to enhance the price of the patriot orator in the court-market for patriots.

The same record, the Strafford Papers, the most important portions of which are the letters between Laud and Wentworth, which lay open the springs of Wentworth's conduct, also reveals fully the character of Laud. The administration of Laud was, in fact, a continuation of that of Buckingham. He had recommended himself to Charles, not by any special aptitude for conducting the government of England, but by having been the adroit adulator of Buckingham, as Buckingham had been of James and Charles. It was a species of oratory exercised on an individual, as Wentworth's oratory exercised on the Parliament in opposition to the court had made the court think that to purchase him would be a good speculation. Laud was a man who specially set up for having a conscience; indeed, the great quarrel between him and the English and Scottish nations was, that he would allow nobody to have a conscience but himself.[2] But notwithstanding this nice

[1] Strafford's Letters and Despatches, i. 34, 35.
[2] Among the MSS. in the State Paper Office there are several papers respecting Laud's procuring the King's interference to put down by authority some opposition to his theological views among the young men at Oxford.

conscience of his, he had casuistry enough to undertake the quieting of some consciences which must have required rather delicate handling. Thus he says in his Diary, " The Marquess (of Buckingham) was pleased to enter upon a near respect to me, the particulars of which are not for paper."[1] Very soon after he became " C. " to Buckingham. It is thus written in his Diary.[2] Some, among whom is his admiring biographer Heylin, call it " Confessor." Prynne says, " Confessor, as himself expounded it. "[3] Archbishop Abbott says, " This man is the only inward councillor with Buckingham; sitting with him sometimes privately whole hours, and feeding his humour with malice and spite."[4] On the death of Buckingham, 23d August 1628, Charles looked upon Laud as his principal minister,[5] and thus " a poor creature who never did, said, or wrote anything indicating more than the ordinary capacity of an old woman "[6] was set up by a creature still weaker than himself to exercise absolute dominion over several millions of human beings, and to forbid them, on pain of imprisonment, mutilation, and ruin, from presuming to discuss either

---

What effect such putting down of theological opinions by authority was likely to produce appears in the case of Sir Henry Vane, who was one of the young men at Oxford subjected to Laud's theological tyranny. Thus may be seen one of the effects of despotism, namely, the despot insisting on doing all the thinking of the nation.

[1] Laud's Diary, p. 5. Prynne says of these words, " Certainly some deep mystery of iniquity, fit to be concealed." Cant. Doom, 416.

[2] Date June 15, 1622. This was the time when James's orgies became more furious than in his younger days—the time when the tyrant, though conscious of failing strength, was still raging with capricious sensuality. See the despatches of the French Ambassador, Count Tillières, in Raumer.

[3] Cant. Doom, 416.

[4] Archbishop Abbot's Narrative.

[5] Heylin's Life of Laud, p. 187. See also Laud's Diary and Strafford's Letters and Despatches.

[6] Lord Macaulay's Essay on Samuel Johnson, contributed to the Encyclopædia Britannica.

religion or politics, on which matters he undertook to do all the thinking himself.

It has been the fashion to contrast Laud and Wentworth; to represent the former as a man of an intellect peculiarly contracted, and a very bad temper; the latter as a man, though of imperious, overbearing temper, of a powerful, capacious, statesmanlike intellect. This contrast has also been applied to the personal appearance of these two men, "the mean forehead, the pinched features, the peering eyes of Laud," being contrasted with "the harsh, dark features of Wentworth, ennobled by their expression into more than the majesty of an antique Jupiter." This description of Laud's face sufficiently agrees with his portraits, which represent a countenance indicative of that combination of the mental qualities which make a man fawn on the powerful and trample on the weak. And as we look on his portraits we can still feel the sensation caused by his presence almost as vividly as those who had to stand out of his way as he passed along the galleries of Whitehall, or saw him in the Star Chamber sentencing his victims to the hangman's knife and red-hot iron.[1]

But as regards this description of Wentworth's face, instead of the "majesty of an antique Jupiter," I could never see in that scowling visage anything but the look and expression of a proud, surly, overbearing, yet mean tyrant, with no trace of the intellectual greatness which is so visibly written on the majestic features of Julius Cæsar, Oliver Cromwell, and Napoleon Buonaparte.

I have looked somewhat minutely into the characters

[1] In the reign of Charles I. the audience assembled to secure places in the Star Chamber at three o'clock in the morning.—Barrington on the Statutes, p. 440. London, 1796.

of those two men, Laud and Wentworth; and the conclusion I have come to is, that they differed less than has been commonly supposed. They were both men of considerable activity and industry, of great pride, of violent, arbitrary tempers, but as statesmen signally deficient in knowledge of human nature and in capacity to understand the spirit of their age. As ministers of Henry VIII. (if, Henry VIII. would have tolerated such ministers) they might have carried their *Thorough*[1] to a triumphant issue, and have ridden rough-shod over the souls and bodies, the estates, goods, and chattels of Englishmen. Though perhaps that is saying too much; for did not even Henry VIII., blinded by his furious passions, and headstrong as he was, understand his age better than they understood theirs? His own position, both from his own strength and the weakness of those he oppressed, was far stronger than theirs. Yet even he, with all his barbarism and brutality, had a modicum of sense and knowledge of mankind sufficient to distinguish him from Laud and Wentworth in their obstinate blindness and deafness to all signs and warnings. For on some occasions Henry, meeting with resistance to his attempts at arbitrary taxation, and knowing that he had no military force ready to put it down, withdrew his demands. A strong, far-sighted statesman, if he cannot make the spirit of his time, will in some measure mould it to his will, will at least somewhat

---

[1] A word used by Laud and Strafford in their correspondence to express what their opponents would have called "*Root-and-branch-work.*" Thus in a letter to Wentworth, dated 9th September 1633, Laud writes, "For the state indeed, my Lord, I am for *Thorough*."—Strafford's Letters and Despatches, i. 111. Again, November 15, 1633, Laud writes to Wentworth, "I am very glad to read your Lordship so resolute." He then hints at what may be done "if the word *Thorough*" [it is in this place printed in italics in the Strafford Papers] "be not left out; if others will do their parts as thoroughly as you promise for yourself, and justly conceive of me."—Ibid., p. 155.

control its action and guide its direction, and, thus controlled and guided, it may carry him to glory and victory. Some men see phantoms where there is nothing but air. Laud and Wentworth went to the other extreme, and where there was something very different from phantoms, would see nothing but what they judged it safe to treat as "phantastic apparitions." "I am confident," writes Wentworth to Laud in December 1633, "that to start aside for such panic fears, phantastic apparitions, as a Prynne or an Eliot shall set up, were the meanest folly in the whole world."[1] To the man blinded by overweening self-conceit and ill-grounded self-confidence, the unflinching courage and heroic self-devotion of a Prynne and an Eliot, though these were but the type of what existed in that age in thousands and tens of thousands of Englishmen, were but "phantastic apparitions," till his dream of a despot's paradise is rudely burst by those phantoms' shout of victory and the gleam of the headsman's axe.[2]

In those very years of the seventeenth century in which

---

[1] Strafford's Letters and Despatches, i. 173.

[2] Besides this inability to comprehend their age, the number of powerful personal enemies whom both Wentworth and Laud raised up seems a proof of the want of political talent of a high order. Laud thus alludes to this defect in Wentworth in one of his letters: "And yet, my lord, if you could find a way to do all these great services and *decline these storms*, I think it would be excellent well thought on."—Strafford's Letters and Despatches, i. 479. Yet Laud was so far from "declining these storms" himself, that even his friend Clarendon gives instances of his insolence and its consequences (see Clarendon's Life, i. 62. Oxford, 1759). And May has thus summed up his character. While he says that Laud "had few vulgar and private vices, as being neither taxed of covetousness, intemperance, or incontinence," he describes him as "a man of an active, or rather of a restless mind; more ambitious to undertake than politic to carry on; of a disposition too fierce and cruel for his coat, which, notwithstanding, he was so far from concealing in a subtle way, that he increased the envy of it by insolence."—May's History of the Parliament, p. 19. Maseres' edition, 1812.

The Administration of Laud and Strafford. 77

Laud and Strafford were striving to do their work in England, Richelieu brought a similar work in France to a complete accomplishment. Richelieu had but to crush what remained of the power of the feudal aristocracy. Now this was a very different operation from that which Laud and Strafford had undertaken. Richelieu had to deal with a power in its old age and decrepitude; Laud and Strafford had to deal with a power in all the vigour of a robust and healthy youth. In France the old feudal barons were as much different as in England; but in France there was then no such race of strong-limbed, strong-hearted, well-fed squires, freeholders, and yeomen as there was in England. In France, to crush the feudal aristocracy was to sweep away every obstacle that stood between France and the absolute dominion of one man, the King or his minister. Moreover, in France there were at that time no materials for any other fabric but an absolute monarchy. Had Richelieu undertaken for the commons of France (where there was no class corresponding to the gentry or squires in England) what he accomplished for royalty, he would, like Laud and Strafford, and unlike the man of genius that he was, have misunderstood his age, and his age in return would have misunderstood and rejected him. Putting the moral aspect of the question altogether aside for the moment, a statesman of real genius and insight would have seen that in England, in the game between the King and the Parliament, the King was the worst card. Although a very able man may do much even for the worst cause, there is no doubt but a large part of the success of successful men is due to the judgment with which they select their cause. But here it is necessary again to bring back into view the moral aspect of the question, in order to guard against my being misunderstood. If a man has taken a side, according, as it may be presumed, to the best of his judgment, he cannot, without the just charge of treachery and perfidy, run over to the other side the moment he fancies he sees unequivocal indications of his own side going to the wall. Marlborough changed from the losing to the winning side. Strafford, with, I thoroughly believe, not a whit less selfish intentions, changed from the winning to the losing side, because he believed that the side he was bribed by place by power and honours to adopt either was, or that he could make it, the winning side.

The objects of Laud and Strafford in England, Scotland, and Ireland so far resembled those of Richelieu in France as regarded making the King absolute and putting down the Puritans and all other sectaries; but they went a step further, and in that step was manifested the rooted incapacity of the men as statesmen. Richelieu was content with destroying the Calvinists as a political party, and he granted them in their religious opinions and worship a wise toleration; as Hume remarks, "the only avowed and open toleration which at that time was granted in any European kingdom." What degree of toleration Laud and Strafford granted we shall see as we proceed.

Most of those who have striven to establish a despotism have probably sought to quiet their own consciences by the assertion made by Strafford, that the absolute power they sought should be "exercised only for public and necessary uses, and never wantonly misapplied to any private pleasure or person whatsoever."[1] This scheme of a despotism assumes the despot to be a Trajan or a Marcus Aurelius, instead of a Charles or a James Stuart. But Strafford's uniform practice, as well as his opinion, distinctly expressed

[1] Strafford's Letters and Despatches, ii. 62.

on many occasions, was totally inconsistent with his words which I have just quoted. And even if an eminently good and wise despotism were admitted to be preferable to any other form of government, the experience of all history teaches us that for one Trajan and one Marcus Aurelius we should have many Tiberiuses, Caligulas, Neros, Domitians, a long succession of monsters of cruelty, wickedness, and folly, inflicting upon mankind a series of evils which turn the world into a hell so horrible that no fear of what may after befall them would deter men from seeking refuge from it even in death. But, as Mr. Mill has shown in his work on "Representative Government," the maxim or common form of speech, that if a good despot could be ensured, despotic monarchy would be the best form of government, though it has been long in use, "perhaps throughout the entire duration of British freedom," is a "radical and most pernicious misconception of what good government is."[1] For the argument assumes "one man of superhuman mental activity managing the entire affairs of a mentally passive people. Their passivity is implied in the very idea of absolute power. The nation as a whole, and every individual comprising it, are without any potential voice in their own destiny. They exercise no will in respect to their collective interests. All is decided for them by a will not their own, which it is legally a crime for them to disobey. What sort of human beings can be found under such a regimen? What development can either their thinking or their active faculties attain under it?"[2]

Parliamentary government has indeed, as Lord Macaulay has observed in a passage I have quoted in my

---

[1] See Mr. John Stuart Mill's "Considerations on Representative Government," chap. iii. London, 1861.   [2] Ibid., pp. 46, 47.

Preface, disadvantages as well as advantages, inasmuch as it is a government where a Charles Townshend or a Windham will have more influence than an Oliver Cromwell or a William the Silent. Most men, however, will probably be of opinion, with Lord Macaulay, "that there would be small gain in exchanging Charles Townshend and Windham for the Prince of the Peace or the poor slave and dog Steenie."[1]

The struggle between the two churchmen, Williams and Laud, for court favour throws light on some dark points in the history of that time. Williams had been chaplain to the Chancellor Egerton. On the death of Egerton he was offered the same office in the family of Bacon. He declined this, and it was by his advice that Bacon was prosecuted for receiving bribes. Buckingham's brother had participated largely in Bacon's iniquitous gains, and Williams's object was not public justice, but his own rise on Bacon's fall. Williams succeeded to Bacon's place.[2] Williams's fall was owing partly to the intrigues of Laud, partly to his own want of obedience to the instructions of Buckingham in the decision of causes in Chancery. For Buckingham's servants used to visit the Court of Chancery for the purpose of overawing the judge and forcing him to determine causes in favour of those suitors from whom they openly received bribes. As soon as Laud, who had a quick and observing eye for such things, saw that the favourite looked coldly upon Williams, "he shunned him as the old Romans walked aloof from that soil which was blasted with thunder."[3]

Williams had obtained from his patron Buckingham a

[1] Lord Macaulay's Essay on William Pitt, contributed to the Encyclopædia Britannica.
[2] Hacket's Life of Williams, part i. pp. 19, 24, 31, 39, *et seq.*
[3] Ibid., pp. 107, 108.

promise of the highest dignity in the Church on the first vacancy. As the death of the then Archbishop of Canterbury, Abbot, might be distant, Williams tried to create the vacancy he desired. Abbot had been so unfortunate as to wound Lord Zouch's gamekeeper with an arrow from his crossbow as he was shooting deer. The wound, which was not mortal in itself, proved so through the unskilfulness of the surgeon. Williams represented in a letter to Buckingham that a man defiled with blood, however innocently, was by the canon law disqualified from approaching the altar, and that he had forfeited not only his office but his movables to the crown.

On the present occasion, Abbot found one or two powerful friends among the members of the commission to which the matter was referred, in Sir Henry Martin, at that time Dean of the Arches, and afterwards Judge of the Prerogative Court, who was moved by gratitude to him for his advancement; and in Andrews, Bishop of Winchester, who himself looked forward to the primacy, and exerted himself to save the accused to defeat Williams's purpose of succeeding him.[1]

After the accession of Charles, Williams was deprived of his office of Lord Keeper and driven from court. But as he was a man of great adroitness as a courtier, he after a time contrived to bring about a reconciliation with Buckingham. Laud's fear of the consequences of this was such, that it haunted his sleep and mingled in those dreams which he recorded in his Diary. Then before Williams's fall from his place of Lord Keeper, and while he was labouring to recover the favour of Buckingham, Laud "dreamt that the Lord Keeper was dead; that he passed by one of his men that was about a monument for him;" and

[1] Hacket, part i. p. 65, *et seq.*; Heylin's Life of Laud, p. 86, *et seq.*

he interpreted this into "dead in the Duke's affections."[1] Again, January 13, Saturday, 1627, he dreamt that "the Bishop of Lincoln desired reconciliation with the Duke of Buckingham." On the following night or morning Williams again haunted the dream-troubled sleep of the prelate. "January 14th, towards morning," he writes, "I dreamed that the Bishop of Lincoln came, I knew not whither, with iron chains; but, returning loosed from them, leapt on horseback and went away, neither could I overtake him." And on the 27th of March he records another dream, in which Sir George Wright, deceased, whose executor he was, appeared to him, and whispered in his ear that he "was the cause why the Bishop of Lincoln was not admitted into favour and to court." His fears of Williams were the chief demon that haunted his sleeping as his waking thoughts. In 1633 he dreamt at Alnwick "that Lord Lincoln came and offered to sit above him at the council table, and that Lord Holland placed him there." He does not write Bishop or even Lord Bishop of Lincoln. He might as well have styled himself Duke, or rather Archduke of Canterbury. It was not altogether without reason that the churchmen of the school of Laud affirmed that the day would come when a priest would be the proudest nobleman in the kingdom.

[1] Laud's Diary for December 14th and 15th, 1623. Many a poor miserable old woman has been burned for witchcraft on much less evidence of a debasing superstition than might be produced from Laud's Diary alone. Besides the importance he attached to the bleeding of his nose, the fall of his picture, and the like, the dreams he recorded about the men he hated or feared might have been construed against him in a way similar to that in which Hobbes, in reference to the power of dreams among savage and rude nations, says that, though reputed witches have no real power, they are justly punished for the false belief they have that they can do mischief, joined with their purpose to do it if they can: "their trade being nearer to a new religion than to a craft or science."—Leviathan, part i. chap. ii.

Though Buckingham's death prevented Williams from deriving any benefit from his reconciliation with the favourite, nothing short of his rival's ruin could satisfy Laud. Williams had proposed to Weston to bring over Sir John Eliot to the side of the court; and as Wentworth did not relish the idea of having such a rival at court as a man of Eliot's abilities would have been likely to prove (assuming that Eliot would have prostituted himself, as Wentworth did), he joined Laud in hunting down Williams.[1]

Williams's real crimes were the same as those of Laud, Wentworth, and the other ministers and courtiers of James and Charles, consequently Laud could only destroy him by inventing some charges of a nature either frivolous or altogether groundless. Accordingly various stories were invented against him, generally representing him as a favourer of Puritans and an advocate of popular rights. How far that representation could be true his sermon at King James's funeral and the general course of his life sufficiently demonstrate. In that court every man whose morals were not of the complexion of those of Tiberius

---

[1] Hacket's Life of Williams, part ii. pp. 17, 67, 82, 83. Williams, trying the effect of submission, proposed to surrender his Bishopric and Deanery of Westminster, on condition of the King's providing for him otherwise. This offer was eagerly seized on both by the King and Laud, and they intimated that if Williams would give in his resignation, he should obtain a living in Ireland. But to this Williams demurred, on the ground that he should then fall under the power of a man, Wentworth, who in six months would find out some old statute to cut off his head,—Strafford's Letters and Despatches, ii. 149; Heylin's Life of Laud, p. 344; Hacket's Life of Williams, part ii. 129. Williams was the only bishop not invited to the christening of the young Prince Charles (afterwards Charles II.), though he professed that he could not have joined in Laud's prayer, which was recommended to all the parish churches, and in which Laud said, "Double his father's graces, O Lord, upon him, if it be possible." Williams truly calls this "three-piled flattery and loathsome divinity."—Hacket, part ii. p. 96.; Clarendon, i. 96, 97.

and Sejanus, of Nero and Sporus, was a Puritan; and nothing could give a more faithful picture of the times than the fact that to accuse a man of favouring Puritans was the way to ruin him at court. Williams was truly little enough either of a Puritan or a favourer of Puritans. But being a somewhat less short-sighted bigot and tyrant than Laud (though he could not have risen to where he was had he not possessed the qualities that render a man by turns a crouching slave and an insolent tyrant), he had advised Charles to show some indulgence to the Puritans. The King approved of the advice, and Williams soon after, in regulating his own courts at Leicester, assigned as the reason of some indulgence to the Puritan party, that it was not his own pleasure only, but that of His Majesty likewise. Laud, having got hold of this, carried it to the King. It is an example of Charles's political ability that he and Laud then formed a resolution to have Williams prosecuted in the Star Chamber for revealing the King's secrets contrary to his duty as a privy councillor. But there were other pretences, particularly his objecting to some of Laud's innovations in the forms of worship. His book upon the holy-table was charged with countenancing Prynne, Bastwick, and Burton. The result was, that Williams, through the devices of the man for whom he had interceded so strongly with King James as to obtain for him high preferment, though against the judgment—as subsequent events showed, a singularly correct one—which that King had formed of him, and who repaid his benefactor with confiscation, imprisonment, and ruin by way of gratitude, was fined £10,000 by the Star Chamber, imprisoned in the Tower during the King's pleasure, and suspended from all his offices and benefices.[1] In rummaging his

[1] Rushworth, ii. 416–449.

Episcopal palace of Lincoln, for the purpose of seizing his furniture and books to pay the fine, two or three letters were found written to him by Osbaldiston, headmaster of Westminster School. In these letters were some obscure expressions, which Laud's jealous and malignant temper interpreted to be intended against himself and the Lord Treasurer Weston. On this ground a new bill was exhibited in the Star Chamber against Williams for divulging scandalous libels against privy councillors; and he was condemned in another fine of £8000. Osbaldiston was also tried, and condemned to pay a fine of £5000 to the King, and £5000 to the Archbishop, to be deprived of all spiritual dignities and promotions (he was a prebendary of Westminster as well as headmaster of Westminster School), to be imprisoned during the King's pleasure, and to stand in the pillory in Dean's Yard before his own school, and his ears to be nailed to the pillory. Osbaldiston made his escape, and left a note in his study in which he said that he was "gone beyond Canterbury." Messengers were sent to the seaport towns to apprehend him, but he remained concealed in a house in Drury Lane till the meeting of the Long Parliament in November 1640, when Laud "ceased from troubling," and his victims "were at rest."[1]

The instruments made use of by Laud in the persecution of Williams were of a nature well suited to such a business. They were Sibthorpe, who maintained in the pulpit the right of kings to take their subjects' money at will and reign as they pleased; Lamb, described as "a creature of dark practices, the most hated of all that trod the earth in the county of Northampton, where he dwelt,"[2] originally a schoolmaster, who having become a proctor,

[1] Rushworth, ii. 803-817.
[2] Hacket's Life of Williams, part i. p. 36., ii. pp. 98, 112, 113.

was made Dean of the Arches; and one Kilvert, a proctor in the Court of Arches, and a man of infamous character. Sibthorpe and Lamb followed the example of Laud in turning round upon Williams, who had been the benefactor of all three, having marked the signs of the times, and observed that their fortunes would be more advanced by the ruin than the defence of their benefactor. Kilvert was one of the most audacious and abandoned of the many practitioners of the law, who in such times had no scruple in resorting to any art of fraud and villany to attain their ends. Williams petitioned the King that he would at least allow the cause to proceed according to the rules of court, and proposed to prove against Kilvert the fabrication of the grossest calumnies, subornation of perjury, intimidation of witnesses, and other "subtle practices." Kilvert went so far as to boast, in the hearing of the Registrar, that he cared not what orders the Lords made, as he would go to Greenwich and have them all altered. Sir Robert Heath, Chief Justice of the Common Pleas, complained that Kilvert had threatened to have him turned out of his place for forwardness, as he termed it, in the cause. The complaint was dismissed, and Heath lost his place.[1] But

[1] Hacket's Life of Williams, part ii. pp. 116-118. In the Remonstrance of the Commons on the state of the kingdom presented to the King in December 1641, one of the points is, "Judges have been put out of their places for refusing to act against their oaths and consciences: others have been so awed that they durst not do their duties; and the better to hold a rod over them, the clause *quam diu se bene gesserit* was left out of their patents, and a new clause, *durante bene placito* inserted." (See May, p. 11, ed. 1812, to the same effect.) "Lawyers have been checked for being faithful to their clients; solicitors and attorneys have been threatened, and some punished, for following lawful suits. And by this means all the approaches to justice were interrupted and forecluded." It appears from this that the statement by Blackstone (1 Com. 267), which would lead to the inference that till the statute 13 Will. III. c. 2, the commissions of the judges were made *durante bene placito*, is incorrect—that form being then a modern innovation.

the persecution had made Williams popular. Wentworth's correspondent Garrard relates, under date February 7, 1637, that Kilvert, supping one night in a tavern in Fleet Street, ordered the driver of a hackney-coach which somewhat hindered his passage in going out to remove his coach. The coachman not doing so, Kilvert struck him once or twice. The coachman struck again. Kilvert, incensed with this, asked who he waited on. The man named some gentlemen who were above in the tavern. Kilvert got a constable and some of the watch, went up into the room, and complained of their coachman to the gentlemen, who bid Kilvert take his course against the man, "who was a hackney-man, theirs to-day, Mr. Kilvert's to-morrow." One of them cried out, "Let us look what we say or do, for he will have us all in the Star-Chamber." Kilvert then, they all being without their hats, clapped on his hat, saying, "he might be covered, for he was as good a gentleman as any there." No sooner were these words out of his mouth, but a lieutenant, one Blagge, a near kinsman of Sir Thomas Jermyn, "soled him well by the ears, and drew him by the hair about the room." They were parted, and by way of making them friends, "wine was called for, and a health to the Bishop of Lincoln [Williams] begun to him, which he pledged, he said, because he durst do no other; he threatens them all with the Star Chamber."[1]

The work of destroying the English constitution had been commenced under Edward IV. and continued under the first Tudors. It had been advancing steadily under the latter Tudors and the two first Stuarts; and it is manifest that Laud contemplated bringing it to completion. By the common law of England no man could

[1] Strafford's Letters and Despatches, ii. 149.

lose his ears in any case ("that I know of," said one of the greatest of English lawyers[1]), nor any member but his hand, and that in case of striking and bloodshed, either in the King's own palace or in the face of the King's courts sitting, the judges therein representing the King's own person. The subjects' members, as well as their lives and goods, were secured by many statutes and fundamental laws of the realm. Before the reign of Queen Mary, as appears by the preamble and first part of the statute 1 & 2 Mary, c. 3, the spreaders abroad of false, seditious, and scandalous news and libels, even though against the King and Queen themselves, were not punishable with the pillory or loss of ears, which was the cause of making the law (suited to that sanguinary reign, and in accordance with the spirit of the Spanish Inquisition, which then governed England), contained in the statute of Mary above referred to. Yet even this statute, made and passed in "those bloody Marian days," did not, for that great offence of scandalous and seditious libels against King and Queen, prescribe the loss of both ears absolutely, but gave the delinquent power to redeem the loss of them within three months next after the sentence was given, and that with the payment only of £100 to the King and Queen's use. Now this affords a measure of the character of Laud, that the ears of his victims were simply and absolutely adjudged to be cut off, without any power of redeeming them in any way within any space of time, with the addition of a fine of £5000 and imprisonment for life, and all this not even for alleged libels against the King or Queen (with the exception of a falsely alleged libel in one case, "Pyrnne's Histriomastix"), but for alleged libels against

---

[1] Prynne's argument in his "New Discovery of the Prelates' Tyranny," London 1641, p. 150, *et seq.*

the bishops, or, as Laud phrased it, against "the hierarchy of the Church." This statute of Mary being only for that Queen's life, a similar statute, 23 Eliz., c. 2, was enacted, which also expired at the death of Queen Elizabeth. And Crompton, in his "Jurisdiction of Courts" (title, *Star Chamber*), produces no precedents of cutting off ears, branding, banishment, perpetual close imprisonment in remote castles, restraint of pen, ink, and books, but only of standing in the pillory, wearing of papers on the head, and riding with the face to the horse's tail through Westminster Hall.

All this sufficiently warrants the conclusion, that if Laud did not burn like Bonner, it was not from the want of will. He was as savage and sanguinary a bigot and tyrant as Bonner and his colleagues, and he carried in some important particulars, which have been referred to above, his violation of the laws of England further even than the bloodstained bigots and tyrants of the reign of Mary had done. He fined, he imprisoned, he cut off ears, he slit noses, he scourged, he set in the pillory, he branded with red-hot iron, he drove by incessant, unrelenting persecution his victims into insanity and death. Laud's own notice in his Diary[1] of the punishment of Leighton, a Scotch divine, the father of Archbishop Leighton, will convey an idea, from an authority that cannot be questioned, of the cruelty of his persecution. "Friday, Nov. 16th, part of his sentence was executed upon him in this manner in the new palace at Westminster, in term time. 1. He was severely whipped before he was put in the pillory. 2. Being set in the pillory, he had one of his ears cut off. 3. One side of his nose slit. 4. Branded on one cheek with a red-hot iron with the letters SS,[2] and on that day seven-night, his sores

[1] Laud's Diary, Nov. 1630.   [2] For sower of sedition.

upon his back, ear, nose, and face being not cured, he was whipped again at the pillory in Cheapside, and there had the remainder of his sentence executed upon him by cutting off the other ear, slitting the other side of the nose, and branding the other cheek." After ten years' imprisonment Leighton was released by the Long Parliament, having by that time lost his sight, his hearing, and the use of his limbs.

William Prynne, a very learned barrister of Lincoln's Inn, and a somewhat rigid Puritan, had written against Arminianism. Laud and three or four other prelates were greatly incensed at Prynne's presuming to differ from them on that subject, and prosecuted him in the High Commission Court. In consequence of prohibitions granted out of the King's Court at Westminster, these prelates being unable to wreak their malice on Prynne for this, they eagerly watched for an opportunity to work his ruin. In 1632–33, Prynne published a book against plays or "common enterludes," as he terms them, entitled "Histriomastix." This book, which extended to 1006 quarto pages, was licensed for the press by the household chaplain to the then Archbishop of Canterbury, Abbot, and published with his approbation after careful perusal of it both in the written and printed copy. This book, being on a subject where Prynne's great legal learning and acuteness were of little or no use, appears to me, after some attempts to read parts of it, whatever attractions it may have possessed for Prynne's contemporaries, of such portentous and unvaried dulness as to entitle its author to a place rather in the "Dunciad" than the pillory. It happened that some six weeks after the publication of this book the Queen acted a part in a pastoral at Somerset House. There being some passages in Prynne's book against women actors among the Romans, Greeks, and Spaniards quoted out of fathers and foreign authors, with this reference to them in the table or index of the book, "Women actors notorious whores," relating to those women actors only whom those authors thus branded, Laud and the other prelates by their instruments, on the day after the acting of the pastoral, carried Prynne's book to the King, showed him some of those passages, particularly the reference above mentioned, and informed his Majesty and the Queen that Prynne had purposely written this book against the Queen and her pastoral; whereas it was licensed, and most of those passages printed, near two years before; and the whole book finished at the press at least three months, and published six weeks, before the acting of this pastoral.[1] But this false information only exasperating the King and Queen against Prynne for the present, and not taking effect to work his restraint, their Majesties being truly informed by others that the book was written and printed long before this pastoral was thought of, Laud caused Doctor Heylin to collect such passages out of the book and digest them into several heads as might draw Prynne into question for supposed scandals therein of the King, Queen, state, and government of the realm.[2] Thereupon Heylin drew up such collections digested into seven heads, with his own malicious inferences upon them, not war-

---

[1] In "the examination of William Prynne, Esq., before William Noy, his Majesty's Attorney-General, the last day of January 1632-33." (Dom. Corresp. Charles I. vol. ccxxxi. No. 77, MS., State Paper Office.) "The examinant saith that the first part of that book was printed before the end of the last Easter Term, the second part was finished in Michaelmas Term last, and the table or index was by that time also finished and printed."

[2] Heylin's account of his mode of proceeding with Prynne's "Histriomastix," as given in his own words (Heylin's Life of Laud, pp. 230, 231), fully confirms the statement given in the "New Discovery of the Prelates' Tyranny," pp. 8, 9. London, 1641.

ranted by Prynne's text, and delivered them in writing to Secretary Cooke and Laud, then Bishop of London. Laud then took Prynne's book and these collections one Sunday morning to Lincoln's Inn to Noy, then Attorney-General, and keeping him both from the chapel and sacrament, showed him the book and collections of some passages out of it, which, he said, his counsel informed him to be dangerous; and charged him on that duty he owed to his master the King to prosecute Prynne for the same. Noy had previously twice read over the book very carefully, and protested that he saw nothing in it that was scandalous or censurable in the Star Chamber or any other court of judicature. He had even commanded a copy of the book (which Prynne had delivered to him) to be put into Lincoln's Inn Library for the use of the Society.[1] He professed to be so discontented at this command of the prelate, that "he wished he had been twenty miles out of town that morning." However this might be (and there is some reason to doubt Noy's alleged unwillingness[2]), a few days after Prynne was called before the Lords to the inner Star Chamber, and on the 1st February 1632-33, was by them sent prisoner to the

[1] This copy is still in Lincoln's Inn Library. At least the copy now there has the words, "Ex dono authoris" written in it in an old hand, though it does not appear to be Prynne's own hand, when compared with his signature in other works of his in Lincoln's Inn Library. The "Histriomastix" is dedicated "To his much honoured friends, the Right Worshipful Masters of the Bench of the Honourable Society of Lincoln's Inn." In this dedication he mentions the ill-effects on many young students and others of stage plays. He states that he had himself, when he first came to London, "been drawn by the importunity of some ill acquaintance to see in four several plays such wickedness, such lewdness, as then made his penitent heart to loath, his conscience to abhor, all stage plays ever since."

[2] Laud thus records Noy's death, which happened soon after, in his Diary: "I have lost a dear friend of him, and the Church the greatest she had of his condition since she needed any such."—Laud's Diary, p. 50.

The Administration of Laud and Strafford. 93

Tower, with a warrant in which no cause of commitment was specified, and to which the hand of Laud, then Bishop of London, and of the Archbishop of York, were subscribed.

By force of this general and illegal warrant, Prynne was kept prisoner in the Tower, notwithstanding his frequent petitions for release, absolute or upon bail, till Noy, on the 21st of June following, exhibited an information against him in the Star Chamber for his book called "Histriomastix," and prosecuted it so that, not permitting Prynne to be bailed, nor yet so much as to repair to his counsel with his keeper, he, on the 17th February 1633-34, procured the following sentence against him,—That he should be committed to prison during life, pay a fine of £5000 to the King, be expelled Lincoln's Inn, disbarred and disabled ever to exercise the profession of a barrister, degraded by the University of Oxford of his degree there taken; and that done, be set in the pillory at Westminster, with a paper on his head declaring the nature of his offence, and have one of his ears there cut off, and in another time be set in the pillory in Cheapside, with a paper as before, and there have his other ear cut off; and that a fire should be made before the pillory, and the hangman should then publicly, in disgraceful manner, cast all the copies of the book which could be produced (to collect which, messengers with special warrants were sent to booksellers into various counties) into the fire to be burnt. No particular passages of the book on which the sentence was grounded were so much as mentioned in this information or decree, as by law they should have been, and no doubt would have been, had they really merited such a censure. Though many of the Lords never dreamed of any execution of this savage decree, and the Queen (whom it most concerned) earnestly interceded with Charles to remit its execution, yet so nearly was the hardness of that King's heart on a level with the weakness of his head, and such were the prelate's power and malice, that on the 7th and 10th of May following it was fully executed with great rigour.[1] Strafford's correspondent, the Rev. George Garrard, writes thus on the 3d June 1634: "No mercy showed to Prynne; he stood in the pillory, and lost his first ear in a pillory in the Palace at Westminster in full term, his other in Cheapside, where, while he stood, his volumes were burnt under his nose, which had almost suffocated him."[2] The suffocation was no part of the sentence; but Laud's malice and cruelty were boundless. While Prynne's wounds were yet fresh and bleeding, within three days after the execution of his sentence, this archprelate of Canterbury, to add more weight to his affliction, against all law and equity, when there was no suit pending against Prynne in the High Commission, and his fine in the Star Chamber unestreated, granted a warrant out of the High Commission for the seizure of the books of his study. Under this warrant a cartload of Prynne's books was seized and carried away, and when Prynne complained of this, the Archbishop in the open court in Star Chamber denied the granting of the warrant, though it was extant under his hand, and has been published by Prynne.[3] Laud also promised present restitution of the books, and nevertheless gave underhand orders for detaining them till they were sold for Prynne's fine in the Star Chamber.

---

[1] Prynne's "New Discovery of the Prelates' Tyranny," pp. 10, 11.

[2] Strafford's Letters and Despatches, i. 261.

[3] New Discovery of the Prelates' Tyranny, pp. 12, 13. There is an abstract of the proceedings in Prynne's case in Rushworth abridged (vol. ii. p. 275, *et seq.*), which publication contains several things which are not in the large copy of Rushworth's collections.

Prynne remained a prisoner in the Tower till new persecution and cruelties were exercised against him.

Although Laud held no ostensible political office except his seat at the Council Board, at the Great Committee of Trade[1] and of the King's Revenue, and as one of the commissioners for the short time the office of Lord High Treasurer was in commission, he had the appointing of Windebank, Secretary of State, and of Juxon, Clerk of the Closet and afterwards Lord High Treasurer.

On the 6th of August 1633 Laud was translated from the diocese of London to the see of Canterbury.

One of the most zealous coadjutors of Archbishop Laud in his systematic violation of the laws of England and encroachments upon the ancient rights and liberties of Englishmen, was Sir John Finch, who had been Speaker of the House of Commons during the last Parliament, who was at this time Lord Chief Justice of the Court of Common Pleas, who in January 1639–40 was appointed Lord Keeper of the Great Seal, and in April 1640 was created Lord Finch. This man's character is an instructive study, as showing by what means lawyers at that time rose into the favour of the court, and into the high places of their profession. He was a fluent, and, it might be added, an adroit rhetorician, if his perversion of the evidence on which he professed to ground his judgments had not been so gross and barefaced as to merit the name rather of clumsy impudence than of adroit villany and baseness. His open attempt to substitute for the English constitution and laws the absolute tyranny of the Cæsars

[1] How much good he did there need not now be a difficult question. "In the reign of Charles I." says Burke, "the Committees of Council were never for a moment unoccupied with the affairs of trade; and even when they had no ill intention (which was sometimes the case), trade and manufacture suffered infinitely from their injudicious tamperings."

was too much even for Clarendon, who informs us that besides his judgments in the case of ship-money, he declared, when he was Lord Keeper, upon a demurrer put in to a bill before him, which had no other equity in it than an order of the Lords of the Council, "that while he was Keeper, no man should be so saucy as to dispute those orders, but that the wisdom of that Board should be always ground enough for him to make a decree in Chancery."[1]

Between eight and nine o'clock in the morning of the 14th June 1637, Prynne was again brought before the Court of Star Chamber, together with John Bastwick, Doctor in Physic, and Henry Burton, Bachelor of Divinity, on the charge of writing and publishing seditious, schismatical, and libellous books against the hierarchy. The Lords having taken their places, Prynne humbly desired their Lordships, before they entered upon the hearing of the cause, to grant him leave to make a short motion to the Court. This being granted, and he beginning to speak, Sir John Finch looking earnestly[2] upon Mr. Prynne, who stood at the bar behind him, interrupted him and began to speak in this manner:—"Is this Mr. Prynne? I had thought Mr. Prynne had had no ears, they being adjudged to be cut off by the sentence of this Court; but methinks he hath ears, and it is fit the Court should take order that the decrees thereof should be better

---

[1] Clarendon, Hist., i. 74, ed. Oxf., 1712. Strafford's words and actions, as well as Laud's, quite agree with these proceedings of Finch, leaving no doubt of the full intention to destroy utterly the English constitution and to treat the English laws as a dead letter. See, among many other proofs elsewhere quoted, Strafford's Letters and Despatches, i. 201.

[2] The word in the contemporary report is "wistly." The book entitled "A New Discovery of the Prelates' Tyranny" is paged on to page 48. Then the paging begins again with page 1, at "A Brief Relation of certain Special and most Material Passages and Speeches in the Star Chamber, 14th June 1637." See also Rushworth, Abrid., ii. 279, and State Trials, iii. 717, 8vo edit.

executed, and see whether Mr. Prynne hath ears or no." This caused many of the Lords to take a stricter view of him, and for their better satisfaction the usher of the Court was commanded to turn up his hair and show his ears, or the places where his ears had been. Upon the sight of the poor man's mutilated head some of the Lords seemed to be displeased that his ears had not been cut closer off, and even carried their brutality so far as to give utterance to some opprobrious words of him, and of the favour shown him in the execution. To this Prynne replied, "My Lords, there is never a one of your honours but would be sorry to have such an ear-mark, and to have your ears cropt as mine are. And I pray, my Lord Finch, give me leave to proceed in my motion without interruption. I hope you will have ears to hear it,—and then say what you please." The Lord Keeper, Sir Thomas Coventry, not perfectly hearing what Prynne said, inquired twice, "What doth he say?" Prynne then repeated his former words with a louder voice, to which the Lord Keeper replied, "In good faith, my Lords, he is very saucy." "I hope," said Prynne, "your honours will not be offended with my words: and I pray God to give you ears to hear us as you ought." "The business of the day is to proceed to the prisoners at the bar," said the Lord Keeper.

Of the three prisoners, Burton appears to have possessed most of the faculty of popular eloquence. When he ended his speech, a great hum was made in the court by many of the audience, "being much affected," says the old report, "with this his Christian resolution." Then the prisoners desiring to speak a little more for themselves, were commanded to silence, and Lord Cottington, Chancellor of the Exchequer, delivered the judgment of the

Court in the following words:—"I condemn these three men to lose their ears in the Palace Yard at Westminster; to be fined £5000 a man to his Majesty; and to perpetual imprisonment in three remote places of the kingdom, namely, the Castles of Carnarvon, Cornwall, and Lancaster." To which Finch added, "Mr. Prynne to be stigmatised in the cheeks with two letters (S and L), for a seditious libeller."[1] This atrocious sentence was rigorously executed in the presence of a vast multitude of people whose sympathies were strongly manifested on behalf of these victims of the tyranny of the Stuart and his hierarchy.

Prynne, after the execution of his sentence, being a close prisoner, and wanting his servant to attend him while he was suffering from his wounds, desired the Lieutenant of the Tower to move the Archbishop of Canterbury either to release or bail his servant (who had been imprisoned only for refusing to accuse his master), upon sufficient sureties, to attend him while his wounds were healing. But the Archbishop utterly rejected this motion, saying that "he intended to proceed against his servant in the High Commission, and he could not call a High Commission Court in the vacation to pleasure Mr. Prynne;" though he could summon two Commission Courts in vacation to suspend Mr. Burton, and might, nay, ought, to have bailed Prynne's servant by law, without calling a court. It was in the case of this servant of Prynne's (who is, in fact, only described as his servant in so far as a barrister's clerk may be so described) that Sir Philip Warwick[2] re-

---

[1] A Brief Relation of Passages and Speeches in the Star Chamber, 14th June 1637, p. 32.

[2] In a work of Andrew Marvell's, intituled "A Seasonable Argument to Persuade all the Grand Juries in England to Petition for a New Parliament" (Marvell's Works, ii. 555; London, 4to, 1776), Sir Philip Warwick is thus

presents Oliver Cromwell as speaking in the House of Commons with an eloquence full of fervour, "aggravating the imprisonment of the man by the Council table unto that height that one would have believed the very Government itself had been in great danger by it." If Sir Philip means by "the Government" the tyranny of Laud and his master, that is of course not what Cromwell meant as being in danger, but Cromwell meant that the English constitution was in danger by it. Cromwell was quite right, and it would have been well for his country and his own fame if he had remained true to the constitutional principles which he then so vehemently expounded. For nothing could exceed the tyranny, the malignity, the violation of law with which Laud proceeded in this case; for though in all cases Laud displayed an extraordinary malignity (insomuch that I think the term Malignant applied to his party by their opponents must have been suggested by him), in this he even surpassed himself. The nature of the duties of a barrister's clerk necessarily makes him acquainted with the most confidential affairs in which his master is engaged, the clerk both knowing what persons frequented his master's chambers, and copying for his master or writing to his dictation. Laud, therefore, who appears to have been desirous of proceeding capitally against Prynne, and of hanging, after torturing and mutilating him, caused this clerk or confidential servant to be frequently examined by the Attorney and Solicitor Generals, who, by threats and great promises, attempted to induce him falsely to accuse and

---

described : "Once secretary to Archbishop Laud, before that a poor singing-boy, got artificially from the Treasurer Southampton and the King £40,000, now Clerk of the Signet; never lies more than when he professes to speak the sincerity of his heart."

betray his master. The man refusing to do so, Laud entered articles against him in the High Commission, and for his refusal to take an *ex officio* oath before sight of his articles, the Archbishop, by a special letter under His Majesty's signet, took the articles against him *pro confesso*, fined him £1000 to the King, taxed him to pay heavy costs of suit (though there was no prosecutor assigned), committed him close prisoner to the Counter, excommunicated him, and after that sent him from prison to prison, ordering his father to pay the messenger's fees, amounting to above £22, under pain of imprisonment, and pretending that he should never be released while he lived, unless he would take his oath to answer the articles, and confess such things as Laud should demand of him touching his master's secrets.[1]

In the course of the month of July 1637, these three victims of Laud's cruelty were sent off from London to their distant prisons. The sub-warden of the Fleet told the King that when Burton was removed from the Fleet towards Lancaster Castle there were not less than 100,000 persons gathered together to see him pass by betwixt Smithfield and Brown's Well, two miles beyond Highgate. His wife followed in a coach, having much money thrown to her as she passed along, which shows that the people whose sympathies were excited were by no means all of the poorest class.[2] On the 27th of July, Prynne, before his wounds were healed, was removed from the Tower to the Fleet about seven in the morning, and within one

---

[1] A Brief Relation, &c., pp. 73, 74; Rushworth, Abrid., ii. 273.

[2] Straff., Let. and Desp., ii. 114. The exact situation of "Brown's Well" or "Brown's Wells" is marked by the Green Man Tavern, a little more than half-way between London and Barnet, which bore on its sign, under "The Green Man," the words, as I can testify, "Brown's Wells," till within the last few years.

The Administration of Laud and Strafford. 101

hour after he was conducted towards Carnarvon Castle. The streets and roads from the Fleet till beyond Highgate were full of people to see and take their farewell of him, whom they thought never to behold again. Some of his friends accompanied him to St. Albans, where he lay the first night. Laud's eye was still upon him, however, and the persons who showed him any civilities on his way to his distant prison were fined, some £500, some £300, and others £250.[1] Some weeks after the arrival of the prisoners at the castles of Lanceston, Lancaster, and Carnarvon, the Christian archprelate, to deprive them of all possibility of comfort or relief from their wives, children, kindred, or friends, procured an order for their exile and close imprisonment in the castles of Guernsey, Jersey, and Scilly; Burton to be removed to Guernsey, Prynne to Jersey, Bastwick to the Scilly Isles.[2] And although, as already observed, there was a clause in the warrants in favour of the prisoners, that, "in regard of their close confinement, His Majesty will give allowance for their diet;" and although the Christian Bishop of London was Lord High Treasurer, there was not so much as one penny given or allowed to any for their diet; and had not their friends and keepers been more charitable than the prelates, they might have starved, notwithstanding this pretended indefinite allowance. Nevertheless, after all this, Laud, in his speech in the Star Chamber, and his Epistle dedicatory prefixed to his answer to Fisher the Jesuit, "desires God

---

[1] A Brief Relation, &c., p. 91, *et seq.*; Rushworth, Abrid., ii. 290. In these proceedings the Archbishop of York and the Bishop of Chester were Laud's zealous coadjutors, the Bishop of Chester acting the part of informer against Prynne's Chester friends, whose persecutions at York originally arose from his information. The Bishop of Chester's three letters to the Archbishop of York on this subject are printed in the work already cited, "A New Dictionary of the Prelates' Tyranny," pp. 218–226.

[2] A Brief Relation, &c., p. 85, *et seq.*

to forgive them," and "forbears to censure them," as if he bore no malice towards them on whom he had wreaked so much. In his confidential correspondence with Wentworth, however, he gives vent to his real sentiments on the subject. "I am verily of your Lordship's mind," he writes, under date August 28, 1637, "that a little more quickness in the Government would cure this itch of libelling, and something that is amiss besides, but, truly, I have done expecting of *Thorow* on this side. . . . What say you to it, that Prynne and his fellows should be suffered to talk what they pleased while they stood in the pillory, and win acclamations from the people, and have notes taken of what they spake, and those notes spread in written copies about the city, and that when they went out of town to their several imprisonments, there were thousands suffered to be upon the way to take their leave, and God knows what else?"[1] Wentworth answered the ecclesiastic in a congenial spirit.[2] Thus these men encouraged each other to acts of cruelty, canting about God, Christ, religion, and justice at the very time while they were committing a crime, compared to which the crimes of ordinary robbers and murderers are as nothing—the crime of attempting to destroy utterly the English constitution, and to reduce to the condition of slaves all the English people of that time, them and their children, and their children's children to all generations.

I have said that Laud, though he could not destroy them by the hands of the hangman, drove, by unrelenting persecution, his victims into insanity and death. I will shortly state one or two cases of ruined fortunes and broken hearts

---

[1] Strafford's Letters and Despatches, ii. 99.
[2] Ibid., ii. 119.

The Administration of Laud and Strafford. 103

that make up the dark history of the administration of Laud and Strafford; for to both these men the expression of Baillie, which calls to mind the retribution that the spirit of the murdered Cleonice predicted to her murderer, is strictly applicable: "Intolerable pride and oppression cry to Heaven for vengeance."[1]

John Workman, lecturer of St. Stephen's Church, Gloucester, had asserted in one of his sermons, which assertion he justified from the "Homilies against the Peril of Idolatry," that pictures or images of Christ, or of any saint, either in a church or a private house, were, "if not flat idolatry, yet little better." Notwithstanding the authority of the "Homilies" themselves of the Church, he was suspended by the High Commission, excommunicated, and obliged to use open recantation in the court at Lambeth, in the cathedral and the church of St. Michael's, Gloucester, condemned in costs of suit, and thrown into prison. Workman was a man of singular piety, learning, and moderation ("as," says the reporter of the case, "the Archbishop himself confessed"), and had been a most diligent preacher and visitor of the sick in the city of Gloucester for above fifteen years; in consideration of which, and of his numerous family, the city of Gloucester had given him an annuity of £20 per annum, under their common seal, a little before his troubles in the High Commission. For this act the mayor, town-clerk, and several of the aldermen were cited before the High Commission and put to £100 charges, and the annuity was cancelled. Having, after some months' imprisonment, with much difficulty obtained his liberty, Workman, to keep himself, his wife and children from starving, set up a little school. The Archbishop, on being informed of this, positively pro-

[1] Baillie's Letters and Journals, i. 272, Laing's edit. Edinburgh, 1841.

hibited him from teaching any children in public or private. The poor minister then attempted to practise medicine for bread. Laud interdicted this too. Workman went mad and died.[1]

Such proceedings as this render the report not incredible that the articles of visitation of Dr. Wren, Bishop of Norwich, contained an article requiring "that the churchwardens in every parish of his diocese should inquire whether any persons presumed to talk of religion at their tables and in their families;"[2] and furnish also sufficient confirmation of the words of Sir Benjamin Rudward in his speech in the debate on grievances at the opening of the Long Parliament: "We have seen ministers, their wives, children, and families, undone against law, against conscience, against all bowels of compassion, about not dancing upon Sundays. What do these sort of priests think will become of themselves when the Master of the house shall come and find them thus beating their fellow-servants? . . . Whoever squares his notions by any rule, either divine or human, he is a Puritan. Whoever would be governed by the King's laws, he is a Puritan. He that will not do whatsoever other men will have him do, he is a Puritan."[3] In pursuance of this system, when great numbers sought refuge in America from such intolerable oppression, Laud's unrelenting tyranny was preparing to follow them, "to send a bishop over to them in New England for their better government, and back him

---

[1] Prynne, Canterbury's Doom, pp. 107, 108.
[2] Neal's History of the Puritans, ii. 273, note.
[3] Parl. Hist., ii. 644, *et seq.* There is in Rushworth, iv. 184-186, a speech of Lord Falkland's which shows to what extent Laud's ecclesiastical tyranny had disgusted men who could not be said to belong to the party of extreme zealots, and also that the peculiar Scriptural phraseology was not confined to those whom Laud and his party called Puritans.

with some forces to compel, if he were not otherwise able to persuade, obedience."[1]

Another case, which I will shortly state, is instructive both as showing the brutality to which Wentworth allowed his violent temper to carry him, and the manner of dealing with evidence by the highest legal functionaries at that time.

Robert Esmond having refused to take the King's timber into his bark, as well because it was before laden with timber for the Lord Chief Justice, as because the King's timber was too long for the bark, the Lord Deputy Wentworth committed him. After about six days' imprisonment in Dublin Castle, Esmond returned home, and within a few days after died, it was said of blows the Lord Deputy gave him when he committed him. There were four witnesses, whose depositions before the Council in England are given in Rushworth.[2] Two of them, Atkins and Holloway, distinctly state they saw the Lord Deputy strike Esmond on the head and shoulders three or four strokes. Atkins "was present when Esmond was brought in. The Lord Deputy was angry with him, and said, 'Sirrah, sirrah,' and struck Esmond on the head and shoulders three or four strokes with a cane, and then committed him. Immediately after Robert Esmond's death, he heard Richard Roach and divers others report that the said strokes occasioned it; he did daily visit Robert Esmond, and he still complained of the blows; and this deponent's wife anointed his shoulders; he often wept and grieved, and he would often say his heart was broken." The other two of the four witnesses, Sir Philip Manwaring and Joshua Carpenter, were servants of the

---

[1] Heylin's Life of Laud, p. 369.
[2] Rushworth, iii. 888, *et seq.*; Rushworth, Abrid., iii. 43, *et seq.*

Lord Deputy, and yet even they do not say that there were no blows given. Now Lord Chief Justice Finch, that member of the Council best qualified from his profession to weigh evidence, has summed up the evidence of these witnesses after a strange fashion. According to Lord Chief Justice Finch's own words, Sir Philip Manwaring was the only witness that "at hearing" was induced to say that he believed in his conscience the Lord Deputy "did not so much as touch him," though in his deposition he said, "whether he touched him or not he cannot depose." Carpenter "doth not know whether he touched him;" and this Lord Chief Justice Finch calls "agreeing with Sir Philip." Holloway "knoweth of no hurt or wrong was done by my Lord Deputy;" but he does not contradict his deposition that "he saw the Lord Deputy strike three or four strokes" (the number specified by Atkins). Of these three witnesses, only one, even by the Judge's own version, states that the Lord Deputy did not commit this act of cruel and cowardly violence upon an unresisting man, who, besides being a prisoner, was sick and infirm; while the fourth witness, Atkins, besides his distinct deposition as to the strokes, also deposes as to the condition of Esmond after receiving them, and that he heard Richard Roach and divers others report that the said strokes caused Esmond's death. That is, of the four witnesses, two swore that Wentworth struck Esmond, a third that he shook his cane at him, but knows not whether or not he touched him. And yet Lord Chief Justice Finch says they have four to one against the strokes, adding, "I wonder whether any man can think there was a stroke." On the other hand, I wonder any man can think there was not. No one can read the case without seeing that all the four witnesses were of the same mind as to what they had witnessed, but that two, being servants of Wentworth, were under duresse as to their testimony.

It would be tedious to attempt an enumeration of the various illegal devices for raising money resorted to by Charles during these years when, there being no Parliament, there could be no legal or parliamentary taxation in England. In addition to the other modes of oppression by taxation, the power of creating monopolies claimed by the crown was more grossly abused than it had ever been. The Roman Catholics, being specially favoured in the grants of monopolies, sold the worst articles at the highest price. "They grow," says Clarendon, "not only secret contrivers in, but public professed promoters of, and ministers in, the most grievous projects, as that of soap, formed, framed, and executed by almost a corporation of that religion."[1] Of this soap Garrard writes to Wentworth January 9, 1633: "Continual complaints rise up that it burns linen, scalds the laundress's fingers, and wastes infinitely in keeping, being full of lime."[2] Another mode of extract-

---

[1] Hist., i. 262.
[2] Strafford's Letters and Despatches, i. 176. Six months later (June 3, 1634) Garrard writes to Wentworth: "The taverns begin to victual again, some have got leave. 'Tis said that the vintners within the city will give £6000 to the King to dress meat as they did before. The proclamation for rating all achates* have done little good; they will not bring them to London as heretofore, so that housekeeping in London is grown much more chargeable than it was before these proclamations were published."—Ibid., p. 262. Again, January 8, 1635, Garrard writes: "Here is a proclamation coming forth to prohibit all hackney-coaches to pass up and down in London streets. Also the Attorney-General hath sent to all taverns to prohibit them to dress meat. Somewhat was required of them, an halfpenny a quart for French wine, and a penny for sack and other richer wines, for the King. The gentlemen vintners grew sullen, and would not give it, so they are well enough served."—Ibid.,

---

* *Cates.* Garrard's mode of writing this word seems to indicate its derivation, which has puzzled Johnson and others, from the French word *achate*, "purchases," and it may thus mean *purchased provisions.*

ing money was to grant licenses to build houses, and then pretend that the houses were built contrary to proclamation, and extort heavy fines. Garrard writes in February 1633: "It is confidently spoken that there are above one hundred thousand pounds" to be got from this source about London, and adds that he speaks much within compass.[1] But some of the proceedings under pretended obsolete forest laws were so extravagant, that it would seem as if the Deity who had determined to destroy Charles had first deprived him of reason. For he would appear, judging from his acts, to have looked upon England as one large hunting-field, where the only difference between the brutes and the human animals was that from the latter were to be selected the whippers-in of his hounds. Of the rest of the human brutes, some were to raise food for the hounds, their master, and his whippers-in; the rest were to supply amusement by being hunted. In reference to the projected new great park or forest for red as well as fallow deer, to extend from Richmond to Hampton Court, even Clarendon admits that "the building of the wall before people consented to part with their land or their common, looked to them as if by degrees they should be shut out from both, and increased the murmur and noise of the people who were not concerned, as well as of those who were, and it was too near London not to be the common discourse."[2] And Garrard writes to Wentworth under date April 14,

p. 507. Under date February 7, 1637, Garrard writes: "The vintners of London have offered to the King a rent of £30,000, to raise Spanish wines twopence in the quart, and the French wines a penny in a quart more than they are usually sold at; they would have had another condition, that the nobility and gentry of the kingdom should have made their provisions from them, and not of the merchant, but that would not be yielded unto."—Ibid., ii. 147, 148.

[1] Strafford's Letters and Despatches, i. 206.
[2] Clarendon, Hist., i. 178. Oxford, 1826.

1635: "All Essex is become forest; and so, they say, will all the counties of England but three, Kent, Surrey, and Sussex."[1] The bounds of the forest of Rockingham were increased from six miles to sixty.[2] Now suppose the brilliant idea of turning all the counties of England but three into forest carried into execution, may not some of the hunted English human brutes—brutes of a nature stubborn even to ferocity—turn round peradventure now and then upon the hunters with "hoofs that trample and horns that gore?"

Wentworth was appointed Lord Deputy of Ireland in 1632, still retaining his office of President of the Council of the North, where he had sufficiently exhibited his inclination to set his own will above the laws of England. But it was in Ireland where the man's tyrannical nature had the finest field for its exercise. In the first place, he assumed the power of deciding causes between party and party, on grounds that left the property, lives, and liberties of the

[1] Strafford's Letters and Despatches, i. 413.
[2] Strafford's Letters and Despatches, ii. 117. Rev. George Garrard to Wentworth, Oct. 9, 1637. In this letter Garrard gives some particulars of the fines levied on trespassers in the royal forests by the Earl of Holland in September 1637, when, assisted by five judges, he held his great court of justice in eyre in Northamptonshire and Oxfordshire. The Earl of Salisbury was fined £20,000; the Earl of Westmoreland £19,000; Sir Christopher Hatton £12,000; and many smaller sums. In the same letter Garrard writes: "Here is at this present a commission in execution against cottagers who have not four acres of ground laid to their houses, upon a statute made the 31st Elizabeth, which vexeth the poor people mightily, is far more burdensome to them than the ship-monies, all for the benefit of the Lord Morton, and the Secretary of Scotland, the Lord Sterling. Much crying out there is against it, especially because mean, needy, and men of no good fame, prisoners in the Fleet, are used as principal commissioners to call the people before them to fine and compound with them." As to the Earl of Holland's holding his court at Winchester for the New Forest, see Strafford's Letters and Despatches, i. 463, where Garrard writes, September 1, 1635, "All goes well as I could wish; yet I should be sorry my Lord of Southampton's manor of Beauly should come to be forest; it would be a great loss unto him."

subject completely at the mercy of despotism. "I know very well," he wrote, "the common lawyers will be passionately against it, who are wont to put such a prejudice upon all other professions, as if none were to be trusted or capable to administer justice but themselves; yet how well all this suits with monarchy, where they monopolise all to be governed by their year books, you in England have a costly experience."[1] And he complains that the lawyers seek "to limit and restrain all causes of prerogative."[2]

Wentworth imagined that he could attain his ends much more completely in Ireland by calling an Irish Parliament and by cajolery, that is, by promises which, like his master and the Borgias, he had no intention of performing, and by threats which he was more likely to make good, making the Parliament a mere instrument of his own and his master's tyranny. But he encountered some difficulty in obtaining the consent of Charles, who hated the very name of Parliament; and when the King at last yielded, he wrote to Wentworth—"As for that hydra, take good heed, for you know that here I have found it as well cunning as malicious. . . . My opinion is that it will not be the worse for my service, though their obstinacy make you to break them, for I fear that they have some ground to demand more than it is fit for me to give."[3] The despatch of Wentworth,[4] in which he sets forth the reasons for calling an Irish Parliament, with the postils[5] made by Charles in

---

[1] Strafford's Letters and Despatches, i. 261.
[2] Ibid., i. 223.   [3] Ibid., i. 233.
[4] Ibid., i. 183, *et seq.*
[5] Usually written *apostyles*, which seems to have come from the French *apostille*. But the word is evidently from the Latin *postilla*. A passage of Bacon, quoted by Johnson under the word "postil," exemplifies the usage of the word: "I have seen a book of account of Empson's, that had the King's hand almost to every leaf by way of signing, and was in some places postilled in the margin with the King's hand."

the margin, enables us now to estimate correctly the truth of the dying words of its author, that "he was so far from being against Parliaments that he did always think Parliaments in England to be happy constitutions of the kingdom and nation, and the best means under God to make the King and his people happy." The sense in which Strafford used these words is now completely laid bare.

Wentworth opened the Irish Parliament with royal pomp, delivered a speech which, for rhetorical swell, might, as has been said of it, have served Milton as a model for the harangue of Lucifer, and demanded and obtained the extraordinary grant of six subsidies. When the second session came, in which the Parliament were to debate upon grievances, they were at once cut short, taunted, reviled, menaced, with all that eloquent insolence of which Wentworth was such a master, and were struck dumb, partly with fear, partly with astonishment, at the amazing effrontery of the man who, after having made them the most solemn promises in the King's name, and by the King's express orders, treated them like criminals when they humbly petitioned for the performance of those promises. Pope Alexander VI. and his son Cæsar Borgia could not have exhibited a finer specimen of " princely intelligence in the transaction of business." When Wentworth wished to continue this Parliament which he had thus cajoled and bullied and cheated, the King refused to yield to his wishes. "My reasons," he wrote, "are grounded upon my experience of them here; they are of the nature of cats; they ever grow curst with age; so that if ye will have good of them, put them off handsomely when they come to any age; for young ones are ever most tractable: and in earnest you will find that nothing can more conduce to the beginning of a new, than the well ending of the former Parliament; wherefore, now that we are well, let us content ourselves therewith."[1]

The villany of Wentworth's proceedings in his treatment of the Irish Parliament will be seen more clearly from this, that the validity of the titles to certain lands formed one of the "graces" to be granted in the second session of the Parliament above mentioned, upon the faith of which the six subsidies had been obtained. Nevertheless, this King and this representative of a King were not ashamed, when they had secured the subsidies, to refuse the price they had solemnly agreed to pay for them. Wentworth and the crown lawyers made out to their own and their King's satisfaction that the King had a good title to all the Province of Connaught, except the county of Leitrim, which had recently been granted away by letters patent, and except church lands, held time out of mind, and the lands of religious houses, which came to the crown by the statute of dissolutions, 33 Henry VIII., and were since granted away by letters patent, and also except such other lands as were held either under letters patent from the crown or under conveyances from Richard de Burgo or his heirs.[2] The Lord Deputy proceeded into the province in question at the head of a commission, summoned juries and held inquisitions in the several counties where the King claimed the lands. The result was such, both as to the nature of it and the mode in which it was brought about, as fully to make good Wentworth's boast that he had made the King "as

---

[1] Letter from the King to the Lord Deputy, London, 22d January $163\frac{4}{5}$. Strafford's Letters and Despatches, i. 365.

[2] See "Brief of His Majesty's Title to the Counties of Roscommon, Sligo, Mayo, and Galway, in the Province of Connaught," in Strafford's Letters and Despatches, i. 454-458.

The Administration of Laud and Strafford.

absolute in Ireland as any prince in the whole world could be."[1]

But arbitrary as Wentworth's proceedings might be in Connaught, his doings in Ulster may be considered as fraught with far more ultimate danger to himself. Several hundred thousand acres had in the preceding reign been planted by new settlers, who were chiefly Scotch, and who, not less by their prudence than their bravery, kept the province in a tranquil state. Wentworth soon found an opportunity of displaying his domineering insolence towards those industrious colonists. Partly in accordance with his own tyrannical nature, and partly in compliance with the constant prompting of Laud, he interfered with the religious worship of the Scotch colonists, threw many of their elders into prison, and banished many of their ministers who would not conform to what they considered an idolatrous form of worship. He thus made for himself "an enemy more terrible," as Clarendon observes, "than all the others, and like to be more fatal,—the whole Scottish nation, provoked by the declaration he had procured of Ireland, and some high carriage and expressions of his against them in that kingdom." It is curious to compare this arrogant braggart's words with his deeds. In one of his despatches he says, "I hope if they [the Scotch in Ireland] should stir (our 8000 arms and twenty pieces of cannon arrived, which I trust now will be very shortly) to give them such a heat in their cloaths as they never had since their coming forth of Scotland, and yet our standing army here is but 1000 horse and 2000 foot, and not fewer of them I will warrant you than 150,000."[2] But at Newburn he found a tenth part of 150,000 a great deal too many for him. The Scotch returned his hatred with interest.

[1] Strafford's Letters and Despatches, i. 344.   [2] Ibid., ii. 328.

After the rout of his force under Lord Conway at Newburn, they peremptorily refused to hold any conference at York, because it was in the jurisdiction of him whom they called that "chief incendiary," their "mortal foe," the Lord-Lieutenant of Ireland. And the saying attributed, I think erroneously, to Pym is true as regards them, for though he kept out of the reach of their shot and swords at Newburn, they may be said to have never left him while his head was upon his shoulders.

Of the measures which Wentworth's eulogists have affirmed to have promoted the commercial prosperity of Ireland, the only one which can be truly said to have benefited that country in any degree was the improvement of the linen manufacture.[1] But even in his mode of doing this the tyrannous cruelty of the man's nature was amply displayed. He interdicted the sale of linen yarn unless it were reeled in a certain mode with which the poor people were unacquainted, and ordered a general seizure of all not prepared for the market according to his dictation, to effect which power was given to break into houses. And the yarn seized, instead of being brought into the exchequer, went to his own looms; he having a direct interest in excluding a competition with his own flax, which he raised in great quantities on his own lands, newly purchased, or rather newly acquired by plunder. The consequence was, that thousands of poor people, debarred the only means of livelihood, for the May rents were paid by the price of the flax and yarn, were absolutely famished. The impression his tyranny left in Ireland may be judged of by the fact that, years after, anything that recalled him might be heard to provoke a curse upon the memory of "Black Tom,"

[1] Strafford's Letters and Despatches, i. 473.

the name by which the Irish peasants long remembered Strafford."[1]

The character and tendency of all Wentworth's measures in Ireland were the same as those of the measures of all tyrants and their tools, with whom the prosperity and well-being of a people are no further considered than as they make them richer plunder to feed the vices of those for whom, according to the creed of Charles and Laud and Strafford, and all such as they, God has created all things on earth. It was thoroughly in this spirit that Wentworth thus wrote to his master: "For this is a ground I take with me, that to serve your Majesty completely well in Ireland, we must not only endeavour to enrich them, but make sure still to hold them dependent upon the crown, and not able to subsist without us; which will be effected by wholly laying aside the manufacture of wools into cloth or stuff there, and by furnishing them from England, and then making your Majesty sole merchant of all salt in Ireland; for thus not only shall they have their clothing, the improvement of all their native commodities (which are principally preserved by salt), and their victual itself from England (strong ties and enforcements upon their allegiance and obedience to your Majesty), but a means found, I trust, much to advance your Majesty's revenue upon salt, and to improve your customs; the wools they grow, and the cloths they weave paying double duties to your crown in both kingdoms; and the salt, outward in England, both inward and outward in Ireland."[2] And in another despatch he thus clenches the argument with regard to salt: "The third ground is the easiness of

---

[1] Rushworth, viii.; Brodie, iii. 73, 74; Forster's Life of Strafford, 353, note 3.
[2] Strafford's Letters and Despatches, i. 93.

making his Majesty sole merchant; salt being so perishable a commodity at sea, and carrying so great a bulk, as it is not easily to be stolen into the kingdom; and yet again of so absolute necessity as it cannot possibly stay upon his hand, but must be had whether they will or no, and may at all times be raised in price so far furth as his Majesty shall judge to stand with reason and honour. Witness the *gabelles* of salt in France."[1]

Witness also some other things which such statesmen as Laud and Strafford left out of their reckoning. If they had carried out all their *thorough*, one consequence of it would have been to change the very nature of the English race; and if this man and his confederate Laud had lived long enough, they might, instead of making a dignified end by the headsman's axe, have terminated their career in a more summary and less dignified style—a style which is the natural result of a long course of plunder and oppression, exasperating a people into a state of phrensy like that in which the Parisian populace hanged De Foulon at the lanterne and tore out the heart of Berthier before it had ceased to beat.

[1] Strafford's Letters and Despatches, i. 93.

CHAPTER IV.

*SHIP-MONEY RESISTED BY JOHN HAMPDEN—PICTURE OF THE
ENGLISH COURT.*

THE first important resistance to the government of Charles which occurred in England was unattended by the slightest particle of violence, and was a declaration in form of law of ancient constitutional rights. A resistance which about the same time arose in Scotland assumed more the violent character of a popular outbreak or insurrection, though it proved far more formidable than popular outbreaks usually are. The resistance in Scotland occurred first in the order of time, being, in fact, simultaneous with the trial and punishment of Prynne, Bastwick, and Burton; but it will be convenient to take the English case first.

The device of ship-money has been attributed to Noy. But in the second year of this reign, while Noy was a strenuous opponent of the court, ships were required from the seaports with the assistance of the adjacent counties. In 1634 the tax had so far assumed a different shape, that the inland counties were assessed as well as the maritime and, instead of ships, money was demanded, under the pretext of fitting out a fleet. A writ was drawn in form of law, and directed to the sheriff of every county in England, "to provide a ship of war for the King's service, and to send it, amply stored and fitted up, by such a day, to such a place." With this writ were sent instructions to each sheriff "that, instead of a ship, he should levy upon his county such a sum of money, and return the same to the treasurer of the navy, for his Majesty's use;" and directions were added in what manner he should proceed against such as refused.[1]

Although the precedents hunted up did not go the length of bearing out the claim now put forward on behalf of the crown, and the tax of ship-money, as levied and employed by Charles, was a flagrant usurpation, this device for raising money succeeded for several years. Heath, who, in the case of Williams, had not shown complete subservience to Laud, was removed from the office of Chief Justice of the Common Pleas, and his place supplied by Finch, who, by much solicitation of the judges, with promises of preferment to some and threats to others, as the judges themselves informed Whitelocke, obtained an extrajudicial opinion, which was to be published, "that in case of necessity, the King might impose this tax, and that he was the sole judge of the necessity."[2]

Laud and Wentworth declared this opinion, thus obtained from the judges by promises and threats, to be the greatest service that profession had done the crown in their time. "But," continues Wentworth, "unless his Majesty hath the like power declared to raise a land army upon the same exigent of state, the crown seems to me to stand but upon one leg at home,—to be considerable but by halves to foreign powers abroad; yet since this, methinks, convinces a power for the sovereign to raise payments for land forces, and consequently submits

---

[1] Parl. Hist., ii. 527; Strafford's Letters and Despatches, i. 438; Rushworth, ii. 259, *et seq.*
[2] Whitelocke, pp. 24, 25.

to his wisdom and ordinance the transporting of the money or men into foreign states, so to carry by way of prevention the fire from ourselves into the dwellings of our enemies, and if, by degrees, Scotland and Ireland be drawn to contribute their proportion to those levies for the public, *omne tulit punctum.*" What follows furnishes a direct and express refutation of the assertion that Charles merely aimed at retaining the ancient prerogative of the crown, and proves conclusively that he and his Ministry contemplated playing the same game in England which Richelieu was playing in France. "Seeing then," Wentworth writes, "that this piece, well fortified, for ever vindicates the royalty at home from under the conditions and restraints of subjects, renders us also abroad, even to the greatest kings, the most considerable monarchy in Christendom, . . . I beseech you, what piety to alliances is there that should divert a great and wise king forth of a path which leads so manifestly, so directly, to the establishing his own throne, and the secure and independent seating of himself and posterity in wealth, strength, and glory, FAR ABOVE ANY THEIR PROGENITORS."[1] These last five words are conclusive as to the question respecting Strafford's intentions to destroy whatever remained of English constitutional rights and liberties, and to make the King absolute.

Many are the proofs of the profound incapacity of the government of Charles and his ministers, but none perhaps is more conclusive than their management of this business of ship-money. A tyrant of great or even of average ability would, by the efficient use he made of some part at least of the money so raised, have furnished himself with some tenable ground for this mode of taxation. There is

[1] Strafford's Letters and Despatches, ii. 61, 62.

ample evidence to show how little Charles did with this ship-money towards the protection of the persons and property of his subjects, and for the honour of the English nation and name.

In 1636, "to sweeten," says Roger Coke, "the judges' opinion for levying ship-money," the King set out a navy, under the command of the Earl of Northumberland; Whitelocke and Coke say of sixty men of war,[1] but there is good reason to believe that many of the vessels were merchant ships.[2] The exploits of this navy are stated to be the seizing and sinking divers of the Dutch busses in the Northern Seas:[3] the result of this proceeding was that the Dutch agreed to give the King for that year £30,000 for licence to fish.[4] Now it appears upon the best authority, that of Charles's own principal ministers, that at this very time the Barbary pirates were landing on the coast of England and Ireland, pillaging the towns and villages, and carrying off the inhabitants by hundreds, nay thousands, into slavery. "The mischief," writes Laud to Wentworth in 1636, "which the most Christian Turks did about Plymouth is most true, and I pray God it do no mischief about our shipping business this ensuing year."[5] To this Wentworth replies, "The pillage the Turks have done upon the coast is most insufferable, and to have our subjects thus ravished from us, and after to be from Rochelle driven over land in chains to Marseilles, all this under the sun, is the most infamous usage of a Christian King, by him suffered, that wears Most Christian in his title, that I think was ever heard of. Surely I am of opinion, that if

---

[1] Whitelocke, p. 25, 1732; Coke's Detection, p. 259, 1697.
[2] Strafford's Letters and Despatches, ii. 56.
[3] Whitelocke, p. 25.
[4] Rushworth, ii. 322; Coke's Detection, p. 259.
[5] Strafford's Letters and Despatches, ii. 24.

this be past over in silence, the shipping business will not only be much backened by it, but the sovereignty of the narrow seas become an empty title, and all our trade in fine utterly lost."[1] Here is a picture drawn by Wentworth, one of those principal ministers, of Englishmen dragged from their homes and driven through France in chains—and all this the result of England's having been subjected first to Buckingham and next to Laud. This had been going on for years. On the 25th of March 1635, Wentworth writes to Mr. Secretary Coke: "The Biscayners have been up the river of Limerick forty or fifty miles within land."[2] In 1633, Wentworth writing on the 9th of June to the Lord Treasurer gives an account of the spoil done by the pirates, which might lead to the supposition that the English Government did not consider the protection of its subjects the duty of a Government at all. "There is one," he says, "lies upon the Welsh coast, which it seems is the greatest vessel. Another is a vessel of some sixty tons, called the *Pickpocket* of Dover, lies in sight of Dublin; and another lies near Youghall, who do so infest every quarter, as the farmers have already lost in their customs £1000 at least; all trade being by this means at a stand."[3]

It appears from Strafford's despatches[4] that the special duty of guarding the seas, of protecting and superintending English commerce, chiefly belonged to Secretary Coke, who appears to have had, from his facilities of communication with the King, the power of directing the Lords Commissioners of the Admiralty. It is perhaps hardly fair to

---

[1] Wentworth to Laud, August 17, 1636, ibid., p. 25.
[2] Ibid., i. p. 392. As to the bold demeanour of the pirates before 1634, see Strafford's Letters and Despatches, i. 68, 90.
[3] Ibid., i. 90. [4] Ibid., i. 137, 151.

judge of a man's general capacity from the extent and accuracy of his geographical knowledge at that time as measured by the standard of the present time. Nevertheless, taking into account the discovery of America by the Northmen in the tenth century, it is beyond a doubt that the enterprise of the navigators of the sixteenth century had placed a considerable amount of accurate geographical knowledge within the reach of inquirers of the seventeenth century who took the trouble to seek it. It appears, however, from the MS. letters in the State Paper Office, that this Secretary Coke, to whom was committed such momentous duties by the King, had no notion whether Iceland was an island or a continent, and that he considered Newfoundland to be a continent. Iceland he calls "a great territory, and unknown," he adds, "whether it be a main continent with Newfoundland or no. Mariners say it is one continent."[1]

With a view to justify the tax of ship-money, or at least to show that the money was expended profitably for the public service, Hume says (1636): "The effects of ship-money began now to appear. A formidable fleet of sixty sail, the greatest that England had ever known, was equipped under the Earl of Northumberland. The Dutch were content to pay £30,000 for a licence [to fish] during this year." Now the Dutch soon resumed their fishing without a licence, and that very year (1636) the *Dragon* and *Katherine*, two English ships of Sir William Courten, valued at £300,000, besides a great amount of property in them belonging to the commanders and others, were set upon by seven Dutch men-of-war as they passed the Straits of Malacca from China, and by them taken, the men tied back to back and thrown over-

[1] Dom. Corresp. Charles I., ccxxix., No. 82, MS., State Paper Office.

board, the goods taken, and the ships sunk.[1] In the latter part of the same year, the English ambassador at Paris states that "the seas are now dangerous by reason of the Dunkirkers," and then goes on to say that the other day his secretary, being in the English passage-boat with Lord Dacres and some other English gentlemen, they were met by the Dunkirkers, who (notwithstanding they were English and provided with good passports) used violence against them and robbed them, taking away from the secretary in particular divers letters directed to the English ambassador, and about £50 in Spanish pistoles, and if the sight of a Dutch man-of-war had not made them go away, they had used them worse.[2] But the best refutation of Hume is the Earl of Northumberland himself. In the words I am about to quote it will be observed that "this summer" means the summer of 1637. His letter is dated February 22, 1636, and as the legal year then commenced on the 25th of March, the date is February 22, 1637. He says—"I know not yet how I shall be disposed of this summer; whether in His Majesty's service at sea or in my own house at Petworth, for it is not declared who shall command the King's fleet. If that charge be committed to any other body, I shall not envy him that hath the honour of it, for I profess to your Lordship, unto whom I shall ever speak freely, that, as it is now managed, it is not an employment fit for any person of honour."[3] On the 24th of the same month, Northumberland again writes to Wentworth thus: "The King hath this day told me privately that he is so well satisfied with my carriage in his service the last

[1] Coke's Detection, p. 259. London, 1697.
[2] Robert Earl of Leicester to Mr. Secretary Coke, Paris, $\frac{2}{23} \frac{\text{Nov.}}{\text{Oct.}}$ 1636, Sydney State Papers, ii. 435.
[3] The Earl of Northumberland to the Lord Deputy, London, February 21, 1636, Strafford's Letters and Despatches, ii. 51.

summer that he intends again to employ me this year, which I should willingly have declined had I known handsomely how to avoid it."[1] The King afterwards made a feeble attempt at a reform of abuses charged against the officers of the navy, which, says Northumberland, in a subsequent letter to Wentworth, "were clearly proved by the testimony of many of the principal commanders in the last fleet."[2] What success attended such attempt appears from the following passage of a letter from Northumberland to Wentworth, dated "From on board the *Triumph*, in the Downs, July 15, 1637:"—"To ride in this place at anchor a whole summer together without hope of action, to see daily disorders in the fleet, and not to have means to remedy them, and to be in an employment where a man can neither do service to the state, gain honour to himself, nor do courtesies to his friends, is a condition that I think nobody will be ambitious of."[3]

As another of the effects of ship-money, Hume states that this year (1636) the King sent a squadron against Sallee, and, with the assistance of the Emperor of Morocco, destroyed that receptacle of pirates. Now for this object England sent only four ships and two pinnaces, and the success of the expedition was entirely due to the accident of Sallee having revolted from the Emperor of Morocco, whose forces attacked the town by land, while the English fleet attacked it by sea.[4] There was great congratulation

---

[1] Strafford's Letters and Despatches, ii. 51. "I perceive some others," he adds, "of whom the King is not very confidant, have been suitors for the employment; and if four pound a day whilst I am abroad be the only reward for my service, truly I could have wished it in another hand."

[2] Ibid., p. 67.   [3] Ibid., p. 85.

[4] Ibid., ii. 115, 116, 118. "The King was very willing and forward to have knighted Captain Rainsborough [who commanded the squadron against Sallee], but he declined it; so order was given that he should have a gold chain and medal of £300 price."—Ibid., p. 129.

between Laud and Wentworth on this action of Sallee, as being "full of honour," and likely to "bring great content to the subject, and help much towards the ready cheerful payment of the shipping-monies."[1] But how far this exploit proved that the ship-money was used in protecting effectively the persons and property of the people of England may be seen from the statement of the Lord Keeper in Parliament on the 21st of April 1640, as "another reason for shipping-writs this year," that the Algerines "are grown to that insolency that they are provided of a fleet of sixty sail of ships, and have taken divers ships, one called the *Rebecca*, of London, taken upon the coasts of Spain, worth at the least £260,000."[2] And Mr. Waller, in a speech to the Lords in November 1640, said: "On every county a ship is annually imposed, and who would not expect but our seas by this time should be covered with the number of our ships? Alas! my lords, the daily complaints of the decay of our navy tell us how ill ship-money hath maintained the sovereignty of the seas; and by many petitions which we receive from the wives of those miserable captives at Algiers (losing between four and five thousand of our countrymen), it doth evidently appear that to make us slaves at home is not the way to keep us from being made slaves abroad; so far has this judgment been from relieving the present or preventing the future necessity, that as it changed our real property into the shadow of a property, so of a feigned it hath made a real necessity."[3]

One might be inclined to infer from the smallness of the sum, twenty shillings, at which Hampden had been assessed for his manor of Stoke Mandeville in Bucks, that

[1] Strafford's Letters and Despatches, p. 138, in answer to Laud, p. 131.
[2] Rushworth, iii. 1139.   [3] Ibid., p. 1339.

the tax of ship-money was extremely small, about one halfpenny in the pound. And Hobbes turns this circumstance into an argument in favour of his view of the question. "Mark," he says, "the oppression; a Parliament-man of £500 a year land taxed at twenty shillings."[1] This would make the tax about one halfpenny in the pound. Whitelocke[2] calls Hampden "my countryman and kinsman, a gentleman of an ancient family in Buckinghamshire, and of a great estate and parts." Though the amount of his estate is not stated by Whitelocke, I think we may conclude that it was more than £500 a year, as Hobbes calls it, from the social position which Hampden held among his contemporary county representatives. The estate which Wentworth inherited from his father was worth £6000 a year,[3] a very large sum at that time; and though Hampden was probably far from reaching that amount, he would hardly have been termed by Whitelocke a gentleman of "great estate," if his estate had not exceeded £500 a year. However that may be, the inference from Hampden's assessment that the tax of ship-money was a light tax can be shown to be erroneous on good authority.

Among the more eminent members of Merton College, Oxford, will not be found the name of the Rev. George Garrard, who nevertheless was a fellow of that college; and if the monthly newsletters which, from 1633 to 1639, he wrote to Wentworth when Lord Deputy of Ireland were published separately from the unwieldy folios bearing the name of "The Earl of Strafford's Letters and Despatches," Garrard's name might be at least as well known as that of

---

[1] Behemoth, p. 60. London, 1682.   [2] P. 25.
[3] Strafford's Letters and Despatches, ii. 105, 106, and Dr. Knowler's Dedication prefixed to the first volume.

Howell, also one of Wentworth's correspondents. The words in which Garrard refers to his having been a fellow of Merton are characteristic. In reference to a story, which does not concern us now, of a certain baronet, whom he describes as a "pretty senseless Master of the Requests," he says: "I may be bold with him, my Lord; he was one of the Fillpots in Merton College when I was fellow there."[1] In his first letter, which is dated "Strand, December 6, 1633," Mr Garrard informs the Lord Deputy that he has settled in London constantly for almost twenty years about "*Allhallentide*;" that since he had the honour first to know his Lordship, his Lordship's great abilities to serve God, his king, and country made him love his Lordship; and that although he had never told his love "until now in this letter," yet long since it had been such that he should be ready to do his Lordship the best service in his power, "either this way of writing, or any other way; proem longer I'll use not, but fall roundly to relate things done here."[2]

The picture of a court presented in these letters of Garrard, though the darker features are carefully kept out of view, reserved for oral communication, is far more a repulsive than an attractive or pleasant one. There are idleness and luxury, and their usual attendants, want of means to continue them without a supply of money. The King is always ready for a present, or, in other words, a bribe; and his courtiers, however high their titles and proud their names, are like a pack of hungry wolves. When any place about court, from the highest to the lowest and most servile, is like to fall vacant, there are hundreds[3] of applicants for it before its occupant is dead.

---

[1] Strafford's Letters and Despatches, i. 176.   [2] Ibid., p. 165.
[3] After a statement of "the little household" settled for the King's eldest

Pardons are sold for the benefit of hungry courtiers, and deeds of ferocious and cowardly violence are resorted to by men of rank for money. Still, in that age, such was the magical influence exercised by rank and title, that women possessed of wealth not only will pay, but make offer of, large sums of money for the privilege of bearing an aristocratic title. One or two examples will convey a more distinct impression than any general description. "I had almost forgot to tell your Lordship," writes Garrard to Wentworth, January 9, 1633, "that the dicing night the King carried away in James Palmer's hat £1850. The Queen was his half, and brought him that good luck; she shared presently £900."[1] In the same letter he writes: "My Lord Savile hath had an high and mighty petition put up against him to the Lords by one Field, a very honest man as I hear, and of your Lordship's country; one much trusted by the old Savile that was wont to be so angry. This young lord is charged by him to have gotten him to his house, whither, when he came, he carried him alone into his study, shuts the door, putting the key in his pocket, goes to a drawer, whence he takes out a dagger, which he puts to his breast, and swears by a most fearful oath that if he did not presently sign and seal that writing lying before him he would kill him in the place. He sealed it." The matter got into the Star Chamber, where Mr. Garrard wishes Field good luck.[2] Mr. Henry Jermyn, in favour at court, at least with the Queen, "hath got the pardon, for which 'tis said he had £500," of a man for the abduction from school of a young lady aged fourteen, and

---

son, from groom of the stole to kitchen-officers, Garrard adds: "These are the chief of his household, yet there stood at least three or four hundred for these places."—Strafford's Letters and Despatches, ii. 167.

[1] Strafford's Letters and Despatches, i. 177.   [2] Ibid., p. 176.

marrying her against her will, for which he was condemned by the King's Bench.[1] "Here are two masks this winter; the King is in now practising his; most of the young lords about the town who are good dancers attend His Majesty in this business. The other the Queen makes at Shrovetide, a new house being erected in the first court at Whitehall, which cost the King £2500 only of deal boards, because the King will not have his pictures in the banqueting-house hurt with lights."[2] Charles had a taste for pictures—a taste which, it would seem, does not go far towards the well-ordering of a commonwealth; and the young lords about town who were good dancers probably figured afterwards among the "gallant cavaliers" who went down before the charge of the grim Puritans, who were neither good dancers nor had much taste for pictures. "This last week the Earl of Sussex was married to Sir Henry Leigh's widow of Dichely by Woodstock, daughter to the old Countess of Devonshire. She pays his debts, £1500, and between them they have £3000 a year to keep them. Here are two other rich women who bid hard for the Earl of Huntingdon; he is next to Sussex, the eleventh earl. The one the day she is married will lay him down upon a table £20,000, which she will freely give him; the other offers £500 a year during his life, and £6000 in money to go to church and marry her, and then at the church door to take their leaves and never see each the other after."[3]

Of the insolence of the lackeys of the nobility, Garrard gives the following example; and if it should be urged that the servants of the Marquis of Hamilton, being mostly Scotch, were less accustomed to a respect of law than the

[1] Strafford's Letters and Despatches, ii. 140.   [2] Ibid.
[3] Ibid., i. 262.

servants of an English peer, it may be answered that there are instances given in these pages of street-quarrels where Englishmen privileged to carry swords not only drew upon men not so privileged but occasionally killed them.

"One Carr, a servant of the Marquis of Hamilton's, was arrested before Wallingford House, which bred a mighty tumult. The serjeant carried him into a house near Charing Cross, whither flocked many of the Marquis's servants and others, broke open the house, setting ladders to it to unglaze and untile it, got in, beat the serjeants so that one of them died since, threatened to blow up the house with gunpowder, took the prisoner, brought him forth, and, with swords drawn, conducted him to Whitehall, and there put him in. The King resented this very ill, and hath caused his proclamation since to be published for apprehending the principals, who were the murtherers and chief causers and fomenters of this unlawful assembly, who in their madness neither regarded the justices, constables, nor any other whosoever."[1]

If such an outrage had been committed under the government of Cromwell, instead of issuing an idle proclamation, he would have hanged the principals among the lackeys.

When a person was pronounced *felo de se*, as his property went to the crown, his unfortunate family not only lost him but their means of subsistence. It was usual for the courtiers to beg from the King the property of the unfortunate man, sometimes before he was dead, and sometimes before there was any ground for pronouncing him *felo de se*. Two cases mentioned by Garrard are curious. In the first a man died worth near £14,000, and

[1] Strafford's Letters and Despatches, ii. 165.

as he had nobody to give it to, he gave it to his servant. "This man, before his master was interred, took the keys to look into the chest where the money was, with the sight whereof he was so overjoyed that he fell mad, crying out, 'All world and no heaven.' *Instantly he* [his property] was begged at court, physicians were sent for, he was blooded; but this joy put him into a fever, that he died within two days after his master, and they were buried both one day, the estate going to his wife and his two children."[1] In this case the court-beggars were disappointed. In the second case it does not appear whether the beggar was successful or not in his zeal to make out a man *felo de se* because he had sought to save his property from a fire. "At a fire lately happened in Queen Street, near to Drury Lane," writes Garrard, "a Popish priest, one Leake, an old man whom I well knew, being loath to part with his money, though once got out, yet when he could get nobody to go into his chamber to fetch out his trunk, in which was £500, and his bonds, he ventures in himself, and was there burnt. The man had some land, and was rich, which caused a courtier to beg his goods and estate, supposing him to be *felo de se;* because had he not gone in he had escaped with his life."[2]

By January 15, 1634-35, Mr. Garrard discovers that, besides his love for the Lord Deputy, he had a love for a hospital—a desire to be "master of a hospital,"[3] "a desire for a grant from the King of the Mastership of Sutton's

---

[1] Strafford's Letters and Despatches, i. 505.   [2] Ibid., ii. 165.

[3] In a subsequent letter to Wentworth (April 14, 1635), Garrard refers to his letter of 15th January, and says, "For my part, I would not be cofferer at court nor Chancellor of the Exchequer, if I were fit for either; my ambition goes no higher than to be master of a hospital where I may pray for my friends; and your Lordship shall oblige me much if you will please to move my Lord's Grace of Canterbury to be my fast friend in that."—Strafford's Letters and Despatches, i. 412, 413.

Hospital when it falls." Accordingly Garrard, in a letter to Wentworth of January 15, 1634-35, after stating several particulars, comes to the point thus: "Which makes me humbly beseech your Lordship that, in a letter to my Lord of Canterbury, you would recommend this, my humble desire, to his Grace. I have been known long to his Grace; the first year King James came to the crown he was proctor and I regent-master, having spent twelve years fellow of Merton College, and I visit his Grace often at Lambeth, and I thank him he useth me well. . . . I am now fifty-five years old, have only one boy. God hath put this humble desire into my thoughts, which if, when it falls, I may chance to have, I shall be better enabled to provide for him by sparing my present fortune."[1] The love of a hospital, being a laudable feeling, as well as the love of a Lord Deputy, was gratified; and, after the letter of March 20, 1637, which is headed in the folio, "The Reverend Mr. Garrard, Master of the Charterhouse to the Lord Deputy," but is still dated from the "Strand,"[2] Mr. Garrard's letters are dated "Charter-

---

[1] Strafford's Letters and Despatches, i. 361.

[2] In this letter of March 20, 1637, Mr. Garrard mentions a circumstance showing that the King was so completely under the dominion of his wife, that even in so small a matter as the Mastership of the Charterhouse he dared not act without her sanction. "My Lord of Northumberland engaged the Queen, who promised to use her power with the King when the place should fall; he died, the King at Newmarket, I instantly writ to that noble Lord, who got His Majesty moved by the Earl of Holland, either to recommend me to the Governors, who all had a good opinion of me, or, according to the institution of the house, to leave it to a free election. This His Majesty did not refuse, but said he would not resolve until he came to London, for the Queen had writ to the King *not to engage himself for any until he spake with her.*"—Ibid., ii. 153. Mr. Garrard had prudently made suit to the Queen—the omission of which might have proved more fatal to his case than even the omission of "getting His Majesty moved." Altogether, Mr. Garrard had no easy task to accomplish in obtaining the Mastership of the Charterhouse. And King Charles's wife would seem to have had an opinion of her husband's judg-

house." These things help to confirm the saying that there is nothing new under the sun, and to show that what some newswriters of the nineteenth century have been to Lord Brougham and to Lord Melbourne, other newswriters of the seventeenth century were to Lord Wentworth, to Lord Cottington, and to Archbishop Laud.

Now Mr. Garrard, being on such terms with the King and Government that imposed the tax of ship-money, his opinions and statements respecting that tax will not be set down to party prejudice. In a letter to the Lord Deputy Wentworth, dated "Strand, January 11, 1634-35," he writes thus: "In my last I advertised your Lordship that the Mayor of London received some reprimand for being so slow in giving answer to the writ sent into the City about the shipping-business; afterward the City Council were called before the Lords, and received some gentle check, or rather were admonished to take heed

ment somewhat similar to that entertained by Mrs. Headrigg for that of her husband Cuddie, "Naebody has better sense than you when ye crack a bit wi' me ower your affairs, but ye suld ne'er do anything aff-hand out o' your ain head." In order to shorten the above extract from Garrard's letter, I omitted those words which follow the word "Northumberland"—"Like a most noble friend, for me, the lowest of his servants"—words expressive of the obsequious style of address in that age from every rank to any rank above it, till we come to the highest, whose style is that of "a mortal God on earth" (to use Bacon's words). Thus Wentworth begins his letters to the King, "May it please your sacred Majesty;" and Garrard begins his to Wentworth, "May it please your Lordship;" while the King begins his to Wentworth, "Wentworth;" but how Wentworth begins his to Garrard we know not, for none have been printed; but we may infer what it would be from this beginning of a letter to the Rev. Charles Greenwood (i. 480), who had been fellow of University College, Oxford, and his "Governour," "Good Mr. Greenwood;" and Greenwood's to Wentworth is "Most honoured Lord" (ii. 338). It is observable that, while the beginning of Garrard's letters is as above stated, the beginning of some of Howell's is "My most honoured good Lord;" and of the first from Howell thanking Wentworth for the reversion of the next attorney's place in York (i. 50), the beginning is "My ever honoured good Lord;" and the beginning of the others slides down from "My very good Lord" to "My good Lord."

how they advised the City in a case so clear for the King, wherein His Majesty had first advised with his learned counsel and with his Council of State. It wrought this effect, that they all yielded, and instantly fell to seizing in all the wards of London. It will cost the City at least £35,000. They hoist up the merchant strangers, Sir William Curtyre, £360; Sir Thomas Cuttcale, £300—great sums to pay at one tax, and we know not how often it may come. It reaches us in the Strand, being within the Liberties of Westminster, which furnisheth out one ship. My Lord of Bedford, £60; my Lord of Salisbury, £25; my Lord of Clare, £40; the Lord Keeper and Lord Treasurer, £20 apiece; nay lodgers, for I am set at 40s. Giving subsidies in Parliament, I was well content to pay to; but I tell my Lord Cottington that I had rather give and pay ten subsidies in Parliament than 10s. this new-old way of dead Noye's."[1]

In September 1635, Garrard writes that the whole sum assessed on England for next spring comes to £218,500. "A notable revenue," he adds, "if it be paid every year, far better than tonnage and poundage, and yet that is paid too."[2]

Cases of hardship and annoyance of course occurred. "Sir John Stanhope was sent for up by a sergeant-at-arms, his misdemeanour thus: The Sheriff demanded of him what he was assessed at for the shipping-money. He answered he had no money, but offered to show him plate or cattle. The Sheriff took some cows to raise the money and drove them away; not putting them off suddenly, he sold them under the money Stanhope was set at, so comes again to drive more. Sir John Stanhope, a cholerick man, withstands the Sheriff's bailiffs, gives them

---

[1] Strafford's Letters and Despatches, i. 358. [2] Ibid., i. 463.

ill words, and he and his men rescue the cattle from them. He is not yet come to answer this; the sergeant returned with affidavits from the neighbour justices that he is so afflicted with the stone and pains of the gout that he cannot stir without danger of his life."[1] So wrote Garrard, January 8, 1635-36.

On the 28th of April 1637, he writes thus of Lord Say's case: "Our term is newly begun, and much term business afoot, of which there is great expectation." Of this business he mentions first, "my Lord Say's trial about the legality of raising the ship-money."[2]

The next extract from Garrard's letters to Strafford serves to show how minute and searching was the tyranny of the Government: "One St. John of Lincoln's Inn, upon some information of the Lords that he should have some hand in drawing Burton's answer, so lawyer-like it was done, had his study searched and all his papers seized on by Sir William Becher, and carried away; which made much noise in the town, because he was of counsel with my Lord Say about that great argument of the writ of gathering the ship-money, which is hereafter to be handled. But Sir William Becher fairly suffered him to send up those papers, which were sent him within two days, and all his other papers shortly after, having found no ground for that information."[3] When Mr. Garrard wrote, "One St. John of Lincoln's Inn," he little thought how terrible an adversary his patron Wentworth would find in this "one St. John of Lincoln's Inn."

In the same letter, which is dated Hatfield, July 24, 1637, Garrard writes: "Before the end of the last term the Lord Say put in his demurrer to the constable's plea, which

---

[1] Strafford's Letters and Despatches, i. 505, 506.   [2] Ibid., ii. 74.
[3] Ibid., ii. 85.

was that by virtue of the King's writ he did distrain the Lord Say's cattle for not paying the ship-money. The Lord Say's demurrer is, that the King's writ is not sufficient warrant to the constable to take distresses; upon this an argument must follow hereafter."[1]

The crown lawyers, however, did not proceed with Lord Say's case. Mr. Forster thinks that they "selected Hampden as a better man to fight it out with than the less affable and apparently more obdurate Lord Say; but here, as everywhere, they were fated to discover their mistake."[2]

Hampden engaged Oliver St. John and Robert Holborne as his counsel, and the case was argued in Michaelmas Term 1637, on the part of Hampden by St. John and Holborne, and on the part of the crown by the Attorney General, Sir John Bankes of Corfe Castle, and the Solicitor General, Sir Edward Littleton. Hampden's counsel contended that the law and constitution of England had sufficiently provided for the defence of the kingdom without the novelty of ship-money. There were the military tenures, which bound the holders of estates in land so held to military service as the price of their estates; there were the Cinque Ports, held by an analogous tenure, and bound to furnish ships or men; there were the King's certain revenues, the fruits of the Court of Wards, and other resources bestowed by the constitution on the King, all which were applicable to the public service and defence of the realm.

The case of ship-money was argued during twelve days in the Exchequer Chamber before the twelve judges. Judgment was given for the crown. Whitelocke says:

[1] Strafford's Letters and Despatches, ii. 86.
[2] The Grand Remonstrance, p. 227, note. London, John Murray, Albemarle Street, 1860.

"All of the judges (except Hutton and Croke) argued and gave their judgments for the King."[1] But Brampston, Chief Justice of the King's Bench, and Davenport, Chief Baron of the Exchequer, pronounced for Hampden, but on technical grounds, agreeing with the majority on the merits of the question. Denham, one of the Barons of the Exchequer, being extremely ill, gave a short written judgment in favour of Hampden. Mr. Justice Hutton was a correspondent of Wentworth's, and gave him a summary of his argument, which contains the law of the case in a very compact form. He says, "The substance of my argument was, that this power of raising ship-money and such charge or taxes was taken away by the statute of 25th Edward I. and the statute of *Tallagio non concedendo*,[2] and the statute of 14th Edward III. c. I. and 1st Richard III. c. 42, and by the statute 3d Car. I.—the *Petition of Right;* and *secondly*, that prerogatives of like nature, inherent to the crown, had, by statutes proceeding from the King's bounty, been granted to his subjects from all times, as I showed by many statutes of old and latter time, as you may see, amongst others, by the statutes made 21st Jac. c. 2, and by another statute the same year, c. 14. I insisted that there was not matter in the writ to manifest that there was a danger of the whole

---

[1] Whitelocke, p. 25. London, fol., 1732.

[2] Blackstone, in reference to the opinion of the judges in the case of ship-money respecting the *Statutum de Tallagio non concedendo*—namely, that it was a separate Act, principally because it was recited as such about nine years before in the preamble to the *Petition of Right*—gives it as his opinion (Tracts, p. 344; Oxford, 4to, 1771) that "upon the whole there is great reason to question the authority of this dubious Act of Parliament otherwise than as a contemporary Latin abstract of the two French charters (of Edward I.), intended (however imperfectly executed) to express the self-same meaning in another language." But that does not invalidate the argument of Judge Hutton, who quotes statutes enough without it.

realm, but of pirates and hindrance of coming in of merchants and trading."[1] How small was the effect produced by Mr. Justice Hutton's argument on the mind of Wentworth appears by the terms in which he writes to Laud, expressing his eager desire that Hampden and others like him "were well whipt into their right senses;"[2] and he then indulges in a jocular vein respecting the handling of the rod by "one Bond, a schoolmaster of the Free School of St. Paul's, London," which, with some more of the brutal pleasantries that passed between him and Laud, might turn out, at no very distant time, a somewhat bitter jest.

Of the independence and honesty of those judges who gave their judgment for the crown in the case of ship-money we may form some idea from the testimony of Clarendon, who, while he will not be suspected of any popular bias, may be considered as able to convey the general opinion of the lawyers of the time regarding the question. Men submitted to the imposition before, "pleasing themselves," he says, "with doing somewhat for the King's service, as a testimony of their affection, which they were not bound to do; many really believing the necessity, and therefore thinking the burthen reasonable; others observing that the advantage to the King was of importance when the damage to them was not considerable, and all assuring themselves that, when they should be weary or unwilling to continue the payment, they might resort to the law for relief and find it; but when they heard this demanded in a court of law as a right, and found it, by sworn judges of the law, adjudged so, upon such grounds and reasons as every stander-by was

---

[1] Strafford's Letters and Despatches, ii. 177.
[2] Ibid., ii. 158. See also p. 138.

able to swear was not law,—by a logic that left no man anything that he might call his own,—they no longer looked upon it as the case of one man, but as the case of the kingdom, which they thought themselves bound in public justice not to submit to."[1]

[1] History, i. 107. 8vo edition. Oxford, 1807.

CHAPTER V.

THE STRUGGLE OF LAUD WITH THE SCOTTISH PRESBYTERIANS—THE FOURTH PARLIAMENT OF CHARLES I.—THE LAST CASE OF TORTURE IN ENGLAND.

WHETHER or not the Presbyterians are to be classed under the general denomination of Puritans, Puritanism is not to be confounded with the ecclesiastical system of Presbyterianism, from which indeed it must be carefully distinguished. It is also certain that, though the number of Presbyterians in the Long Parliament exceeded that of those Puritans who were not Presbyterians, the Puritans of the Long Parliament who led in battle as well as in debate were not Presbyterians but Independents. The Scots, however, were mostly Presbyterians, and differed from the Episcopalians of the Anglican Church in this, that while at least such representatives of the Anglican Church as Laud were willing to lick the dust at the feet of a human tyrant, provided they could set their own feet on the neck of all other men, the Presbyterians, on the one hand, demanded that their system of theology should be accepted on pain of death[1] on earth and damnation afterwards, and, on the other hand, were prepared to offer an armed resistance to all other human tyrants; herein agree-

---

[1] Lord Macaulay concludes his account of the case of Thomas Aikenhead—the last case, I believe, of theological murder in Britain—with these words: "Wodrow has told no blacker story of Dundee."—History of England, iv. 194.

ing with the pretensions of the Roman Pontiff, even while they professed to regard the Pope as the Beast, the Antichrist, the Man of Sin. A strange exhibition of human arrogance is thus presented by a body of men, whose mental faculties were in such a state that it was a part of their creed that old women were in the habit of riding through the air on broomsticks, imagining that they were competent to compose a creed or confession of faith which was to rule the minds of all succeeding generations of mankind. The arrogance of these men is signally exhibited in their pretensions to the possession of a power "to deliver over to Satan, to lock out and debar from the kingdom of heaven,"[1] which is a manifest usurpation of the power of their God, whom they represented as making a hell, and predestinating or foredooming to it nine-tenths of the human race from all eternity.

Charles, both in accordance with his father's favourite project and with the views which Laud was constantly urging upon him, was very desirous of bringing the Church of Scotland, in point of government and ceremonies, to a conformity with that of England. But to do this required large funds, and the funds of the Church in Scotland had been almost all seized by the nobility. To meet this difficulty the King and his counsellors resolved, by one sweeping act of revocation, to resume to the crown all the tithes and benefices which had been given to or taken by laymen at the Reformation. The persons in Scotland who had obtained possession of the Church property differed in the general character of the class to which they belonged from the same class of persons in England. In England, where the ancient nobility was almost extinct and the King was almost absolute, the Church property mostly got

[1] Calderwood, p. 347.

into the hands of new men, often the mere domestics of the favourites of Henry VIII., which favourites themselves were new men also. In Scotland the case was somewhat different, the ancient nobility not having been extinguished (as they had been in England by the wars of York and Lancaster), and the King not being nearly so absolute as in England, that is, being more checked, not indeed by any constitutional checks, but by the power of the nobility, which was still sufficiently great to enable them to lay their hands on so tempting a prize as the Church property. In Scotland, therefore, the persons who got grants of the Church property from the crown, and who were called titulars of tithes, which phrase corresponds to the English term impropriators, were not to the same extent as in England new men, but they were the ancient nobles and gentry of that land, at least, a considerable portion of them. Yet there was a remarkable similarity in the two countries in regard to the grounds for making these grants. As in England the revenue of a convent had been granted by Henry VIII.[1] to a woman as a reward for having made 'a pudding that pleased his palate, and, according to Fuller, " not only all the cooks but the meanest turnbroach in the King's kitchen did lick his fingers," so in Scotland, at least according to Knox, "the patrimony of the Kirk, bishoprics, abbeys, and such other benefices, were disposed by the Queen to courtiers, dancers, and flatterers. The Earl of Bothwell, whom the Queen preferred above all others after the decease of David Rizzio, had for his part Melrose, Haddington, and New Bottel."[2] These persons used the privileges which they had acquired in a manner which sufficiently proved that the zeal for religion which they,

---

[1] Fuller's Church History, p. 337.
[2] Knox's History of the Reformation, p. 396; Brodie, i. 391.

or at least many of them, professed as the main cause of their hostility to the Church of Rome was but a very shallow pretext; for although they had engaged to take upon themselves the support of the clergy, they paid them at a rate as low as possible, while they appropriated to their own use all those endowments for the support of learning which in England the universities and other establishments were suffered to retain. They also exercised their rights of tithe with far more severity than had been done by the Roman Catholic clergy, who usually accepted a certain reasonable sum of money as a compensation for their claim, whereas they would not suffer the farmer to remove a sheaf of corn from the field till the tithe had been selected and taken. "To our great grief," said the reformed clergy, "we hear that some gentlemen are now more rigorous in exacting tithes and other duties paid before to the Church than ever the Papists were, and so the tyranny of priests is turned into the tyranny of lords and lairds."[1]

On the other hand, the Protestant clergy by no means acquiesced in the measure of primitive apostolical poverty which the lords and lairds meted out to them. They had avowedly looked for the property of the Church, or "patrimony of the Kirk," as they called it, as the reward of their piety.[2] As they made pretensions to spiritual power equal to that of the Church of Rome, they also laid claim to the temporal possessions of that Church. Thus, in the second "Declinature" of Black, it is said that God has given the keys of the kingdom of heaven to the Church, and that the clergy were empowered "to admonish, rebuke, convince,

[1] Spottiswoode, p. 164.
[2] See Brodie's History, i. 388, and the notes with the authorities there cited.

exhort, and threaten to deliver unto Satan, to lock out and debar from the kingdom of heaven."[1] Black, after citing a great number of misapplied texts of Scripture, concludes that the phrase of sheep and pastors is to be understood literally, that the laity have no more power to judge the conduct of the clergy than the sheep to judge the conduct of the shepherd. "My commission, the discharge and form of delivery thereof, should not, nor cannot be lawfully judged by those to whom I am sent, they being as both judge and party, sheep and not pastors, to be judged by this word, and not to be judges thereof."[2] Well might Mr. Brodie say, "Did ever Papal arrogance—did ever anything in any age or nation surpass this?"[3]

In this struggle for wealth and power, the lords and lairds, being much the stronger party, got all the wealth, and turned a deaf ear to the demands of the clergy for restitution and a repeal of the act of annexation. It was in vain that the clergy declared that unjust possession was no possession before God, and that those of whom they acquired the right were thieves and murderers, and had no power to alienate the patrimony of the Church.[4] The lords and lairds retained their prey, and seemed perfectly satisfied with the goodness of their title. It was in vain, also, or too late, that the Assembly enacted that all ministers who dilapidated their benefices should be excommunicated.[5] As for the power, if they left to the clergy some portion of that control over the morals of the people, such as enforcing certain penances for certain offences, which had been exercised by their Popish predecessors, they took care that

---

[1] Calderwood, p. 347.   [2] Ibid., pp. 347, 348.
[3] Hist., i. 398-405, note. Mr. Brodie supports the account of Spottiswoode and others by the authority of the other side, namely, Calderwood, and James Melville's Memoirs in MS. in the Advocates' Library.
[4] Spottiswoode, pp. 164, 165.   [5] Calderwood, p. 91.

it should not interfere much with their own freedom of action, or with the indulgence of any vices to which they might be inclined. Such men as Morton and Huntly cared mighty little for the censures of Maister John Knox, and much less for those of any of his brethren, on their indulgence in the sins, tyranny, cruelty, rapacity, sensuality, which did most easily beset them. And if they did consent to occupy occasionally in the face of the congregation, at the command of their pastor, the stool of repentance for fornication, the stool of repentance was probably as little an object of terror to them as it was to a certain venerable Scottish peer of the last generation, or to the old Earl of Eglinton, who, according to the story told by the Duke of Hamilton to Lord Dartmouth, and inserted among his notes in Bishop Burnet's "History of his Own Times," declined to leave the stool of repentance on which he had sat three successive Sundays for fornication, on the ground that it was the best seat in the kirk, and he did not see a better man to take it from him. We must now endeavour to learn how this transfer of so large an amount of property as that which belonged to the Roman Catholic Church in Scotland [1] affected the great body of the people of Scotland.

There are various ways in which this seizure of the Church property by the nobility would affect the people. In the first place, there cannot be a doubt that at least some portion of the produce of that property was, under

[1] "The Scottish clergy paid one-half of every tax imposed on land, and as there is no reason to think that in that age they would be loaded with any unequal share of the burden, we may conclude that, by the time of the Reformation, little less than one-half of the property in the nation had fallen into the hands of the Church."—Robertson's History of Scotland, i. 141, 142. 4th edition. London, 1761. This estimate would make the amount larger than in England, where it has been estimated that about one-third of the land had fallen into the hands of the Church of Rome.

the old management, applied to the relief of the poor, even though the Roman Catholic Church may have somewhat neglected its duty in that and other works for which the property had originally been granted, as is indicated in a petition in 1560 from the clergy to the Parliament "that the Pope of Rome's usurped authority should be discharged, and the patrimony of the Church employed for the sustentation of the ministry, the provision of schools, and entertainment of the poor, of a long time neglected."[1] In the second place, the churchmen were usually mild and easy landlords, and they had a vast number of small tenants. These were in great numbers dismissed by the lords and lairds who succeeded the churchmen, and those who were not dismissed were treated with an oppressive severity and a grinding rapacity that rendered their lives very wretched. One of the accounts, and that too from the richest district of Scotland, says that the countrymen were so enslaved to their lords that they were kept in a state of the greatest poverty, and that many of their women did not wash their linen above once a month, nor their hands and faces above once a year.[2] There were, however, even then, says a Scottish writer of authority, some large leaseholders.[3] The same writer observes, in regard to the above charge of want of personal cleanliness, that filth in a people may be considered the most infallible test of penury and misery, since they who are bereft of a sufficient supply of wholesome food generally want the spirit to attend to cleanliness which is within their reach.[4] From the oppression of their feudal

[1] Spottiswoode, p. 150.   [2] Whitelocke's Memorials, p. 468.
[3] Brodie's History, i. 433, note.
[4] Ibid., p. 434. I have somewhat altered Mr. Brodie's words. He says, "bereft of other comforts." To those poor oppressed people at that time, "comforts," in the sense in which the word is now used in Scotland as well

lords these poor people had no escape but death. Some writers indeed say that a part found a resource in emigration, which is reported to have been great; but I fear that was more in the shape of kidnapping than of free emigration. I have said there was no refuge from the oppression of their lords, because by the hereditary jurisdictions they could only appeal from the lords' tyranny and injustice to the lords' courts. Even in the supreme or King's courts, to which few had access, the corruption was extreme.[1] There the maxim was, " Tell me the man and I will tell you the law." In the lords' courts, justice was a very rare and dear, and human life a somewhat cheap commodity. James Boswell, in his "Letter to the People of Scotland," tells a story of a man who was tried for his life, before the abolition of the heritable jurisdictions, in the court of one of these small feudal tyrants. The jury were going to bring him in not guilty, when some one whispered them that "the young laird had never seen an execution," whereupon the verdict was death, and the man was hanged. Whether this individual story be true or not, the very repetition of it by a man like Boswell, so proud of his character of a Scotch laird, is one among many proofs of the existence in Scotland of a "deep traditional horror, the record, as it were, of that confused mass of cruelty and suffering which has left no other memorial."[2]

as in England, were out of the question. But it is generally true that people who cannot get food care little for washing.

[1] Till about the middle of the last century the judgments of the supreme court were written out in the President's chamber, and often altered after they were pronounced. President Forbes procured the abolition of this practice by a provision that they should be subscribed openly, in presence of the whole court.—Brodie's Hist., i. 429, note.

[2] The "pit and gallows," the "fossa et furca" of the "Regiam Magestatum," were the especial characteristics of feudal power. The fossa is said by Du Cange to have been a pit filled with water. The furca or gallows was

To give another instance. There is a tradition still existing in Forfarshire that Alexander Lindsay, Earl of Crawford, called the "Tiger Earl," when he reached his castle after the loss of a battle, in his savage rage killed the groom who took his horse as he dismounted. The perpetration with impunity of such an act of cowardly barbarity shows that the condition of a servant to a feudal baron in Scotland at that time was similar to that of a negro slave in states where the life of the slave is in the power of his master, and is not under the protection of the law.[1]

As I have said, the nobility having swallowed the whole of the property of the Roman Catholic Church in Scotland, were by no means disposed to disgorge any portion, however small, to form a Church Establishment. It was the project of Charles I. and Archbishop Laud to resume a considerable part of the Church property in order to form an ecclesiastical establishment in Scotland, bearing some resemblance to that of England, that arrayed the Scottish nobility and gentry in fierce opposition, and ultimately in open rebellion. These potentates had very small regard for what is understood in England by the

throughout Europe the mark of a lordship or manor. "Voltaire," says the Honourable Daines Barrington, "has so many of them on the estate which he has lately purchased in Burgundy, that he has declared he can accommodate half the kings in Europe, but that he thinks them hardly high enough for the purpose. This is an anecdote, however, which I cannot pretend to warrant any further than that I have seen it in print."—Observations on the Statutes, p. 350, note [x]. 5th edition. London, 1796.

[1] A further illustration is afforded by the story, told by Sir Walter Scott in the Malagrowther Letters, of the Scottish baron who had a sort of pillory, called in Scotland the *jougs*, on each side of the gate of his castle. Riding out one morning, he observed a marauder in one of those places of punishment. On his return, finding the other similarly occupied, he inquired whether another thief had been caught. The official to whom he put the question answered "No," but added, that as he thought the single fellow looked awkward on one side of the gateway, he ordered one of the labourers to be stuck up on the other for the sake of uniformity.

Struggle of Laud with the Presbyterians. 149

terms "liberty of the subject," as far as it related to all classes of men below the rank of lords and lairds, but they saw with great satisfaction the measures adopted by Charles and Laud to excite the fury of the people, whom they were willing enough to use now, as they had done at the Reformation, for their own ends. Indeed, though the zeal of the great body of the people of Scotland for the Covenant, and all that it contained, might be thoroughly sincere (and subsequent events, particularly in the reigns of Charles II. and James II., abundantly proved its sincerity), it must never be forgotten that at that time in Scotland oligarchical power, the power of the nobility great and small, was very great, almost absolute, while popular or democratical power, the power of the people beyond the circle of the nobility and landed gentry, was non-existent. Moreover, what we understand now in England by public opinion had then no existence in Scotland.

When I say, however, that at that time the power of the nobility was almost absolute, the expression requires some explanation. The Parliaments of Scotland, where, as all the estates sat in one chamber, the representatives of boroughs were completely overawed by the haughty nobles,[1] had early adopted the plan of selecting a committee to prepare the bills or articles (hence called Lords of the Articles), which were to be discussed. By the mode of electing the Lords of the Articles and some additional contrivances, a bill disagreeable to the King could not even be the subject of discussion. After the accession of the

---

[1] In the case of England, "the Commons," said Coke, "sitting in presence of the King and among the nobles, disliked it, and found fault that they had not free liberty to speak. And upon this reason, that they might speak more freely, being out of the royal sight of the King, and not amongst the great lords, so far their betters, the house was divided, and came to sit asunder."—D'Ewes, p. 515.

King of Scotland to the English throne, the bishops nominated eight noblemen for the articles, the nobles eight bishops, and these sixteen nominated eight representatives of shires and eight burgesses.[1] This plan placed the nomination altogether in the power of the crown. The prelates thus obtained the command of the legislature. Some great civil offices were also, in accordance with the policy pursued by Charles and Laud in England, bestowed upon ecclesiastics, which still further disgusted the nobility. Moreover, the statute 1594, c. 222, by which no bill obnoxious to the court could ever even reach the Lords of the Articles, since it had to pass first an officer of the crown, and secondly a committee nominated by the crown, was resorted to in 1633 by Charles as an apt engine for the accomplishment of his designs. But though the King might thus appear to be absolute as far as regular parliamentary opposition could be taken as a measure, he was far from being so in reality. According to this measure, the King might appear to possess not only as much power in Scotland as he did in England, but a vast deal more. Practically, however, the matter was not so. The Scottish nobles knew that if they could not successfully resist the King in Parliament, they could set him at defiance in their strong and remote castles, and even in the field if they only kept united. The fate of the Ruthvens, indeed, the Earl of Gowrie and his brother, showed that they were little inclined to assist one of their own order when they might gain more by destroying than by saving or avenging him. But the case was different when what they considered the rights of all of them were threatened. In such a case they resolved even on resistance in Parliament, though not altogether in a parliamentary way.

[1] Brodie's Hist., i. 430, 431.

They were disposed to defend their plunder by the same means by which they had acquired it. When assembled in Parliament, or the Convention of Estates, as it was termed, they determined that, rather than yield to the act of revocation proposed by the King, Charles I., they would massacre the royal commissioner, the Earl of Nithsdale, and his adherents, in the face of the assembly. With this view Lord Belhaven, an old blind man, placed himself close to the Earl of Dumfries, a supporter of the measure, and keeping hold of his neighbour with one hand, for which he apologised, as being necessary to enable him to support himself, he held in the other the hilt of a dagger concealed beneath his dress, that, as soon as the general signal should be given, he might plunge it into Dumfries's heart. Nithsdale learning something of this resolution, gave up for the time the proposed measure of revocation, and returned to court. The King, however, at length succeeded in obtaining a partial surrender of the tithes into the power of the crown. The power of levying them in kind was suppressed. Every season's tithe might be retained on the payment of a modified sum, and the entire right might be purchased from the titular at a sum restricted to ten years' rent. Moreover, with a view to the endowment of a National Church, with the power and splendour which Laud might consider not only befitting but necessary, the Abbey of Arbroath was recovered from the Hamilton family for the See of St. Andrews, and the Lordship of Glasgow for the See of Glasgow, but on terms which made the surrender a good bargain to those surrendering. Several estates of less value were also purchased for the several sees; but none were recovered without compensation, though the restitution was given out to be an act of gratuitous piety.[1] These proceedings, though they did not amount to anything like a restoration to the nation of the national property which had been seized, had more effect in arraying the Scottish oligarchy in opposition to Charles than all that King's acts of misgovernment, and all his attempts to render himself absolute master of the lives, the liberties, and the consciences of his subjects; and, together with an attempt to reverse some of the attainders that had taken place in the preceding reign, in consequence of which the Lords of Buccleuch and Cessford were compelled to surrender a part of their spoils arising from the forfeited property of Stewart, Earl of Bothwell, enraged them so much, that some wild schemes were entertained among them for dethroning Charles and placing the Marquis of Hamilton on the throne.

Two tyrannies, a monarchical and an oligarchical, were at that time contending for the dominion of Scotland. Neither of them having a regular standing army to support its pretensions, the question which should be successful depended upon which should be able to array the bulk of the people upon its side. Now, though the intense devotion to Presbyterianism which, in the subsequent reign, manifested itself in Scotland was in a great measure owing to the persecution exercised in that reign, even at this time the people at large rather preferred Presbyterianism to Prelacy; at least they objected to such a form of Episcopacy as Laud and Charles sought to introduce. The light in which the innovations sought to be introduced by Laud were viewed by the most intelligent of the Scottish clergy at that time may be seen in the correspondence of Robert Baillie, minister of Kilwinning in

[1] Burnet's Memorials of the Dukes of Hamilton, p. 30; History of his Own Times, i. 20.

Ayrshire, and afterwards Principal of the University of Glasgow. In a letter dated "Kilwinning, January 2, 1637," he says, "Bishops I love; but pride, greed, luxury, oppression, immersion in secular affairs, was the bane of the Romish prelates, and cannot have long good success in the Reformed."[1] The intermission of English Parliaments in this dark time appears to have been felt in Scotland as well as in England. Baillie says in a letter dated January 29, 1637, "It's our hearty prayer there might be a Parliament in England which might obtain all misorders there redressed."[2] Though it might appear from the first of the above extracts that Baillie was at one time in favour of a moderate kind of Episcopacy, he afterwards adopted the opinion of such of his brethren as were for a total abolition of an Episcopal Church Government. In this state of things the people of Scotland, not being in a condition to stand up for themselves, and having never really known either civil or religious liberty, had no choice but to take part with their native oppressors against the foreign tyrants who sought to obtrude "English-Popish"[3] ceremonies (a compound word which comprehended what they most hated) upon the Kirk of Scotland.

The Presbyterian mode of worship had given so much offence to Laud, that he was determined, at whatever risk, to change it, and introduce in its place a ritual approaching nearer to the Romish than the English did, and therefore still more repugnant to the Presbyterians, though the word Presbyter was allowed in Scotland as a great concession

---

[1] Baillie's Letters and Journals, i. 2. 3 vols. Edinburgh, 1841. Edited by David Laing, Esq.

[2] Ibid., i. 11.

[3] A book, characterised by Mr. Brodie as "a work of great learning and ability" (ii. 463), by Gillespie, an eminent divine, was intituled "A Dispute against the English-Popish Ceremonies obtruded upon the Kirk of Scotland."

to the prejudices of the people, instead of its derivative, priest, which had been lately introduced with much pomp into England.¹ But the expression of King James himself, who, when courting the favour of the Presbyterian party, had called the English service an ill-mumbled mass, though Laud might not have heard of it, or, if he had, might utterly disregard it, was not forgotten and not likely to be forgotten, in Scotland. Laud's biographer, Heylin, may be considered as giving expression to the opinion of his hero as to the necessity of introducing into Scotland the English ritual when he says, that in "the Kirk of Scotland, for want of some such public forms of prayer, the ministers prayed so ignorantly, that it was a shame to all religion to have God spoke to in that barbarous manner, and sometimes so seditiously that their prayers were plain libels against authority, or stuft with lies made up of all the false reports in the kingdom."² Scotland had successfully resisted all attempts to conquer her by kings very different from Charles, and by bishops clad in mail who charged at the head of their men-at-arms. Though fallen, it might seem, upon evil times since her old heroic days, with her warlike aristocracy degenerated into

---

[1] Brodie's Hist., ii. 446, note; Heylin's Life of Laud, p. 348. Argyle in a letter to Wentworth, dated "Inveraray, February 20, 1638-39," says, "So, with your Lordship's good leave, I must say still your Lordship is mistaken if you think the book that was offered and pressed here was only the English service, for in the very reading any man may see the contrair." And in the next paragraph he mentions "His Majesty's paternal care of his own children," and their being "the loather to come under the hands of indiscreet pedantis or rude taskmasters, that want the affection and moderation of a father."—Strafford's Letters and Despatches, ii. 291. The Rev. G. Garrard in a postscript to a letter to Wentworth, July 3, 1638, says, "They grow foolish at Oxford, for they had a question about the legality of ship-money; as also whether the *addita* and *alterata* in the Scottish Liturgy did give just cause of scandal; but my Lord's Grace of Canterbury [he was Chancellor of the University of Oxford] hearing of it, forbade them such questions."—Ibid., ii. 181.

[2] Heylin's Life of Laud, p. 235.

a selfish, a factious, and venal oligarchy, with her national property plundered wholesale, she was still strong enough to set at defiance the attempt to subdue her by an old woman in a mitre, who must needs traverse in a coach, and consider that a great feat, the road by which Edward Plantagenet had led to destruction his long and formidable array.[1]

The Scottish nobility showed good generalship in the way in which they began the conflict. They assembled at

---

[1] When Charles visited Scotland in 1633, for the purpose of being crowned, he was attended by Laud, like his evil demon. Laud was then Bishop of London, and just on the eve of being made Archbishop of Canterbury. In Laud's Diary there is the following curious entry in reference to this journey:— "July 8 [1633], Monday.—To Dumblain and Stirling—my dangerous and cruel journey, crossing part of the Highlands by coach, which was a wonder then."—Laud's Diary, p. 48. Laud's digestion, and consequently his temper, would have been improved if he had made the journey on foot or on horseback, instead of in his coach. It appears from some parts of his correspondence with Wentworth, that Laud was somewhat addicted to what the Presbyterians would have called gluttony, and that his friends considered venison pies, hung beef, dried fish, &c., as acceptable presents to him. In a letter dated Croydon, September 10, 1638, he thus writes to Wentworth: "I find by your letters you are gone on hunting. I hope you will find a time to go on fishing too, for I mean to be a very bold beggar, and desire you to send me some more of the dried fish which you sent me the last year." Then, after saying that the dried fish was the best, and some hung beef which Wentworth had sent him out of Yorkshire the worst, that he ever tasted, he adds, "But since you are for both occupations—flesh and fish—I wonder you do not think of powdering or drying some of your Irish venison, and send that over to brag too."—Strafford's Letters and Despatches, ii. 213. There is also an original letter, of which I made a copy, in the Harleian MSS. in the British Museum, dated "Lambeth, June 3, 1634," in which he thanks Sir William Bellasys, Sheriff of the Bishopric of Durham, for "twoe younge roebucke pyes," which did not reach him, however, in the condition intended, but "as moldye as if they had been sent from a farre countrye." Laud's temper, naturally bad, must have been made worse by indigestion, arising from feeding on such things as venison pasties, without taking enough exercise, as is evident from his telling Wentworth that he considered his ride in his coach from his London house, then in St. Paul's Churchyard, to Whitehall, as exercise, and that when translated to Canterbury he would have no exercise but to slide over in a barge from Lambeth to the court and Star Chamber.—Strafford's Letters and Despatches, i. 110.

the house of Nicholas Balfour, in the Cowgate, Euphemia Henderson, Bethia and Elspa Craig, and several other matrons, and recommended to them that they and their adherents should give the first affront to Laud's Service-book, assuring them that men should afterwards take the business out of their hands.[1] On Sunday, the 23d of July 1637, the Dean of Edinburgh prepared to read the new service before a numerous concourse of persons in the High Church of St. Giles in Edinburgh. There are many contemporary accounts bearing testimony to the violence of the tumult which followed, but the story which has gained most currency and has received the adoption of one great novelist, after having been manufactured by another, is not to be found in any of the authentic contemporary narratives. All the authorities admit that one stool was thrown at the head either of the Dean or of the Bishop, who, on the failure of the Dean to obtain a hearing, mounted the pulpit, expecting greater reverence from his office. But the adroit romance-writer would seem to have compounded his story of two parts, which did not belong in point of fact to the same incident. A certain godly woman hearing a young man behind her sounding forth "Amen," turned quickly round, and after she had warmed both his cheeks with the weight of her hands, increased by the weight of her Bible, she thus shot against him the thunderbolt of her zeal: "False thief," said she, "is there na other pairt of

---

[1] Memoirs of Henry Guthry, late Bishop of Dunkeld, p. 23. 2d edition. 1747. Mr. Brodie says (ii. 451), "Some Episcopal writers assert that there was a preconcerted plan to obstruct the service by violence, but though it would be too much to deny the assertion, there does not appear sufficient evidence to authorise the belief of it." Yet he adds afterwards (ii. 456), as a conclusion from the evidence he has himself quoted, "that the Episcopal faction were not far wrong in imputing a participation of the tumult to people of a higher class than was acknowledged by the opposite party."

the church to sing mess in, but thou must sing it at my lug?"[1]

A wild tumult instantly commenced. The Bishop was assailed with missiles and with vehement exclamations of "A pope! a pope! antichrist! stone him! pull him down!" while the windows were broken with stones thrown from without. The Bishop, on his way to his lodgings, was assaulted in the street, his great corpulency rendering his progress slow, as well as procuring for him the epithet of "beastly belligod," in addition to those of "false antichristian wolf and crafty fox." One woman cried, "Fye, if I could get the thrapple [windpipe] out of him." And when some one replied that though she obtained her desire there might presently come a much worse in his room, she answered, "After Cardinal Beaton was sticked, we had never another cardinal since; and if that false Judas the Bishop were now cut off, scarce any man durst hazard to be his successor,"—a remark which has been thought to afford proof, among other things, that the Episcopal faction were not far wrong in imputing a participation of the tumult to people of a higher class than was acknowledged by the opposite party. Precautions

---

[1] Balfour's Stonie Field-Day. The circumstance of the weight of her hands increased by that of her Bible is from Gordon of Straloch's MS., as cited by Mr. Brodie, ii. 454. Mr. Brodie adds in his note: "This is the circumstance which gave rise to the story of a woman beginning the tumult by throwing a stool—a story which I can only trace to De Foe's "Memorials of the Scottish Church." Yet Mr. Laing quotes Gordon of Straloch's MS., along with De Foe, for it. The uproar was predetermined and instantaneous. The story alluded to is thus told by Sir Walter Scott: "As the reader of the prayers announced the collect for the day, an old woman, named Jenny Geddes, who kept a green-stall in the High Street, bawled out, The deil colick in the wame of thee, thou false thief! dost thou say the mass at my lug?' With that she flung at the Dean's head the stool upon which she had been sitting, and a wild tumult instantly commenced."—History of Scotland, continued in Tales of a Grandfather, i. 414. Edinburgh, 1846.

were taken which secured the service from interruption in the afternoon. The Bishop, not considering himself safe in his own lodgings, was conveyed to Holyrood House in the Earl of Roxburgh's coach, surrounded by the Earl's retinue with drawn swords. The populace were thus prevented from rushing in upon the carriage that they might drag forth the Bishop and tear him to pieces; but they pelted the carriage with stones till its arrival at Holyrood House.[1]

This tumult at Edinburgh seemed the signal for a general resistance to the reception of the Service-book throughout Scotland. In Baillie's "Letters and Journals" there are some curious particulars. "At the ingoing of the pulpit, some of the women in his ear assured Mr. John Lindsay that if he should twitch the Service-book in his sermon he should be rent out of the pulpit." And Mr. William Annan going to visit the Bishop after supper, "is no sooner on the causey, at nine o'clock, in a mirk night, with three or four ministers with him, but some hundreds of enraged women of all qualities are about him. . . . They beat him sore; his cloak, ruff, hat, were rent. However, upon his cries, and candles set out from many windows, he escaped all bloody wounds; yet he was in great danger, even of killing." This was at Glasgow. Baillie adds: "This tumult was so great that it was not thought meet to search, either in plotters or actors of it, for numbers of the best quality would have been found guilty."[2]

---

[1] See Brodie, Hist., ii. 455, 456. Mr. Brodie cites various MS. accounts (in the Advocates' Library) of this remarkable riot.

[2] Baillie's Letters and Journals, i. 20, 21. It is worth remarking that Bishop Guthry always represents the women as having been set on by men of mark. In one place (p. 29) he says: "And so these matrons disbanded for that day, having nothing more committed to them at that time by those that hounded them out." The number of the "matrons assembled on the street" is, on one

The resistance in Scotland now rapidly acquired strength and organisation. More than thirty peers and a very large proportion of the gentry of Scotland, together with the greater number of the royal burghs, had, before the month of December, agreed not merely to oppose the Service-book, but to act together in resisting the further intrusions of Prelacy. In pursuance of this object, a species of engagement called the National Covenant was drawn up and sworn to by the bulk of the population of Scotland, 1st March 1637–38. There was afterwards a new edition or modification of this document, which was accepted with some alteration by the English Parliament, and received the title of the Solemn League and Covenant. The adoption of the Covenant by a large portion of the Scottish nobility and gentry is a fact that demands some explanation, and such explanation will throw light both on the nature of the Scottish Government and of the leading transactions of that time.

The fact that, at a subsequent period, the Covenanting oligarchy of Scotland rejected the invitation of the English Parliament to model their government into a republican form, while they were so determined in their adherence to a republican form of government in their church, is only an apparent anomaly, being produced by the uniform operation of the same cause, the same law of human nature. They were naturally desirous to keep what they had got, and they judged the best way to do that was to have monarchy in the state, and what they called a truly Christian poverty of republicanism in the Church.

On the 21st of November 1638 the Covenanters, as they

occasion, stated at three hundred. And on the occasion of this tumult at Glasgow, Baillie, it will be observed, speaks of "some hundreds of women of all qualities."

soon began to be called, held at Glasgow a general assembly of the Church, at which the Marquis of Hamilton attended as Lord Commissioner for the King. There Episcopacy was abolished, the existing bishops were deprived of their power, and eight of them excommunicated for divers alleged irregularities. It is worthy of remark that it was at this time that the Earl of Argyle first openly joined the Covenanters, among whom his political talents enabled him to take at once a leading part among the Covenanting nobility, the chief of whom were the Earls of Rothes, Cassilis, Montrose, Loudon, and Lothian, and Lords Lindsay, Yester, Balmerino, and Cranston. It has been supposed by some writers that Argyle's accession to the Covenanters was caused by his discovery of a plan for depriving him of his lands by an invasion from Ireland by the Earl of Antrim, who pretended a title to part of Argyle's estates.[1]

The Covenanters took arms to support these measures.[2] They recalled to Scotland many of the officers who had been trained in the wars of Germany, and gave the chief command to Field-Marshal Alexander Leslie of Balgony. Alexander Leslie had served under and been honoured with the friendship of Gustavus Adolphus, who promoted him to be his Lieutenant-General. He returned to Scotland in 1638, and was created Earl of Leven in 1641. His military talents do not appear to have been equal to those of David Leslie, who served under him as Lieutenant-

---

[1] See an account of this plan in Strafford's Letters and Despatches, ii. 300-305, in a despatch from Wentworth to Mr. Secretary Windebank, dated Dublin, 20th March 1638. Wentworth does not seem to have much approved of the plan.

[2] In Charles's letters to Hamilton, he bids him always grant concessions (saying, "I give you leave to flatter them with what hopes you please"), but gain time, that he might arm and recall them all. But the Scots were too quick for him; they armed first.—See Burnet's Mem., p. 55, *et seq.*

General, and was afterwards General of the Scottish army at Dunbar. Baillie says that Montrose had entertained hopes of being appointed to the chief command of the Scottish armies, and that when that honour was conferred upon Leslie, Montrose immediately began to deal with the King.[1] The Covenanters soon made themselves masters of the castles of Edinburgh, Dalkeith, and other national fortresses.

In the meantime, King Charles made preparations for the invasion of Scotland by land and sea. Of the popular feeling in England against the war in which Charles had involved himself with the Scots an idea may be formed from the following statement of Wentworth's correspondent, Garrard: "The pressed soldiers, who were taken out of Norfolk, Suffolk, Essex, and Kent, to go with Marquis Hamilton in the ships, went very unwillingly; one cut off his toe, another hanged himself—both of Suffolk—rather than they would go to the wars; and much ado had the Earl of Warwick and Lord Maynard to get them take shipping at Harwich when they knew with whom they were to go."[2] Charles's fleet, thus manned, and commanded by the Marquis of Hamilton, who had as much talent for commanding a fleet as Archbishop Laud, lay idle in the Firth of Forth, while Charles in person advanced at the head of an army of 23,000 men.[3]

[1] Baillie's Letters and Journal, ii. 261. Baillie says (i. 213), "Such was the wisdom and authority of that old, little, crooked soldier [Alexander Leslie], that all, with an incredible submission, from the beginning to the end, gave over themselves to be guided by him." But how does that agree with the facts respecting the interference both of the nobility and clergy at Kilsyth, Dunbar, and elsewhere, and with Lieutenant-General Baillie's statement, which will be quoted in a subsequent page?

[2] Rev. G. Garrard to the Lord Deputy, May 20, 1639, Strafford's Letters and Despatches, ii. 351. May fully corroborates this; see Hist. of the Parl., book i. chap. v.

[3] Charles attempted to gain adherents by proclaiming a pardon for the past,

On the other side, the Scottish Covenanters had raised an army of twenty-four or twenty-five thousand men, among whom a considerable degree of military discipline had been introduced. The highest Scottish nobles acted as colonels, the captains were gentlemen of rank and fortune, and the inferior commissions were given chiefly to certain officers who had served abroad. They lay encamped on Dunse Law, a hill close by the town of the same name, which rises with a gentle slope, terminating in a level of nearly thirty acres, and still bears on its broomy top marks of the encampment of the Covenanters.

Instead of a decisive battle, only one very slight action took place, when a few English cavalry retreating hastily and in disorder from a still smaller number of Scots, seemed to show that the invaders had not their hearts engaged in the war. A treaty was entered into. The King granted a declaration, in which, without confirming the Acts of the Assembly of Glasgow, he agreed that all matters concerning the regulation of Church government should be left to a new convocation of the Church. The Covenanting Lords disbanded their forces, and restored to the King's troops the strong places which they had occupied; but they held themselves ready to take arms and seize upon them again on the slightest notice. The General Assembly of the Church, convened according to the treaty, confirmed all that had been done by their predecessors at Glasgow. The Scottish Parliament on their part demanded several privi-

and offering the conditions proposed to the Assembly at Glasgow; but denouncing as traitors all who should refuse to submit on such terms, and disposing of their lands to their tenants or vassals who embraced the King's side, and the feudal holdings of the vassals to the superiors of whom they held, and likewise the property of tenants who adhered to the Covenant to the landlords who took the opposite side. "This wise plot," says Baillie, "proved as pedantic a policy as all the former had done; not a man regarded the favour; all were more enraged with that lawless condemning and alienating of lands."

leges necessary to freedom of debate, and required that the estates of the kingdom should be convened at least once every three years. On receiving these demands the King prepared to renew the war.

But the difficulty of raising money, and the general disorder and embarrassment of his affairs, determined the King to send for Wentworth, who had on the 12th of January 1640 been created Earl of Strafford. Accordingly Strafford came over from his government of Ireland, and it was resolved to call a Parliament in England for the first time for eleven years. The House of Commons met on the 13th of April 1640, determined to redress grievances which were great and manifold. But the King wished them to vote the supplies before they occupied themselves with the redress of grievances. Long discussions arose on this subject. The Commons showed themselves resolved to make the grievances take precedence of the supplies. The King had recourse to the interference of the Lords. The Lords voted that the supplies ought to precede the grievances.[1] The Commons then after a long debate resolved that the vote of the peers was a violation of their privileges.[2] The King sent a message to the Commons, that if they would grant him twelve subsidies, payable in three years, he would engage not to continue to levy the tax of ship-money without the consent of Parliament.[3] The sum appeared immense; it was more, they said, than all the money in the kingdom. However, notwithstanding their repugnance to suspend the inquiry respecting grievances, they took the message into consideration. They were on the point of deciding that they would grant subsidies without fixing the amount of them, when the Secretary of State, Sir

[1] Parl. Hist., ii. 562.   [2] Ibid., 563.
[3] Ibid., 570, 571.

Henry Vane (the elder), rose and said, that unless they admitted the whole of the message, it was not worth while deliberating, for he had authority to tell them that the King would only accept what he had demanded. Herbert, the Solicitor-General, confirmed the assertion of Vane. On the following day, the 5th of May 1640, the Parliament was dissolved, three weeks after it had assembled.

As soon as the Parliament of Scotland heard that the King was again collecting his army, they reassembled theirs, with such speed that it was plain they had been occupied during the short suspension of arms in preparing for a new war. They did not now wait till the King should invade Scotland, but at once crossed the Tweed on the 20th August 1640, their horse troops standing in the water to break the force of the stream, their foot all wading in order up to their middle. On this occasion a man who was afterwards to make himself very famous had an opportunity of showing the qualities of an active and hardy officer. "The lot," says Baillie, "gave the van that day to Montrose; to whom I think it was very welcome. He went on foot himself first through, and returned to encourage his men; yet one of his sojours, and he only of all the army, did drown. All our foot crowners[1] went through on foot, except one or two, being employed to break the water on horse."[2] The Scots advancing to the banks of the Tyne, found Lord Conway posted at Newburn with 6000 men, having batteries of cannon in his front, and prepared to dispute the passage of the river. On the 28th of August the battle of Newburn was fought. The Scots, after silencing the English artillery by their

---

[1] Colonels of foot regiments.

[2] Baillie, i. 256. I have modernised Baillie's spelling. He spells "water" "watter," according to the Scotch mode of pronouncing the word.

superior fire, entered the ford, girdle deep, and made their way across the river. The English fled with disorder, and almost without resistance. Monk commanded a regiment on this occasion, and had for his own guns but one ball and one charge of powder. He applied for ammunition to Major-General Astley, and received for answer that there was no more. Whereupon posting his soldiers along the hedges, armed with muskets, he imposed so well upon the enemy, that they did not venture to attack him, and he succeeded in carrying off the English artillery to Newcastle, where, however, with the place itself, it very soon fell into the hands of the Scots. Long afterwards Monk used to speak with indignation of the weak and cowardly counsels which in 1640 had thrown away an army fitted to produce a very different result.

On the 11th May 1640, a mob, consisting almost entirely of youths and apprentices, attacked Archbishop Laud's palace at Lambeth. Laud thus notes the result in his Diary:—"May 11, Monday night, at midnight, my house at Lambeth was beset with 500 persons of the rascal riotous multitude. I had notice, and strengthened the house as well as I could, and, God be blessed, had no harm." It is observable that when Laud afterwards makes another entry in his Diary respecting this affair, he omits altogether one very important part of it, namely, the use of the rack in violation of the laws of England, even as declared by the judges of his master, Charles I. He says, "One of the chief being taken, was condemned at Southwark on Thursday, and hanged and quartered on Saturday morning following." The inhuman punishment of treason was awarded to the victim by the crown lawyers because there happened to be a drum with the mob, and the marching to beat of drum was held to be a levying of war against the King. But the inhuman execution on Saturday for what was termed treason was not all; for on Friday, notwithstanding the solemn decision of the judges in the case of Felton against the use of torture, as always and in all circumstances contrary to the law of England, John Archer, the unhappy man who had been arrested as one of the rioters, was racked in the Tower to make him confess his companions; and the King's serjeants, Heath and Whitfield, took his examination on the rack. The warrant has been printed by Mr. Jardine in his valuable tract on the "Use of Torture in England."[1] Mr. Jardine, after stating that on the 21st of May 1640 a warrant was issued under the King's signet, directing the Lieutenant of the Tower and two of the King's serjeants to examine one John Archer, who was charged with having been concerned in the tumultuous attack upon Archbishop Laud's palace, and "if upon sight of the rack he does not make a clear answer, then they are to cause him to be racked as in their discretion shall be thought fit," says, "This is the last recorded instance of the infliction of torture in England, and, as far as I have been able to discover, the last instance of its occurrence."

[1] Pp. 108, 109.

CHAPTER VI.

MEETING AND FIRST PROCEEDINGS OF THE LONG PARLIAMENT.

ON the 3d of November 1640, the fifth Parliament of Charles I.—that Parliament which, from the length of its duration, is known as the Long Parliament—met at Westminster.

Although the very word Parliament implies talking, the Long Parliament is not famous for what it said, but for what it did. All that could be said on the great constitutional questions had been said more than ten years before in the debates on the Petition of Right by the greatest constitutional lawyers that England has ever seen—by Coke, by Selden, by Prynne, by Noy, by Maynard, by Glanville. The King, who, after many evasions, had passed the Petition of Right, had afterwards acted in open defiance of the law to which he had given his solemn consent, and had governed without Parliaments, and solely according to his own absolute will, and had then attempted to vindicate that course by the sword. The chances of war had gone against him, and now, under the pressure of circumstances, he had again recourse to a Parliament, because for the time he saw no other means of supplying his want of money.

In the House of Commons the leaders of the opposition to the court were Pym, Hampden, and St. John. At the opening of the Long Parliament many opposed the court who neither belonged to the party of Pym and Hampden, nor to the party of those who, after the deaths of Pym and Hampden, became the leaders of the Long Parliament. In those winter months of 1640 we see men acting together in Parliament who afterwards never met but on fields of battle. We see Falkland speaking and voting on the same side with Hampden; and more than that, we see men acting together who afterwards evinced towards each other a more envenomed hatred than that of the combatants on the opposite sides of a field of battle. For we see Hyde and Holles speaking and voting on the same side with the men whom they afterwards hated with a hatred surpassing that of ancient mortal enemies—a hatred impelling them to seek to destroy them while they lived, and when they were dead to blacken their memories. But Hyde requires something more than a passing notice.

Edward Hyde, afterwards the celebrated Earl of Clarendon, was the son of Henry Hyde, a younger son of Lawrence Hyde, of West Hatch, Esquire. This Lawrence Hyde was the younger son of Robert Hyde of Norbury, in the county of Chester, Esquire, which estate of Norbury had, according to Clarendon, continued in that family and descended from father to son from before the Conquest. Edward Hyde was born at Dinton in Wiltshire, six miles from Salisbury, on the 18th February 1608. He was educated in his father's house at Dinton under the care of a schoolmaster, to whom his father had given the vicarage of that parish, till he was thirteen years of age, when he was sent to Magdalene College, Oxford.[1] Although at that time students went to the English universities at a much earlier age than they do at present, Hyde appears to have gone to Oxford at an age earlier than the average

[1] Clarendon, Life, i. 1–7. Oxford, 1827.

age. Thus Pym went to Oxford at fourteen,[1] Hampden[2] and Vane[3] at fifteen. It seems also to have been a usual practice at that period to leave the university without taking a degree. Hampden, Pym; and Vane all appear to have done so, as well as many more of the eminent men of that time.

Edward Hyde went from Oxford to the Middle Temple, with the intention of really devoting at least a part of his time to the study of the law. He took care, however, so to distribute his time as to reserve some portion of it for the pleasures of society. He had laid it down as a rule, as he has himself informed us in his Life, always to be found in the best company, and to aim at intimacy with the persons most considerable for their fortune, rank, or personal endowments, though that portion of his time which, in the earlier period of his residence in the Temple, was passed in the society of the young officers who filled the town on the breaking out of war with Spain and France, and which he appears to have looked back upon with feelings of dissatisfaction and even of terror, may perhaps be regarded as an exception to the rule. The list of his early intimacies, including the names of Ben Jonson, Selden, May, Sir Kenelm Digby, Morley, Hales, Chillingworth, and Sir Lucius Cary, afterwards Lord Falkland, attests the judgment of his selection. But Hyde's view of advantage from the judicious distribution of the portion of his time he did not devote to study went farther than that. Favourable circumstances enabled him to acquire the patronage of the most powerful personages about the court, of the Marquis of Hamilton, and of Archbishop Laud. Their countenance, and "the familiarity used

---

[1] Wood's Ath. Oxon., title, "Pym." [2] Ibid., title, "Hampden."
[3] Ibid., title, "Vane."

towards him," as he himself informs us,[1] by the Earl of Pembroke, Lord Chamberlain, the Earl of Holland, and many other lords and ladies, and other persons of interest in the court, made him be looked upon by the judges in Westminster Hall with much "condescension."[2] The nature of the professional advantages derived from such patronage may be inferred from a passage of a letter from Hyde to Whitelock in 1637, in which he says, by way of excuse for the shortness of the letter—" My pen is deep in a Star-Chamber Bill."[3]

[1] Clarendon, Life, i. 68. Oxford, 1827.

[2] The nature of this "condescension" is thus explained by Roger North, speaking of the favour shown by the Lord Chief Justice Hyde to Francis North, afterwards the Lord Keeper Guilford—"This judge was industriously favourable to his Lordship, calling him cousin in open court, which was a declaration that he would take it for a respect to himself to bring him causes." —Life of Lord Keeper Guilford, i. 78. 3d edition. London, 1819.

[3] Whitelock's Memorials, p. 26. London, 1732. Mr. Sanford (Studies and Illustrations of the Great Rebellion, p. 402) says that "the compilation published after his death, entitled Whitelock's Memorials, is manifestly a bookseller's speculation, and founded on some rough notes of Whitelock, eked out by scraps from the newspapers, and other much more doubtful sources of information; and edited by some Royalist who had little personal knowledge of the general events of the Civil War, and who has not only made sad confusion in dates, but (as in the case of Strafford's trial) has also introduced certain passages which may be safely pronounced to be absolute forgeries." And in a note at p. 324 he refers to pp. 40, 41 of the edition of 1682 of Whitelock's Memorials, as to Whitelock declining to undertake the conduct of the 24th Article, of which there is not a trace in Rushworth or any other account of the trial that he has seen. Mr. Sanford's long and laborious researches on this period of English history give, no doubt, weight to his opinion; but such a case as that of the words I have here quoted in my text from Whitelock's Memorials—words from a private letter of Hyde to Whitelock, which he had inserted in his Journal—seems to me to prove that Whitelock kept a regular journal, in which he set down things as they occurred. It would be perhaps impossible to prove that the edition even of 1732 is in the precise condition in which Whitelock left his Journal. The edition of 1682 is admitted to have been spurious, by whomsoever Whitelock's papers had been tampered with. I have not compared the two editions of Whitelock's Memorials, but have always used that of 1732, regarding that of 1682 as untrustworthy. And to me the edition of 1732 has not looked like a compilation from newspapers, but like notes written from day to day by a man

Clarendon has displayed great ability both in his utterances and in his reticence—both in what he has told and in what he has forborne to tell. If he had told all or even half of all he knew of the history of the men and women, particularly the court men and women, of that time, his revelations would have been as strange and startling as those of Tacitus, or even as those of Suetonius and Juvenal. Though he might be inferior to some of his contemporaries as an eloquent and adroit speaker, both at the bar and in Parliament, he was, as a writer, a consummate advocate; and his History and his Life, taken together, may be truly viewed as a long, an elaborate, and most adroit defence of the court and the policy of the Stuarts. What a strange, dark history, for instance, is half revealed, half kept back in sombre shadow and fearful mystery, in what he tells us of the Bruce and Sackville duel; and in his History, taken together with what he lets out in his Life, of the habits and instincts of Sir Edward Sackville, Earl of Dorset, and of his own means of obtaining an intimate knowledge of them; of his having, when a young man in the Temple, spent much time "in the eating hours with the Earl of Dorset, the Lord Conway, and the Lord Lumley, men who excelled in gratifying their appetites;" of Dorset's[1] "person, beautiful and

---

who had special means of information which his position gave him. At the same time there may be many passages even in the edition of 1732 which were not written by Whitelock. For example, I consider it absolutely impossible that the account of the battle of Marston Moor could have been written by Whitelock, for reasons which I have shortly stated in a note to a subsequent chapter (Chapter XIV.)

[1] The account given by Aubrey of Venetia Stanley, who, after having been the mistress of Richard Sackville, Earl of Dorset, the elder brother of this Edward Sackville, whom he succeeded in 1624, became the wife of Sir Kenelm Digby, is very characteristic of that time. See Aubrey's Letters and Lives, vol. ii. p. 330, note. London, 1813.

graceful and vigorous, his wit pleasant, sparkling, and sublime, and his other parts of learning and language of that lustre that he could not miscarry in the world;" of the full and unrestrained scope he gave to his appetites in the pursuit of all sensualities which that season of life— the latter years of the reign of James I., when the court of England was a scene of drunkenness and of infamous vices, such as had seldom if ever been exhibited in a Christian country—could suggest to him; of the savage duel in which he killed the Lord Bruce under the walls of Antwerp, " upon a subject very unwarrantable;" of his subsequent life, not altogether undarkened by remorse, yet remorse so ineffective that it did not " make that thorough impression upon him, but that he indulged still too much to those importunate and insatiate appetites, *even of that individual person, that had so lately embarked him in that desperate enterprise.*"[1] Well might Clarendon say of himself, that when he looked back to those days of his own early life, when he herded with such associates, he had much more cause to be terrified upon the reflection than the man had who viewed in the morning Rochester Bridge, which he had galloped over in the night, and saw that it was broken.[2] Such might have been the feelings of many

[1] Clarendon, Hist., i. 106, 107. Oxford, 1826.
[2] Clarendon, Life, i. 75. Oxford, 1827. Clarendon's sentence here is a remarkable instance of the dislocation of grammar which frequently occurs in his writings—" The man who viewed Rochester Bridge in the morning that it was broken and which he had galloped over in the night." Dante has an image somewhat similar :—

"E come quei, che con lena affanata
Useito fuor del pelago alla riva,
Si vulge all' acqua perigliosa, e guata;
Cosi l' animo mio, ch' ancor fuggiva,
Si volse 'ndietro, a rimirar lo passo,
Che non lasciò giammai persona viva."
Inferno, c. i. v. 22.

a man who survived to die quietly in his bed after having in any, even the slightest degree, come in contact with that hideous court or any of its inmates—of any man, at least, who retained enough of the nature of man to feel horror of crimes branded by the laws of God and man—of crimes which the records of antiquity represent as having been punished by fire from heaven, by the direct and dreadful vengeance of the Omnipotent.

When all the difficulties of the case are taken into account, it may be doubted whether full justice has ever been done to Clarendon's talents as an advocate. The case committed to or undertaken by him resembled those "delicate investigations" in which the characters of persons of high rank or in high place are most intimately involved, and in which the most consummate advocates at the bar are retained with the highest fees. The fee which Clarendon ultimately received was no doubt a very large one—but never, perhaps, was a heavy fee better earned by the exquisite tact and adroitness of the advocate in marshalling the strong points of his case and keeping the weak points as much as possible out of sight. Those writers who attribute all this to a fondness for mystery, which they impute to Clarendon, take a very superficial view of the matter. Thus, in his account of the Bruce and Sackville duel, as the lady referred to under the phrase "that individual person" was not a public character, it might be as fruitless as impertinent to attempt to identify her. But, in a subsequent passage of his "History" (vi. 191), it is at least very probable that, by "some persons who were wonderfully fearful that the King should make his escape and dreaded his coming into France," he meant the Queen, who had at that time very cogent reasons for not desiring her royal husband's society. Clarendon wrote his "History" as if he appeared at the bar of the world as counsel for Charles II., for Charles I. and his Queen, and also for James I. If, as I have elsewhere remarked, the imperial power at Rome had been settled on one family, as the royal power in England was on the family of Stuart for the greater part of the seventeenth century, Tacitus could not have written as he has done respecting the characters of Tiberius, Caligula, Claudius, Nero, Messalina and Aggripina. When we read, therefore, Clarendon's characters of the Stuarts, as well as of their adherents, from Strafford to Montrose, and of their opponents, from Hampden to Cromwell, we must ever bear in mind that we are reading the discourse, however able, adroit, and even subtle, in its analysis of human character, of the avowed advocate of the Stuarts before the tribunal of posterity.

There is a writer, like Clarendon, the historian of a great war of which he was the contemporary, whose fame is still growing after more than 2000 years, between whom and Clarendon a comparison naturally suggests itself. The result of such a comparison is certainly not favourable to Clarendon, even in regard to that most important quality of a historian, a devotion to truth, in which we might have hoped that an Englishman would have been at least equal to a Greek. I will quote from a recently published "History of Greece" the ablest estimate of Thucydides as regards his truthfulness as a historian which I have ever met with, and we shall see as we proceed how far Clarendon is from even approaching such a standard. "The political judgments of Thucydides," says Mr. Cox, "are unfortunately not always to be trusted. Least of all are they to be trusted in the cases of Nikias and of Kleon; but it is the happiest thing that his exact and scrupulous truthfulness has in each case preserved to us the facts

which show how far or why his censures are undeserved."[1]
I fear that Clarendon, like Thucydides, a contemporary historian, and, like him, also an actor in some of the transactions he relates, will be found not to come up to the standard of "exact and scrupulous truthfulness" which Mr. Cox, after the most careful examination, has considered Thucydides to have attained. I fear that Clarendon, unlike Thucydides in his treatment of Nikias and Kleon, in his treatment of Vane and Cromwell, so far from recording the facts in such a shape as to show that his censures are undeserved, has suppressed some facts and distorted others in the way that seemed best adapted for his purpose of blackening the memory of the men he hated. In that most important part, too, of the historian's labour, the management of the perspective of history, the superiority of Thucydides over Clarendon is immense. "Those skirmishes on which Clarendon dwells so minutely would have been told by Thucydides with perspicuous conciseness, while important battles and events would have been told with minuteness without prolixity."[2]

There was a class of persons at that time in the House of Commons very different from either the fine speakers or the fine gentlemen—a class denominated by Mrs. Hutchinson the "worsted-stocking men."[3] These men might be taken as the representatives of that large portion of the English nation whose position and pursuits in life did not permit them to devote that amount of time and attention either to rhetoric or to fencing which was

[1] G. W. Cox's History of Greece, ii. 422. London, 1874.
[2] Lord Macaulay's Essay on History, Miscellaneous Writings, pp. 111, 130. London, 1875.
[3] "A certain mean sort of people in the House, whom, to distinguish from the more honourable gentlemen, they called *worsted-stocking men*."—Memoirs of Colonel Hutchinson, p. 279. Bohn's edition. London, 1854.

absolutely necessary for that degree of skill and dexterity in the use of the tongue or of the rapier[1] which would have given them any chance of victory in a war of words with such fine speakers as Pym or Strafford, or Hyde or St. John, or any chance of life in a hand-to-hand encounter with such fine gentlemen as Sir Edward Sackville. And Sackville, be it observed, though perhaps rather above the average in bodily strength and activity, was but one of a numerous class. The fact of the great amount of time and practice—years of incessant labour—absolutely necessary for the acquisition of the art of fencing in any degree of perfection, might, in the event of an appeal to the sword, appear likely to give much the best chance of success to those who had devoted most time to the use of the rapier—a far more deadly weapon in a close hand-to-hand single combat than the broad sword; and those would be rather found among the courtiers and fine gentlemen than among the "worsted-stocking men." Nevertheless, among these men, whose worsted stockings, ill-made cloth suits, plain collars and small bands, and somewhat neglected hair, formed a strong contrast to the silk and lace and embroidery and perfumed curls of the fine gentlemen, there were men who, if they had not devoted quite so much time to the use of the rapier as Sir Edward Sackville, had by no means neglected either that or the other bodily exercises fitted to make men formidable in war.

[1] The use of the rapier, which had upon the Continent long superseded in private duel that of the sword and buckler, was introduced into England towards the end of the sixteenth century, according to Fuller, by Rowland Yorke, who betrayed the fort of Zutphen to the Spaniards. One effect of this change would seem to have been to diminish the advantage of mere bodily strength, since there is a complaint in a comedy printed in 1599, "The Two Angry Women of Abingdon," that if sword and buckler fight be once gone, "this poking fight of rapier and dagger will come up; then a tall man and a good sword and buckler man will be spitted like a cat or rabbit."

Proceedings of the Long Parliament. 177

There was one of those men of whom, though I shall have to speak of him more in detail hereafter, I would here say a few words.

He was a man about the middle height—about two inches under six feet—of a person strong and well knit, but, though not awkward like a timid, ill-made man, neither graceful nor courtly, rather abrupt and clownish in his movements. His features were strongly marked, and his face was rough and reddish, like that of a man who passed much of his time in the open air and took much violent exercise. Though his forehead was well arched and massive, and his head large and well shaped, and his mouth told quite a history in its singular power of expression, indicating at once deep thought and indomitable resolution, combined with enthusiasm, with pity, with melancholy, these things are apt to escape the casual observer; and the general expression of his strong features, roughened and reddened by wind and sun, might have seemed to men accustomed to live in courts and cities that of simplicity of character and ignorance of the world. In a word, the whole impression conveyed by the countenance, joined to an ungainly address and harsh voice, might be to a stranger, at least one who was a courtier, that the man was a farmer or small squire, who, by some accident, had emerged out of his own element and found his way into Parliament. The consequence was that a stranger, if a cunning man, who might have occasion to talk with him on business of importance, might be apt to leave him with the impression, if not with the firm conviction, that he had outwitted him. But the cunning man of the world might soon find that he had been somewhat premature in his conclusion, and that he had been thoroughly checkmated by the rough-looking, rough-spoken rustic, and into the air "hoist with his own petard." For this man who looked such a mere clown was not only daring as Cæsar but crafty as Sulla and inscrutable as the grave. And though the courtiers and fine gentlemen of the House, who prided themselves on their fine clothes and fine manners, might think but lightly of him then, before many years had passed their contempt was to change into a very different feeling. For that clown was the man who was to lead the charge at Naseby, and at Marston Moor bring up the cuirassiers who were to scatter Rupert's chivalry to the winds. The name of this member was Oliver Cromwell —a man by birth a gentleman, who had followed not very successfully the business of farming his own land, but who was destined to attain a much greater measure of success in the occupations of his after-life, those of a soldier and a statesman.

On the 7th of November, the first day on which the House entered upon business, Pym opened the debate on grievances, and was vehement in his exposure of the many acts of tyranny under which the nation had suffered during the long intermission of parliaments.

On the 7th of November the Commons passed a resolution that those victims of Star Chamber and High Commission tyranny and cruelty, Mr. Prynne, Dr. Bastwick, and Mr. Burton, who, after having been barbarously mutilated, had been sent to distant prisons, should be brought up forthwith by warrant of the House, and made to certify by whose warrant and authority they had been mutilated, branded, and imprisoned. Within a month after the return of Prynne, Bastwick, and Burton, their business was referred to a committee, upon whose report it was voted by the House that their several judgments were illegal, unjust, and against the liberty of the subject;

and about a month after it was further voted that they should receive damages for their great sufferings, and that satisfaction should be made them in money, to be paid by the Archbishop of Canterbury, the other high commissioners, and those lords who had voted against them in the Star Chamber, and that they should be restored to their callings and professions of divinity, law, and physic. The damages were fixed for Burton at £6000, for Prynne and Bastwick at £5000 each. But though the Parliament could thus restore those persecuted men to liberty, and even make some compensation for their pecuniary losses and fines, it could not restore their mutilated bodies; and though it could punish the murderers, it could not bring back the murdered Eliot from the tomb.

Upon the 11th of November a motion was suddenly made by Mr. Pym, who declared that he had something of importance to make known to the House, and desired that the outward room should be cleared of strangers, and the outer doors upon the stairs locked. This being done, Pym rose and began by alluding to the grievances under which the nation laboured, and which had formed the subject of discussion on former occasions. He inferred from those grievances that a deliberate plan had been formed of entirely changing the frame of government, and subverting the ancient laws and liberties of the kingdom. Then entering into some commendation of the nature and goodness of the King, he thus continued: "We must inquire from what fountain these waters of bitterness flow, what persons they are who have so far insinuated themselves into his royal affections as to be able to pervert his excellent judgment, to abuse his name, and wickedly apply his authority to countenance and support their own corrupt designs. Though he doubted not there would be many found of their class who had contributed their joint endeavours to bring this misery upon the nation, yet there was one who, both by his capacity and inclination to do evil, enjoyed an infamous pre-eminence; a man who, in the memory of many present, had sat in that House an earnest vindicator of the laws, and a most zealous assertor and champion of the liberties of the people; but he had long since turned apostate from those good affections, and, according to the custom and nature of apostates, was become the greatest enemy to the liberties of his country, the greatest promoter of tyranny that any age had produced." He then named "the Earl of Strafford, Lord-Lieutenant of Ireland, and Lord President of the Council of York, who, he said, had in both places, and in all other provinces wherein his services had been used by the King, raised ample monuments of his tyrannical nature, and that he believed if they took a short survey of his actions and behaviour, they would find him the principal author and promoter of all those counsels which had exposed the kingdom to so much ruin."[1] He then instanced some high and imperious actions done by him in England and Ireland, some proud and over-confident expressions in discourse, and certain passionate advices he had given in the most secret councils of state, adding, says Clarendon, "some lighter passages of his vanity and amours, that they whose patriotism did not arouse in them alarm and indignation at the actions of the violent and despotic minister, might at least be moved to aversion and contempt towards the bold and unprincipled libertine;" and so concluded "that they would well consider how to provide a remedy pro-

[1] Clarendon, i. 300, 301. 8vo edition. Oxford, 1826.

portionable to the disease, and to prevent the further mischief they were to expect from the continuance of this great man's power and credit with the King, and his influence upon his counsels."[1]

While the debate still continued respecting the Earl of Strafford, a message came from the Lords concerning a treaty with the Scots, desiring a meeting by a committee of both Houses that afternoon. Pym and some other members, suspecting that the Lords, surprised and perhaps alarmed at hearing of the extraordinary precautions just taken to exclude strangers, had sent these messengers with an object very different from the professed one, quickly despatched them with the following answer,—" That the House hath taken into consideration the message from the Lords, but that at this time the House is in agitation of very weighty and important business, and therefore they doubt they shall not be ready to give them a meeting this afternoon as they desire; but as soon as they can, they will send an answer by messengers of their own." They then resumed the consideration of the "weighty and important business" to which they had alluded.[2] In conclusion, it was moved and carried, with the consent of the whole House, that the Earl of Strafford might be forthwith impeached of high treason; Lord Falkland alone modestly desiring the House to consider "whether it would not suit better with the gravity of their proceedings first to digest many of those particulars which had been mentioned by a committee before they sent up to accuse him, declaring himself to be abundantly satisfied that there was enough to charge him." Which, says Clarendon, was very ingeniously and frankly answered by Pym, " That such a delay

[1] Clarendon, i. 300, 301.   [2] Rushworth, iv. 43, fol. 1721.

might probably blast all their hopes, and put it out of their power to proceed further than they had done already; that the Earl's power and credit with the King, and with all those who had most credit with King or Queen, was so great, that when he should come to know that so much of his wickedness was discovered, his own conscience would tell him what he was to expect, and therefore he would undoubtedly procure the Parliament to be dissolved, rather than undergo the justice of it, or take some other desperate course to preserve himself, though with the hazard of the kingdom's ruin; whereas, if they presently sent up to impeach him of high treason before the House of Peers, in the name and on the behalf of all the Commons of England who were represented by them, the Lords would be obliged in justice to commit him into safe custody, and so sequester him from resorting to council, or having access to His Majesty, and then they should proceed against him in the usual form with all necessary expedition." These reasons for haste being by all considered satisfactory, it was voted unanimously, "that they should forthwith send up to the Lords, and accuse the Earl of Strafford of high treason, and several other crimes and misdemeanours, and desire that he might be presently sequestered from the Council, and committed to safe custody." Mr. Pym was chosen the messenger to perform that office, and the doors being opened, most of the House accompanied him on the errand. Accordingly, at the bar of the House of Lords, and in the name of all the Commons of England, he impeached Thomas Earl of Strafford (with the addition of all his other titles) of high treason, and other heinous crimes and misdemeanours, of which he said the Commons would in due time make proof in form; and in the meantime he desired, in their

Proceedings of the Long Parliament. 183

name, that he might be sequestered from all council, and be put into safe custody.[1]

As soon as Pym and the Commons withdrew, the Lords entered upon a debate on the message. In the meantime Strafford, who was with the King, being informed of these proceedings, went hastily to the House, and "with a proud, glooming countenance," made towards his place. But he was at once with some clamour called upon to withdraw, and was then committed to the custody of the Keeper of the Black Rod, the sudden change in his fortunes being accompanied by as sudden a change in fortune's votaries; "no man capping to him before whom that morning the greatest in England would have stood uncovered."[2]

A few days after his arrest Strafford petitioned the Lords to be admitted to bail, but this was refused; and on the 25th of November the House of Lords ordered that he should forthwith be committed to the Tower.[3] On the 30th of January he was sent for by the Lords. He came from the Tower by water, with a guard of musqueteers, the people, "at his going out and coming in, shouting and cursing him to his face." In the House of Lords his long charge, on many sheets of paper, was read to him, sitting for a while on his knees before the bar. Afterwards he

---

[1] Clarendon, i. 303-305, 8vo edition. Oxford, 1826. A story is told by some writers (see "Echard's History of England," vol. ii. book i. ch. 2. p. 82, fol. 1718) of Pym's saying to Strafford the last time they met, which was just before Strafford's taking office, "Remember that though you leave us now, I will never leave you while your head is upon your shoulders." The strongest proof of the improbability of the truth of this story appears to me to be that, had Pym really used such words to Strafford, it is not likely that a man who possessed so much power as Strafford did for many years, and who was so unscrupulous and unsparing in the exercise of it, would have left Pym's own head on his shoulders till such time as he could make use of it to cut off Strafford's.

[2] Baillie's Letters and Journals, i. 272, 273. Laing's edition. Edinburgh, 1841.

[3] Parl. Hist., ii. 735, 739.

was permitted to sit down at the bar, for it was eight o'clock before all was read.¹

On the 18th of December Laud was impeached of high treason by Holles, in accordance with a resolution of the House of Commons to that effect. The Lords ordered the commitment of the Archbishop. But he was permitted to go to his house for some papers to enable him to make his defence, and a book or two to read.²

The Commons having appointed a committee, of which Pym was the most active member, to collect and arrange the charges and evidence against Strafford, next proceeded against some of the inferior instruments of the King's tyranny. Sir Francis Windebank, one of the Secretaries of State, the creature of Laud, and a concealed Roman Catholic, was charged with illegally releasing Romish priests from prison. He avoided arrest and trial by flight, and escaped to Paris, where he eventually made a public profession of Romanism.³ The Lord Keeper Finch was proceeded against as a procurer of the judgment against Hampden in the matter of ship-money, and for his many abuses of power. Finch was a very dexterous rhetorician, and he petitioned to be heard for himself at the bar of the House of Commons. His prayer having been granted, he made a very eloquent and ingenious speech in his own defence: but though his deportment was very humble and submissive, and his speech full of persuasive rhetoric, it did not prevent the Commons from voting him a traitor. On the next day his impeachment was carried up to the Lords, who ordered his commitment; but Finch had fled into Hol-

---

¹ Baillie, i. 297.
² Parl. Hist., ii. 680; Lords' Journals; Laud's Diary, p. 60.
³ Parl. Hist., ii. 682, *et seq.*; Whitelocke's Memorials, p. 37; Sanderson's Life of Charles I., p. 332.

land.¹ Clarendon hints that Finch had come to a compromise with the popular party; and he expresses surprise at their suffering Windebank to escape their justice, "against whom," he says, "they had more pregnant testimony of offences within the verge of the law than against any person they had accused since this Parliament, and of some that it may be might have proved capital, and so their appetite of blood might have been satiated." But the Commons of England were (to their honour) not bloodthirsty. They wanted only the heads of Strafford and Laud, and they probably connived at the escape of the subordinate instruments of those two cruel tyrants. The rapidity with which the Commons shivered to pieces Charles's fabric of tyranny, proves what a false measure of the circumstances in which they were placed he and his prime advisers Laud and Strafford had taken. "Within less than six weeks," says Clarendon, "for no more was yet elapsed, these terrible reformers had caused the two greatest counsellors of the kingdom, whom they most feared, and so hated, to be removed from the King, and imprisoned under an accusation of high treason; and frighted away the Lord Keeper of the Great Seal of England, and one of the principal Secretaries of State, into foreign kingdoms for fear of the like; besides preparing all the Lords of the Council, and very many of the principal gentlemen throughout England, who had been high-sheriffs and deputy-lieutenants, to expect such measure of punishment from their general votes and resolutions, as their future demeanour should draw upon them for their past offences."

They next sent up a message to the Lords with respect to the judges who had upheld ship-money, and their Lordships forthwith ordered that Bramston, Davenport, Berkeley,

¹ Parl. Hist. ii. 685, *et seq.*

Crawley, Trevor, and Weston should find heavy bail to abide the judgment of Parliament.[1] Berkeley, who had been very conspicuous for his slavish and unconstitutional doctrines on the bench in the case of ship-money, was arrested while sitting on the bench, but after some time he was permitted to withdraw himself.

The Parliament now set to work on those great constitutional measures which have made its name so famous. The first of these was the Act for Triennial Parliaments.[2] By this Act every Parliament was to be *ipso facto* dissolved at the expiration of three years from the first day of its session, unless actually sitting at the time, and, in that case, at its first adjournment or prorogation. The Chancellor or Keeper of the Great Seal was to be sworn to issue writs for a new Parliament within three years from the dissolution of the last, under pain of disability to hold his office, and further punishment; in case of his failure to comply with this provision, the peers were enabled and enjoined to meet at Westminster, and to issue writs to the sheriffs; the sheriffs themselves, should the peers not fulfil this duty, were to cause elections to be duly made; and in their default, at a prescribed time the electors themselves were to proceed to choose their representatives. No future Parliament was to be dissolved or adjourned, without its own consent, in less than fifty days from the opening of its session. The passing of this most important statute was welcomed by the nation with bonfires and such marks of joy as showed that the people in some measure at least understood its value.

---

[1] Parl. Hist., ii. 700.
[2] Stat. 16 Car. I. c. 1. As this Act was repealed in the sixteenth year of Charles II., and therefore is not to be found in the statutes at large, the reader will find an abstract of it in Parl. Hist., ii. 718. It is printed at large in Rushworth, iv. 189, and in Scobell, an. 16 Car. I. c. 1.

The Commons then passed a bill declaring ship-money illegal, and annulling the judgment of the Exchequer Chamber against Mr. Hampden.[1] In an Act granting the King tonnage and poundage, it is declared that it is and hath been the ancient right of the subjects of this nation that no subsidy, custom, impost, or other charge whatsoever may be laid or imposed upon any merchandise exported or imported by subjects, denizens, or aliens, without common consent in Parliament.[2] "This," observes Mr. Hallam, "is the last statute that has been found necessary to restrain the crown from arbitrary taxation, and may be deemed the complement of those numerous provisions which the virtue of ancient times had extorted from the First and Third Edwards."[3] The arbitrary taxation thenceforth was to be perpetrated by the Parliament, and it is this which it remains for the "virtue" of modern times to restrain, and, if possible, obtain redress and compensation for.

Another important measure of the Long Parliament was the abolition of the Star Chamber.[4] The Act abolishes all jurisdiction, in the strict sense, whether of a civil or criminal nature, of the Privy Council as well as of the Star Chamber; and it is enacted that every person committed by the Council, or any of them, or by the King's special command, may have his writ of *habeas corpus*, in the return to which, the officers in whose custody he is shall certify the true cause of his commitment, which the court whence the writ has issued shall within three days examine, in order to see whether the cause thus certified appear to be just and legal or not, and do justice accordingly, by delivering, bailing, or remanding the party.

[1] 16 Car. I. c. 14.
[3] Constitutional History of England, chap. ix.
[2] 16 Car. I. c. 8.
[4] 16 Car. I. c. 10.

At the same time there was abolished the English Inquisition, the illegal and tyrannical Court of High Commission.[1] Although the greatest of English lawyers had shown the illegality of fining and imprisoning by the High Commission,[2] there being no such power conferred by the statute of Elizabeth[3] which created this court, and had actually expunged this clause out of the Commission, which made Williams, Bishop of Lincoln, when Lord Keeper, complain to his patron the Duke of Buckingham, that Coke had left them "nothing but the rusty sword of the Church—excommunication,"[4] rather more than enough, we should think, these illegal powers were again usurped under the fostering hand of Laud and Charles. How they were exercised has been seen.

With the Star Chamber (by a clause in the Act abolishing that court) fell the court of the President and Council of the North, where Strafford had exhibited so much of his insolent tyranny; the court of the President and Council of Wales and the Welsh marches, which had arrogated a jurisdiction over the adjacent counties of Salop, Worcester, Hereford, and Gloucester; and those of the Duchy of Lancaster and County Palatine of Chester (except the jurisdiction of the two last in matters relating to what was called the King's private estate, though probably the land came rather under the head of folcland than bocland).

---

[1] By stat. 16 Car. I. c. 11.
[2] Coke, 4 Inst., 324, *et seq.*   [3] Stat. 1 Eliz. c. 1.
[4] Cabala, p. 103. A few pages further on (p. 113) we find Laud (November 18, 1624) in one of his fawning letters to his patron Buckingham, appearing as "an humble suitor" to be in the High Commission, on the ground "that there is never a bishop that lives about London left out of the Commission but myself, and many that live quite absent are in, and many inferiors to bishops. I think the Commission is a place of great experience for any man that is a governor in the Church." It certainly proved a place of some experience to him of one kind or other.

The usurpation of these various courts had deprived one-third of England of the privileges of the common law. Another Act remedied abuses in the Stannary Courts of Cornwall and Devon.[1] Others limited the prerogative of purveyance, and abolished that of compulsory knighthood.[2] Another determined the boundaries of royal forests.[3] Another Act of this Parliament is important in recognising the military tenures as being then the provision made by the laws for the defence of the kingdom. In the preamble of an Act empowering the King to levy troops by the compulsory method of pressing for the special exigency of the Irish rebellion, it is recited that, " by the laws of the realm, none of His Majesty's subjects ought to be impressed or compelled to go out of his county[4] to serve as a soldier in the wars, except in case of necessity of the sudden coming in of strange enemies into the kingdom, or except they be otherwise bound by the tenure of their lands or possessions."[5]

[1] 16 Car. I. c. 15.   [2] 16 Car. I. cc. 19, 20.   [3] 16 Car. I. c. 16.
[4] In some editions of the statutes this is printed "country," but county is the correct reading.
[5] 16 Car. I. c. 28.

CHAPTER VII.

TRIAL AND EXECUTION OF STRAFFORD.

ON the 22nd of March 1640-41, the trial of the Earl of Strafford commenced in Westminster Hall. At the upper end of the hall were a throne for the King and a chair for the Prince. The throne was unoccupied. There were two cabinets or galleries with trellis-work upon each side of the throne. The King, the Queen, and their court occupied one of these, the foreign nobility the other. The King broke down the screens with his own hands, so that they sat in the eyes of all. Before the throne lay a large woolsack, covered with green, for the Lord High Steward, the Earl of Arundel, and a little lower two other woolsacks for the Lord Keeper and the judges, who were all in their scarlet robes. Beneath this sat the peers in their robes of scarlet and ermine. In front of the benches where the peers sat was a bar covered with green, at one end of which stood the managers of the trial appointed by the Commons; at the opposite end the witnesses entered, and between was a small desk at which the prisoner might stand or sit, with the Lieutenant of the Tower beside him, and behind him four secretaries at another desk. Behind these, at a long desk close to the wall, were Strafford's counsel, some five or six able lawyers who drew his answer, and were allowed to assist him in points of law, but not of fact. On both sides of the hall were erected scaffolds

Trial and Execution of Strafford. 191

eleven stages high, the highest almost reaching to the roof. In two ranks of these, divided from the rest by a rail, sat the Commons, together with the Commissioners of Scotland[1] and the Lords of Ireland, who had joined with the Commons of England as the accusers. The rest of the long galleries were filled with such an audience as no English orator had ever before addressed. There, with the other men of that time eminent for ability and learning, sat May, the accomplished translator of Lucan and historian of the Long Parliament, and Rushworth, the laborious and faithful[2] collector of state papers, who has devoted the whole of one of his folio volumes to a report of this trial. There were assembled, with pen, ink, and paper in their hands to take notes of the trial, the ladies noble by birth if not by character, whose grace and beauty still live on the canvas of Vandyke. There, we may surmise, sat Vandyke himself, who died in the following December. There were the two most celebrated women whose features his pencil has preserved—Henrietta Maria de Bourbon, Queen of England, and Lucy Percy, Countess of Carlisle.

Strafford came from the Tower about seven o'clock, accompanied by six barges, in which were 100 soldiers of the Tower. At his landing at Westminster he was met by

---

[1] Among these was Baillie, who in his quaint manner has given the most graphic description we possess of the scene.

[2] Not the least significant words in Rushworth's long titlepage are these: "Faithfully collected and impartially published without observation or reflection. By John Rushworth of Lincoln's Inn, Esq." As a contrast to Rushworth's Collections may be mentioned Nalson's Collections, which last work is, to borrow an important remark of Mr. Forster, "an utterly untrustworthy gathering of the most violent party pamphlets and libels got together towards the close of Charles II.'s reign for the special delectation of His Majesty, and as an antidote to Rushworth, by a compiler who had himself no personal knowledge of the men or the events over which he exercised an unlimited right of the grossest abuse and most unwearied misrepresentation."—Debates on the Grand Remonstrance, p. 393.

200 of the trained bands, who guarded him into the hall. The prisoner entered the hall and advanced to the bar. The King had expressly forbidden that the axe should be carried before him according to the custom in such cases. Strafford was not handsome; but his countenance was stern, dark, and manly, and his person tall and well formed.[1] He naturally stooped much; but this being now attributed to his bodily infirmities (for his old enemies, the gout and stone, had revisited him in the Tower), excited sympathy. He was dressed in deep mourning, which corresponded with his present fortunes, and his bearing now, very unlike what it had been some months before, was at once modest and dignified. Nothing could altogether smooth the contraction of his brows; but as that no longer indicated the hard, insolent, domineering haughtiness which had raised up against him so many implacable personal enemies, it imposed a sort of mysterious awe, by suggesting the idea at once of deep abstraction, and firm and calm self-collectedness, becoming in a man who had fallen from such a height of power.

As soon as Strafford entered the dock, the Earl of Arundel, as Lord High Steward of England, commanded the proceedings to be commenced. Then the impeachment, consisting of twenty-eight articles, was read, with Strafford's answer to it, in two hundred sheets of paper. This occupied the first day. The Queen left the hall about eleven o'clock, but the King and Prince Charles stayed till the court rose, which was after two, when Strafford was sent back to the Tower, and appointed to return upon the following morning at nine o'clock. The crowd saluted the fallen states-

---

[1] "Il était laid, mais assez agreable de sa personne, et la Reine me contant toutes ces choses, s'arrêta pour me dire qu'il avait les plus belles mains du monde."—Mem. par Motteville, tome i. p. 251.

man as he passed, and he returned their salutes with great humility and courtesy. On the following day at the appointed hour Strafford again appeared at the bar, and again (as, indeed, on all the successive days of the trial), the King, Queen, and Prince, and the rest of the great audience, were in their seats. The Lord High Steward then commanded the committee of the Commons appointed to manage the evidence to proceed; and Pym, the chief manager, rose. "My Lords," he began, "we stand here by the commandment of the knights, citizens, and burgesses now assembled for the Commons in Parliament, and we are ready to make good that impeachment whereby Thomas Earl of Strafford stands charged in their name, and in the name of all the Commons of England, with high treason. This, my Lords, is a great cause, and we might sink under the weight of it, and be astonished with the lustre of this noble assembly, if there were not in the cause strength and vigour to support itself, and to encourage us. It is the cause of the King; it concerns His Majesty in the honour of his government, in the safety of his person, in the stability of his crown. It is the cause of the kingdom; it concerns not only the peace and prosperity, but even the being of the kingdom. We have that piercing eloquence, the cries, and groans, and tears, and prayers of all the subjects assisting us. We have the three kingdoms, England, and Scotland, and Ireland, in travail and agitation with us, bowing themselves, like the hinds spoken of in Job, to cast out their sorrows."[1] After some more words of exordium, Pym proceeded to enumerate and comment upon the various points of Strafford's answer to the charges of the impeachment. In answer to Strafford's plea that he had executed his commission with moderation, Pym

[1] Rushworth, viii. 102, 103.

said: "If you compare his courses with other parts of the world, he will be found beyond all in tyranny and harshness; but if you compare them with his mind and disposition, perhaps there was moderation; habits, we say, are more perfect than acts, because they be nearest the principle of actions. The habit of cruelty in himself, no doubt, is more perfect than any act of cruelty he hath committed; but if this be his moderation, I think all men will pray to be delivered from it: and I may truly say that is verified in him, *The mercies of the wicked are cruel.*"[1] In regard to his plea, "that many orthodox and learned preachers had been advanced by his means, and the doctrine and discipline of the Church of England by his means protected and defended," Pym said: "My Lords, I shall give but two or three patterns of the clergy that he hath preferred. If you will take Dr. Atherton; he is not to be found now above ground, for he was hanged for many foul and unspeakable offences. Dr. Bramhall hath been preferred to a great bishopric; but he is a man that now stands charged with high treason: he hath been but few years in Ireland, and yet he hath laid out at least £30,000 in purchases. I shall name but one chaplain more, and that is one Arthur Gwyn, who, about 1634, was an under-groom to the Earl of Corke in his stable: in the year after, Dr. Bramhall preferred him to be a clergyman; and a parsonage and two vicarages impropriate were taken from my lord of Corke and given to this Arthur Gwyn. I shall add no more patterns of his clergy."[2]

Pym then called his witnesses. The remonstrance of the Irish Parliament was then read, to which Strafford replied in a long and able speech. Pym replied to this, and the

---

[1] Rushworth, viii. 105.   [2] Ibid., 107.

court was then adjourned to the following day; on which, and the next succeeding days, the charges were chiefly managed by two able lawyers, Glynne and Maynard, both members of the House; though the whole House of Commons, having put themselves into a committee, had liberty to charge the prisoner, every man as he saw occasion. "Many foul misdemeanours," says May, "committed both in Ireland and England were daily proved against him; but that ward which the Earl, being an eloquent man, especially lay at, was to keep off the blow of high treason, whatsoever misdemeanours should be laid upon him; of which, some he denied, others he excused and extenuated with great subtlety, contending to make one thing good, that misdemeanours, though never so many and so great, could not, by being put together, make one treason, unless some one of them had been treason in its own nature. Every day, the first week, from Monday to Saturday, without intermission, the Earl was brought from the Tower to Westminster Hall, and arraigned many hours together; and the success of every day's trial was the greatest discourse or dispute in all companies. For by this time the people began to be a little divided in opinions. The clergy in general were so much fallen into love and admiration of this Earl, that the Archbishop of Canterbury was almost quite forgotten by them. The courtiers cried him up; and the ladies, whose voices will carry much with some parts of the state, were exceedingly on his side. It seemed a very pleasant object to see so many Sempronias with pen, ink, and paper in their hands, noting the passages, and discussing upon the grounds of law and state. They were all of his side, whether moved by pity proper to their sex, or by ambition of being thought able to judge of the parts of the prisoner. But so great was the favour and love which they openly expressed to him, that some could not but think of that verse—

> "Non formosus erat, sed erat facundus Ulysses;
> Et tamen æquoreas torsit amore Deas."

In regard to Strafford's advice about the King's acting as absolved from all rules of government, there were five articles taken together—the 20th, 21st, 22d, 23d, and 24th: That he had advised an offensive war with Scotland, alleging that the demands of the Scottish Parliament justified it, before the commissioners of that Parliament had been heard in vindication of their proceedings: That he had declared his readiness to supply His Majesty by extraordinary ways, unless the English Parliament should grant twelve subsidies; and had, for wicked ends, in confederacy with Sir George Radcliffe, raised an army of 1000 horse and 8000 foot in Ireland: That he had declared openly to several people that the King ought first to try the affections of his people in Parliament; but, if that failed, then he might use his prerogative in levying what he required; and that, when Parliament disappointed his hopes of twelve subsidies, he advised the dissolution, declaring that His Majesty was free from all rules of government; adding that he had an army in Ireland with which he might reduce the kingdom to obedience. These points were proved by various witnesses, the King having reluctantly yielded to a demand of the Commons to release the council from their oath of secrecy. The first point in regard to Scotland was proved by the Earls of Morton and Traquair, by Juxon, Bishop of London and Lord Treasurer, and by Sir Henry Vane. Traquair swore, too, that, at the council of peers at York, the prisoner, in regard to Scottish affairs, declared that the unreasonable demands of subjects in a parliament were a ground for the King's putting himself in a posture of war. Lord Conway deposed that having, before the meeting of the short Parliament the preceding year, asked the prisoner how the troops were to be paid, he answered that he confidently expected twelve subsidies from the Parliament; but from Conway's saying, "What if the Parliament would not give that assistance," the Earl of Strafford replied, "The cause was very just and lawful, and if the Parliament would not supply the King, then he was justified before God and man if he sought means to help himself, though it were against their wills." The Earl of Bristol deposed that, after the dissolution of the short Parliament, Strafford said to him that the times did not admit of so slow and uncertain a remedy as a Parliament; that he had already been denied from that quarter, and, using the maxim *salus reipublicæ suprema lex*, said, "That the King must provide for the safety of the kingdom by such ways as he should think fit in his wisdom; that he must not suffer himself to be mastered by the frowardness and undutifulness of his people, or rather, as he conceived, by the disaffection and stubbornness of particular men." The Earl of Northumberland deposed that he heard Strafford tell His Majesty, before the meeting of the short Parliament, that if the people refused to supply him, he was absolved from rules of Government and acquitted before God and man.[1] Sir Henry Vane deposed that he heard the prisoner say this to

---

[1] The Earl of Northumberland deposed to other interrogatories "that, though the Earl of Strafford said that His Majesty might use his power when the kingdom was in danger or unavoidable necessity, he did after say that that power was to be used *candide et caste*, and an account thereof should be given to the next Parliament, that they might see it was only employed to that use." But even according to this addition, if the King might levy money upon any plea of necessity which one Parliament has denied, with the profession that he would give an account of it to the next Parliament, which he might call or not as he thought fit, Parliament evidently became a mere farce.

the King after the dissolution: "Your Majesty having tried all ways, and been refused, in this case of extreme necessity, and for the safety of your kingdom and people, you are loose and absolved from all rules of government; you are acquitted before God and man; you have an army in Ireland; you may employ it to reduce this kingdom."

Strafford contended that it was strange that no one heard the words relative to the Irish army but Sir Henry Vane; that he might easily mistake *this* for *that* country; and that, as the army had been raised to reduce Scotland, and the Scottish business was then agitated, the remark had necessarily reference to it; that, accordingly, the Earl of Northumberland and others deposed that they understood the army was intended for Scotland; and that, as there was no war in England which called for it there, it necessarily followed that it never could be meant to introduce it into this kingdom.

The minutes of council had all been destroyed by the command of the King; but Sir Henry Vane the elder, being absent from London and in want of some papers, sent the key of his study to his son, Sir Henry Vane the younger, who, in executing his father's orders, found notes of a council, which, among other opinions delivered by other privy councillors, contained the following words spoken by Strafford to the King: "Your Majesty having tried the affections of your people, you are absolved and loose from all rules of government, and to do what power will admit. Your Majesty having tried all ways, and being refused, you shall be acquitted before God and man. And you have an army in Ireland that you may employ to reduce this kingdom to obedience, for I am confident the Scots cannot hold out five months." These notes the younger Vane showed to Pym, who, on the 10th of April, produced them to the House of Commons.[1] On the 13th of April the notes were read by Pym in Westminster Hall. This additional evidence was finally admitted against Strafford, and he was called upon to make his general defence against the facts, the law being left to his counsel.

The principal articles of impeachment against Strafford may be summed up in the charge—an endeavour to subvert the fundamental laws of the kingdom. In the enumeration of treasons contained in the Statute of Treasons,[2] which then constituted the English law of treason (the statutes of Henry VIII. creating so many new treasons having been repealed in the first year of Mary),[3] there is no mention of such a treason as this. And since the laws against treason in England were made to protect the King not the subject, it was not to be expected that any law could be found which should include in its enumeration of treasons, that offence of which Strafford was undoubtedly guilty, an attempt to increase the power of the King and to depress the liberty of the subject. Although, therefore, Pym and the other managers for the Commons in Strafford's trial displayed much eloquence as well as much skill and dexterity, it must be admitted that Strafford had the best of it both for eloquence and law.

Strafford began by adverting to the painful and adverse position in which he stood, alone and unsupported against the whole power and influence of the Commons; his health shattered, his memory impaired, his thoughts unquiet and

---

[1] See an elaborate account given by Mr. Sanford, by collating the three separate reports of D'Ewes, Gawdry, and Verney, of what took place in the House of Commons on the 10th of April, when Sir Henry Vane the younger and Mr. Pym were enjoined by the House to declare how they came to know the latter part of the twenty-third article.—Studies and Illustrations of the Great Rebellion, p. 327, *et seq.*

[2] 25 Edw. III. stat. 5, c. 2.   [3] By stat. 1 Mary, c. 1.

troubled; and he prayed of their lordships to supply his many infirmities, by their better abilities, better judgments, better memories. He then argued with great force and acuteness against the doctrine of arbitrary and constructive treasons, and concluded with a peroration which has been justly admired for its pathetic eloquence.

"My Lords," he said, "it is hard to be questioned upon a law which cannot be shown. Where hath this fire lain hid so many hundred years, without smoke to discover it, till it thus burst forth to consume me and my children? That punishment should precede promulgation of a law, to be punished by a law subsequent to the fact, is extreme hard. What man can be safe, if this be admitted? My Lords, it is hard in another respect,—that there should be no token set, by which we should know this offence, no admonition by which we should avoid it. My Lords, be pleased to give that regard to the peerage of England, as never expose yourselves to such moot points—such constructive interpretations of laws: if there must be a trial of wits, let the subject-matter be of somewhat else than the lives and honours of peers. It will be wisdom for yourselves, for your posterity, and for the whole kingdom, to cast into the fire these bloody and mysterious volumes of constructive and arbitrary treason, as the primitive Christians did their books of curious arts, and betake yourselves to the plain letter of the law and statute, that telleth us what is and what is not treason, without being more ambitious to be more learned in the art of killing than our forefathers. It is now 240 years since any man was touched for this alleged crime, to this height, before myself. Let us not awaken these sleeping lions to our destructions, by raking up a few musty records, that have lain by the walls so many ages, forgotten or neglected. May your Lordships please not to add this to my other misfortunes,—let not a precedent be derived from me, so disadvantageous as this will be in its consequence to the whole kingdom. Do not, through me, wound the interest of the commonwealth;— and howsoever these gentlemen say they speak for the commonwealth, yet, in this particular, I indeed speak for it, I show the inconveniences and mischiefs that will fall upon it; for, as it is said in the statute 1 Henry IV., 'no one will know what to do or say for fear of such penalties.' Do not put, my Lords, such difficulties upon ministers of state, that men of wisdom, of honour, and of fortune, may not with cheerfulness and safety be employed for the public. If you weigh and measure them by grains and scruples, the public affairs of the kingdom will lie waste, no man will meddle with them who hath anything to lose. My Lords, I have troubled you longer than I should have done were it not for the interest of those dear pledges a saint in heaven hath left me." Here[1] (says the reporter) his weeping stopped him, then he went on: "What I forfeit myself is nothing, but that indiscretion should extend to my posterity woundeth me to the very soul. You will pardon my infirmity; something I should have added, but

[1] Hume, by way of heightening the effect of the scene, uses these words for which there does not appear to be any authority—"Here he pointed to his children"—nor is there any good evidence that his children were present. The effect is really heightened by the absence of his children and by the fact of this burst of emotion having been unpremeditated and forced upon him by a sudden tide of overwhelming recollections. The presence of his children would have savoured of that appeal to the pity of the judges common at Athens which Socrates disdained to submit to, saying that though he had three children not one of them should appear before the Dikasts to weep and beg his life. And though Strafford could hardly be said to possess that clear consciousness of a blameless life which, added to a naturally fearless temperament, enabled Socrates thoroughly to silence what Plato calls "the child within us who fears death," yet Hume would seem to do his hero injustice in imputing to him the rhetorical artifice, amounting to stage trick, of parading before the court his children to weep, beg, and entreat for his life.

am not able; therefore let it pass. Now, my Lords, for myself I have been, by the blessing of Almighty God, taught that the afflictions of this present life are not to be compared to the eternal weight of glory which shall be revealed hereafter. And so, my Lords, even so, with all tranquillity of mind, I freely submit myself to your judgment, and whether that judgment be of life or death, *Te Deum laudamus.*"[1]

A great orator is by the very nature of his art a great actor. It is in that, as in other arts, the perfection of art to conceal the art, to make art look like nature. Where a man is defending himself, too, as Strafford was, he is necessarily so sincere in desiring his own acquittal, that his art is exercised under great and peculiar advantages. This is expressed in the description of an eyewitness, Baillie: "In the end he made such ane pathetic oration for ane half hour as ever comedian did upon a stage. The matter and expression was exceeding brave."[2]

Yet it would hardly be a correct description of that, perhaps the most eloquent speech, "everything considered, that has yet been printed in the English tongue," to say that after all it was but a masterly piece of acting. That pause, those tears in the "proud glooming countenance" at thought of "those pledges a saint in heaven had left him" —there is no need to suppose that those did not come from the heart, even had it been the heart of a man every way worse than Strafford. Even of the worst it has been said,

---

[1] This is from the report in Whitelocke's Memorials, which Mr. Forster has characterised (Life of Strafford, p. 396, note) as the most complete report that has been given. I have followed Rushworth's words in regard to the sudden stop caused by the recollection of his second wife. Whitelocke's words, "Here he stopped awhile, letting fall some tears to her memory," have the air of a stage direction which should regulate the quantity of tears by tale.

[2] Baillie's Letters and Journals, i. 347. Edinburgh, 1841. Edited from the author's MSS. by David Laing, Esq.

"none are all evil," and the train of recollections which the mention of his young and innocent children was calculated to call up, was linked with some of the deepest and most overpowering emotions that have their dwelling in the heart of man. As there is in truth no greater grief[1] than, in misery, in misfortune, in bereavement, to be reminded of brighter and better days that can return no more, so there is nothing more potent to overthrow the proudest and sternest nature than to have suddenly presented to the mind some beloved and lost object between all the images and recollections of whom and some present misery, humiliation, and disaster there exists a strange and most startling repugnance. Strafford was a tyrant—in his family, as well as beyond it. Few if any were the checks Strafford had received till he received that check, once for all, that sent him to prison and the block. He was a rich man's eldest son, and pampered and spoiled by fortune from his earliest years. However false the charge mentioned by Baillie of his having struck his second[2] wife so as to cause her death might be, the very invention of such a report in connection with Strafford's name, and other charges of the truth of which there is but too much evidence of a kind to show an intemperate and unmanly excess of passion, such as that of his having caused or hastened the death of Esmond by striking him, a sick, infirm, and defenceless man, some violent blows with his cane, have an undoubted significance. The age of Strafford was an age of great crimes and great

[1] "Nessun maggior dolore,
Che ricordarsi del tempo felice
Nella miseria."—Dante, Inf. c. v. v. 121.

[2] Baillie calls her his first wife (vol. i. p. 347, Laing's edition), but that is a mistake. Strafford was married first at the age of eighteen to a daughter of the Earl of Cumberland; and ten years after he married his second wife, Arabella Holles, a daughter of the Earl of Clare, a lady, says Sir George Radcliffe, the friend and biographer of Strafford, "exceeding comely and beautiful, and yet more lovely in the endowments of her mind."

retributions, and as I think that Strafford certainly had his full share in the crimes, I think also that he was entitled to his full share of the retributions. Such things place men in situations, forcing out ebullitions of feeling which, though to us of another age and other habits they may appear strained and theatrical, were in them, though in some sense they might be forced, really natural and sincere. If, with the sudden recollection of that beloved though unuttered name, bringing back for a moment from the grave her who once bore it in all her well-remembered beauty, there flashed across his brain the thought that had *she* lived his fate might have been different, that under her influence a nobler ambition might have conducted him to a goal very different from that which was now looming darkly before him, he might well weep over that vision of early and better days.

Great as was the eloquence of this conclusion of the defence of Strafford, there are passages in Pym's reply hardly inferior in eloquence. "My Lords," said Pym, "many days have been spent, in maintenance of the impeachment of the Earl of Strafford, by the House of Commons, whereby he stands charged with high treason; and your Lordships have heard his defence with patience, and with as much favour as justice would allow. We have passed through our evidence, and the result of all this is, that it remains clearly proved that the Earl of Strafford hath endeavoured by his words, actions, and counsels, to subvert the fundamental laws of England and Ireland, and to introduce an arbitrary and tyrannical government. This is the envenomed arrow for which he inquired in the beginning of his replication this day, which hath infected all his blood; this is that intoxicating cup (to use his own metaphor) which hath tainted his judgment, and poisoned his heart:[1] from,

---

[1] Rushworth, viii. 661. In the report of this speech of Pym's, printed in one of the King's pamphlets in the British Museum, the passage given as above in

hence was infused that specifical difference which turned his speeches, his actions, his counsels, into treason; not *cumulative*, as he expressed it, as if many misdemeanours could make one treason; but *formally* and essentially. It is the end that doth inform actions, and doth specificate the nature of them, making not only criminal, but even indifferent words and actions to be treason, being done and spoken with a treasonable intention." In the course of this speech Pym said: "Those that live so much under the whip, and the pillory, and such servile engines as were frequently used by the Earl of Strafford, they may have the dregs of valour, sullenness, and stubbornness, which may make them prone to mutinies and discontents: but those noble and gallant affections, which put men to brave designs and attempts for the preservation or enlargement of a kingdom, they are hardly capable of. Shall it be treason to embase the King's coin, though but a piece of twelvepence, or sixpence? and must it not needs be the effect of a greater treason to embase the spirits of his subjects, and to set a stamp and character of servitude upon them, whereby they shall be disabled to do anything for the service of the King and commonwealth?"[1]

Pym thus concluded his long speech: "The forfeitures inflicted for treason by our law are of life, honour, and estate, even all that can be forfeited; and this prisoner, having committed so many treasons, although he should pay all these forfeitures, will be still a debtor to the commonwealth: nothing can be more equal than that he should perish by the justice of that law which he would have subverted; neither will this be a new way of blood.

Rushworth is given thus: "This, my Lords, is that poisonous arrow that hath tainted his blood; this is that cup of deadly wine that hath intoxicated him."   [1] Rushworth, viii. 665.

There are marks enough to trace this law to the very original of this kingdom: and if it hath not been put in execution these 240 years, it was not for want of law, but that all that time hath not bred a man bold enough to commit such crimes as these; which is a circumstance much aggravating his offence and making him no whit less liable to punishment, because he is the only man that in so long a time hath ventured upon such a treason as this. It belongs to the charge of another to make it appear to your Lordships that the crimes and offences proved against the Earl of Strafford are high treason by the laws and statutes of this nation, whose learning and other abilities are much better for that service."[1]

A circumstance mentioned by Baillie, which has given rise to some comment, may perhaps be accounted for by supposing that Pym could not help feeling the great lameness of the strictly legal argument, and that this caused the apparent failure of his memory, and looking in vain to his papers for a point or two, towards the close of his speech. Baillie says that Pym "made one of the most eloquent, wise, free speeches that ever we heard or I think shall ever hear;" and then adds, "To trouble the man, God let his memory fail him a little before the end. His papers he looked on; but they could not help him to a point or two, so he behoved to pass them. I believe the King never heard a lecture of so free language against his idolised prerogative."[2]

Strafford said in the course of his defence, "It is now full 240 years since treason was defined," alluding no doubt to the statute of Edward III., though if he had said 290

---

[1] Rushworth, viii. 669, 670.
[2] Baillie's Letters and Journals, i. 348. Edinburgh, 1841. Edited by David Laing, Esq., from the author's MSS.

he would have spoken more accurately; and he affirmed truly that in that definition of treason nothing which he had done was contained. If the word "King" in the statute of treasons could have been proved to mean "Sovereign" in the strict and proper sense of the word, and according to that sense to comprehend the Commons of England, Strafford might have been justly charged with treason under that statute. But at that time it was not pretended that such a construction could be given to the words of the statute. This view is supported by the line of argument adopted even by some of the ablest lawyers themselves who spoke on behalf of the managers for the Commons, and this may probably be considered as the chief reason which induced the Commons to abandon the impeachment and bring in a bill of attainder.[1] "Why should he have law himself," said St. John, in arguing the bill of attainder before the Peers, "who would not that others should have any? We indeed give law to hares and deer, because they are beasts of chase; but we give none to wolves and foxes, but knock them on the head wherever they are found, because they are beasts of prey."[2]

St. John here argues the case as a statesman rather than

---

[1] Mr. Forster in his valuable work, "The Debates on the Grand Remonstrance," pp. 133, 134, has shown, on the evidence of a MS. note of Sir Simonds d'Ewes, that both Pym and Hampden were of opinion that a bill of attainder was unnecessary, and that it would be better to obtain judgment on the impeachment. Lord Macaulay had come to this conclusion as to the opinion of Hampden from a very obscure note of one of his speeches by Sir Ralph Verney. Mr. Sanford says: "It is clear that the object of the bill of attainder was to give to the whole proceedings against Strafford as national a character as possible, some of the Commons showing a jealousy at the decision of such a question, which they considered involved the fate of the country, being left to the House of Lords alone, constituted as we have seen that House to have been."—Studies and Illustrations of the Great Rebellion, p. 347.

[2] Rushworth, abr., iv. 61; Clarendon, i. 407.

as a lawyer, contending that as at that time the law of treason in England had been made to protect the King and not the subject, a man whose proved purpose had been to deprive Englishmen of any law but the will of a tyrant, should be destroyed as a public enemy, or a dangerous and noxious beast of prey. In the case of Laud, which came on *after* the battle of Marston Moor, Serjeant Wild and others were sent by the Commons to show the Lords in a conference that a man might incur the guilt of high treason as much by offences against the nation as by offences against the King. The scene which Marston Moor presented to royal contemplation was somewhat different from that of such insurrections against royal oppression as those headed by Jack Straw and Wat Tyler. The King's best troops—Rupert's Life Guards and the picked men of his cavalry borne down and driven into headlong flight by the onset of Cromwell's cuirassiers—princes and noblemen and knights and royal gentlemen and their lackeys slain or scattered by a brewer and his men. Before such an event as this who shall imagine the royal indignation and scorn, even at the most delicate and distant hint that high treason could be committed against a beast of burden—a thing created only to pay taxes and to be the slave of the caste privileged to commit crimes with impunity?

When the Lords, before passing the bill of attainder, consulted the judges as to whether the 15th and 19th articles of the impeachment amounted to treason, the judges unanimously declared that those offences amounted to treason, and accordingly out of the forty-five Peers who were present, twenty-six voted him guilty on the 15th article, for illegally levying money in Ireland by force; and on the 19th, for imposing an unlawful oath on the

Scots.[1] But these judges had been bred in a bad school, and they were now as obsequious to the Parliament as they had before been to the King.

On the same day on which the Commons resolved that a bill should be prepared to assure their own continuance, namely, the 5th of May 1641, they ordered "that all the knights of shires, citizens and burgesses of every county, should meet this afternoon to consider in what state and condition their several counties, cities, and boroughs are in respect of arms and ammunition; and in what condition for lord-lieutenants, or deputy-lieutenants, whether they be persons well affected to religion and to the public peace; and to present the names of them to the House; and likewise to consider what forts and castles there are in their several counties, &c.; and who are the governors of them; and who are the governors of the islands, and the castles and forts there."[2] It is evident from this that the Commons already saw that the dispute between them and the King would come to the issue of the sword; and it is probable that this proceeding was hastened by information of certain desperate designs against the Parliament, by some officers of the King's army (from which the affair was known as the army plot), communicated to the House by Mr. Pym, two days before, namely, on the 3d of May.[3]

The first trace of the army plot that appears in the Journals is on the 28th of April 1641, when Mr. Hyde was sent up to the Lords with a message that the Commons had received information which led them to fear that the Earl of Strafford might have a design to escape, wherefore

---

[1] Whitelocke, p. 45. Parl. Hist., ii. 757, 758.
[2] Parl. Hist., ii. 782, and see Sir Ralph Verney's Notes, pp. 71, 72.
[3] Parl. Hist., ii. 776, and see Sir Ralph Verney's Notes, pp. 66, 67, 71, 72, 73.

they desired the guard over him might be strengthened. On the 3d of May Pym communicated to the House of Commons all the particulars of the plot which had come to his knowledge. These particulars involved persons very near to the King and Queen in schemes not only for the release of Strafford, but for procuring the interference of the army to overawe the Parliament. A committee of ten of the Lords examined the suspected persons in the presence of a committee of seven of the Commons, consisting of Holles, Pym, Hampden, Strode, Fiennes, Clotworthy, and another member whose name does not appear. Their proceedings were conducted under a protestation of secrecy;[1] but on the 7th of June Hampden was sent to the Lords with a request that they would give the Commons leave to make use of the examinations taken by the committee, and upon their consent, Mr. Fiennes made a report to the House of which Sir Ralph Verney's note (under date "Tuesday, 8th June 1641") contains some particulars, "which," observes Mr. Bruce, "will not be found in Rushworth, Nalson, or, as I believe, anywhere else." Mr. Fiennes reported three heads—1. Concerning the Tower guard, and Strafford's escape; 2. A design to engage the army against the Parliament; 3. Bringing the French into England.[2]

From various passages in the Notes of Sir Ralph Verney,[3] as well as from other evidence, it appears that the Queen had been particularly active in this plot. Indeed the chief conspirators were young courtiers attached to the Queen's interest, one of them, Mr. Henry Jermyn, Jarman, or

[1] Commons' Journals, ii. 135. I have availed myself of the assistance of Mr. Bruce's valuable notes to his edition of the Notes of Sir Ralph Verney, printed for the Camden Society, 1845. See p. 86, *et seq.*
[2] See Sir Ralph Verney's Notes, pp. 87, 88, 89, 90, 110, 111, 133.
[3] Sir Ralph Verney's Notes, pp. 87, 88, 89. See Rushworth, iv. 257.

German (for we find the name written in all these ways), being her special favourite, and ultimately becoming her husband. The Queen-mother also, Mary de Medici, was suspected of being engaged in this intrigue, as well as in all other intrigues which had for their end the destruction of the English constitution and the substitution of despotism in its place. Defeated in all her political intrigues in France by a far greater politician than herself, Cardinal Richelieu, forbidden to return to France, and declining to follow the Cardinal's advice to make Florence the place of her retreat (for the widow of Henry IV. shrank from making her native city witness of her misfortunes and her fall), she had, after having made Brussels and Holland successively "too hot for her," came in 1638 to England, where, says Whitelock, "the people were generally discontented at her coming and at her followers, which some observed to be the sword and pestilence, and that her restless spirit embroiled all where she came."[1] The populace of England, excited by the many rumours of plots in which the Queen-mother was supposed, not without reason, to be engaged, began to treat her with the same insults which she had met with elsewhere. Upon this the King sent a message to the Commons, who, while they expressed their readiness to assist His Majesty in all just ways for her protection, humbly beseeched him, that as their precautions might prove insufficient to save her from insult, he would move her to leave the kingdom. She soon after returned to the Continent, and died at Cologne in 1642, a few months before the great Cardinal, whom she had first raised to power, and who had for "reasons of state" repaid that favour with exile from the country where she had once worn a crown, and what is more, had once held a sceptre.

[1] Whitelock, 29.

The result of these plots, together with the King's obstinate refusal to disband the Irish army, tended to confirm the majority of the Commons in their determination to carry out the capital charge against Strafford. When some of the party called Straffordians privately urged a judgment against Strafford as for a minor offence, and not high treason, in which judgment they would have concurred, it was answered, that were he voted guilty of a misdemeanour, and doomed to banishment from the royal presence, and incapacity to serve in a public station, as well as to fine and imprisonment, the King would immediately, on a dissolution of Parliament, remit the punishment, and, with a general pardon, restore him to favour and place, when he would act over again all and more than all that had been so justly complained of.[1]

Charles, when he refused to permit Strafford to retire to his government of Ireland, had pledged himself by a solemn promise that "while there was a king in England, not a hair of Strafford's head should be touched by the Parliament." And again he had written to him in his prison in the Tower, a letter in which were these words—"I cannot satisfy myself in honour or conscience without assuring you that upon the word of a king you shall not suffer in life, honour, or fortune." Whether the "word of a king" was at any former time of more sanctity, one would not infer that it ever in England, at least within the period not fabulous of her history, was a thing very safe to trust to. For was not Magna Charta confirmed in all thirty-two times? And does not every one of these confirmations imply the breach of a king's word, nay, of a king's oath? And if it be said that a king is not bound by the word or oath of his father or grandfather, it may be

[1] Clar., i. 241, *et seq.*

Trial and Execution of Strafford. 213

answered that this piece of casuistry, if admitted, would not explain the fifteen confirmations, or rather the necessity for them, in the reign of one king alone, the chivalrous Edward III.[1] It is also not unworthy of remark that almost at this very time in France, Cinq-Mars, in consequence of the treatment he had met with at the hands of Louis XIII., might well have exclaimed with Strafford, "Put not your trust in princes." The defence of such conduct in kings seems to need such a line of argument as that adopted by one[2] of the bishops, who told Charles on this occasion that kings had two consciences—a private and a public conscience.

On Friday the 7th of May, the Lords, in a thin House,[3] passed the Bill of Attainder. On the next day, the 8th of May, the Commons requested the Lords to join with

---

[1] Sir Walter Raleigh, in the dedication of his "Prerogative of Parliaments" to King James, has made as bold a defence of royal perjury as might be looked for in an address of Machiavelli to Borgia. He says: "The bonds of subjects to their kings should always be wrought out of iron, the bonds of kings unto subjects but with cobwebs. Thus it is (most renowned sovereign) that this traffick of assurances hath been often urged, of which if the conditions have been easy, our kings have as easily kept them; if hard and prejudicial, either to their honours or estates, the creditors have been paid their debts with their own presumption. For all binding of a king by law upon the advantage of his necessity makes the breach itself lawful in a king." Poor Sir Walter! And yet all this availed him not. But when such doctrines were thus stated by such men, it was high time for those who were to fight the great battle of Armageddon to be looking to their swords, pikes, and muskets, and to be "keeping their powder dry."

[2] Williams, Bishop of Liucoln, see next page.

[3] Parl. Hist., ii .757, 758. The Bill of Attainder against Strafford was *passed by only* 26 against 19. The bishops had declined voting in the matter of Strafford, as being ecclesiastical persons, and so prohibited by the Canons from being concerned "*in agitatione causæ sanguinis;*" and the Catholic Peers kept away. The numbers stated above, and given by Nalson and Whitelock, agree with the Lords' Journals. Clarendon, who is very inaccurate in such matters, says, "And so in an afternoon, when of fourscore who had been present at the trial, there were only 46 lords in the House (the good people still crying at the door for justice), they put the bill to the question, and, 11 lords only dissenting, it passed that House."

them to move His Majesty for his consent to the Bill of Attainder. The Lords agreed, and sent a certain number of Peers to wait upon His Majesty. On the following day, Sunday, the King summoned his Privy Council at Whitehall, called in some of the judges and bishops, and asked their opinions. Juxon, Bishop of London, who had held the staff of Lord Treasurer "without reproach and laid it down without regret," honestly advised him not to consent to the shedding of the blood of a man whom in his heart he believed to be innocent. According to Clarendon, Williams, Bishop of Lincoln, and soon after Archbishop of York, told the King "that there was a private and a public conscience; that his public conscience as a king might not only dispense with, but oblige him to do that which was against his private conscience as a man; and that the question was not whether he should save the Earl of Strafford, but whether he should perish with him; that the conscience of a king to preserve his kingdom, the conscience of a husband to preserve his wife, the conscience of a father to preserve his children (all which were now in danger), weighed down abundantly all the considerations the conscience of a master or a friend could suggest to him for the preservation of a friend or servant; and by such unprelatical, ignominious arguments, in plain terms, advised him, even for conscience' sake, to pass that act."[1] These "unprelatical" arguments have been supposed to have been suggested to Williams by his intense, and, though not ungrounded, somewhat "unprelatical" hatred of Laud, and of Strafford as the sworn friend and ally of Laud—two men whose destruction he is said to have ardently desired. It has even been said that it was on the motion of Williams that the

---

[1] Clarendon, Hist., i. 451.

bishops had withdrawn from attendance at Strafford's trial, on the ground that they were prohibited by the canons from having their hands in blood. It is curious and instructive to see by what causistry or Jesuitry two such "ecclesiastical persons" as Williams and Laud could hunt after each other's blood. Three other bishops advised Charles to guide his conscience by the opinion of his judges. The judges, it is said, declined to give any reasons for their opinion, and merely stated that the case, as put to them by the Lords, was treason. It is not difficult to conjecture the result when Charles's conscience began to stand in need of this sort of assistance. Though, as he was to make a stand soon, it would have been a wiser as well as a braver and more honourable course for him to have made it here. But Charles had neither the strength of head nor of heart to enable him to act such a part. The majority of the council pressed upon him the votes of both Houses of Parliament, and the imminent danger of a refusal; and late on Sunday evening Charles reluctantly subscribed a commission to give his assent to the Bill of Attainder; and, at the same time, to a bill which had been introduced into the Commons on the 6th, passed by them on the 7th, and by the Lords on the 8th of May, "to assure the continuance of this present Parliament from adjourning, proroguing, or dissolving, without the consent of both Houses."[1]

It is stated by Whitelock that Charles sent Secretary Carleton to Strafford to inform him of what had been done, with the motives which had influenced the King, among which was particularly mentioned Strafford's own request, contained in a letter he had written to the King; that Strafford then asked whether His Majesty had passed

[1] Parl. Hist., ii. 758, 759, 784, 786, 787.

the bill or not, as if astonished and as not believing that the King would have done it; and that being again assured that the bill was really passed, he rose from his chair, lifted up his eyes to heaven, laid his hand upon his heart, and uttered these words, "Put not your trust in princes, nor in the sons of men, for in them there is no salvation,"—an expression of emotion natural in a man who had done and risked so much to make the power of Charles absolute; even while we remember the words in the letter which Strafford had just before written to the King: "Sir, my consent shall more acquit you herein to God than all the world can do besides; to a willing man there is no injury done."

Nothing now remained for Strafford but to prepare for death. Every man who dies a public and violent death for political crimes, real or imputed, in his own estimation, and even in that of most of his friends, passes for a martyr. The pride that supports most men in such a situation was not found wanting in the fallen but still haughty earl. To the obstinacy of a stern spirit, which will often enable even a common felon to die like a hero, there was added in Strafford that mixture of personal and aristocratical pride which had distinguished him through life, and attended him to the scaffold and the grave.

Of the many similar scenes which London had witnessed, there was probably none that had so many spectators as this last scene of the life of Strafford; for it is stated, though probably with some exaggeration, that not less than 100,000 persons had assembled on Tower Hill. Though within the circuit of those walls that surrounded old London had been shed by the public executioner the most heroic as well as the noblest blood, the blood of heroes like Wallace and his captains who died for Liberty, of martyrs like Sir Thomas More who died for Conscience, the blood of the noblest of this earth, according to the measure of earthly nobility, of the last of the Plantagenets,[1] and some of the greatest of their peers; yet did not all these spectacles so move the people as this. And the cause might be that now for the first time were they to behold a man whom they believed to be their mortal enemy, a man who had laboured to make their king absolute, and them and their children and their children's children to all generations slaves, now (and it was the first time such an event had been recorded in their country's annals) were they to behold this man, lately so powerful and so formidable, brought, as it seemed, by them or their representatives, to die by the hand of the public executioner for his crimes and his treasons against the ancient rights and franchises of Englishmen. There was indeed a terrible significance in the very numbers of that vast multitude that gathered in a dark, grim, but silent circle round the block that was to be the final goal of so many daring projects and such towering ambition.

Strafford, in his walk from the Tower to the place of execution on Tower Hill, took off his hat frequently and saluted the assembled multitude; and received not a word of reproach or insult. His step and manner are described by Rushworth, the clerk of the Parliament and indefatigable collector who was on the scaffold, to have been those of "a general marching at the head of an army to breathe

[1] Edward Plantagenet, Earl of Warwick, son and heir of George Duke of Clarence, and grandson of Warwick the kingmaker, was beheaded on Tower Hill in the reign of Henry VII., and his sister, the Countess of Salisbury, in that of Henry VIII. The slaughter of the English nobility on the field and the scaffold, which accompanied and followed the wars of York and Lancaster, and made way for the prerogative government of the Tudors and the Stuarts, almost affords a parallel to that of the Roman nobility which was at once a cause and consequence of the imperial tyranny.

victory, rather than those of a condemned man to undergo the sentence of death." From the scaffold he addressed a speech of some length to the people; and it is melancholy to reflect that like some other men (such for instance as Lord Lovat) who have died in the same place in the same manner, his dying professions of pure and patriotic intentions were strangely at variance with the tenor of his life, and even the written evidence of his own words, as subsequently revealed by the publication of his letters and despatches.

Having ended his speech[1] to the people, he turned to take leave of the friends who had accompanied him to the scaffold. His eloquence, like that of many others of the remarkable men of that remarkable time,[2] was conspicuous to the very last. Seeing his brother weeping, he said, "Brother, what do you see in me to cause those tears? Does any innocent fear betray in me guilt? or

---

[1] The paper containing these heads of his speech, written by his own hand, was afterwards found lying on the scaffold, and was printed by Rushworth, viii. 761. The following is a copy of it:—
1. I am to pay the last debt we owe to sin.
2. Rise to righteousness.
3. Die willingly.
4. Forgive all.
5. Submit to what is voted justice but my intentions innocent from subverting.
6. Wishing nothing more than great prosperity to King and people.
7. Acquit the King constrained.
8. Beseech to repent.
9. Strange way to write the beginning of reformation and settlement of a kingdom in blood on themselves.
10. Beseech that demand may rest there.
11. Call not blood on themselves.
12. Die in the faith of the Church.
13. Pray for it, and desire their prayers with me.

[2] Particularly of his enemy, Sir Henry Vane the younger, whose speech on the scaffold, like Strafford's, was remarkable for its noble eloquence, and deep and solemn yet quiet pathos.

any innocent boldness atheism? That block must be my pillow, and here I shall rest from all my labours. No thoughts of envy, no dreams of treason, nor jealousies, nor cares, for the King, the State, or myself, shall interrupt this easy sleep. Remember me to my sister and to my wife; and carry my blessing to my eldest son, and to Ann, and Arabella, not forgetting my little infant, that knows neither good nor evil, and cannot speak for itself; God speak for it, and bless it!" While undressing himself, and winding his hair under a cap, he said, looking on the block, "I do as cheerfully put off my doublet at this time as ever I did when I went to bed." The executioner struck off his head at one blow..

Strafford was beheaded on the 12th of May 1641, and in the forty-ninth year of his age. Within a few weeks after his death, the Parliament mitigated the penalties of his sentence to his children. In the succeeding reign the attainder was reversed, and his son was restored to the earldom. Though that earldom was but fourteen months old, and Wentworth had been created Baron and Viscount Wentworth only in 1628, even those to whom the preamble of a patent or the inscription of a tomb may not appear conclusive evidence on the point either of personal merit or of family antiquity, must admit that his family was at that time one of the most considerable of the class known in England under the name of gentry. The estate which he inherited from his father was worth £6000 a year, a very large sum at that time.[1] He had received part of his education at St. John's College, Cambridge. From his early years he was of studious and regular habits. He appears to have taken almost as much pains with his ora-

---

[1] Strafford's Letters and Despatches ii. 105, 106, and Dr. Knowler's Dedication prefixed to them.

torical education as the great orators of antiquity. Sir George Radcliffe informs us that the excellence possessed by him in speaking and writing was attained by reading well-penned authors in French, English, and Latin, and observing their expressions; by hearing of eloquent men; and by a very great care and industry which he used when young in penning his epistles and missives of what subject soever. "I learned one rule of him," adds Sir George, "which I think worthy to be remembered. When he met with a well-penned oration or tract upon any subject or question, he framed a speech upon the same argument, inventing and disposing what seemed fit to be said upon that subject before he read the book; then reading the book, he compared his own with the author's, and noted his own defects, and the author's art and fulness; whereby he observed all that was in the author more strictly, and was better able to judge of his own defects and the way to supply them."[1] Upon his early habits further light is thrown by some advice which he gave to his nephew, Sir William Savile, in a letter dated Dublin Castle, 29th September 1633.[2] With respect to the greater part of this advice, particularly what regards economy and regularity in the management of his private affairs, temperance in drinking and abstinence from gaming, it was the rule by which Strafford shaped his own conduct, and to which, according to Radcliffe, his old and intimate friend, he strictly adhered. The part of the advice to which he himself least adhered was that recommending calmness and courtesy of demeanour; for even his most intimate friend, Sir George Radcliffe, admits that "he was naturally exceeding choleric," and the actions of his life show that in that particular he was never able thoroughly to subdue nature.

[1] Strafford's Letters and Despatches, ii. 435.   [2] Ibid., i. 169.

Among Strafford's good qualities Sir George Radcliffe especially extols his fidelity to, and zeal for, his friends. "He never had anything in his possession or power which he thought too dear for his friends; he was never weary to take pains for them, or to employ the utmost of his abilities in their service." Radcliffe also describes him as "exceeding temperate in meat, drink, and recreations. Beef or rabbits was his ordinary food, or cold powdered meats, or cheese and apples, and in moderate quantity. He was never drunk in his life, as I have often heard him say." In Ireland, where drinking "was grown," says Radcliffe, "a disease epidemical," he never suffered any health to be drunk at his public table but the King's, Queen's, and Prince's, on solemn days. "His chief recreation was after supper, when, if he had company which was suitable unto him, that is, honest, cheerful men, he would retire into an inner room, and sit two or three hours, taking tobacco and telling stories with great pleasantness and freedom: and this he used constantly with all familiarity in private, laying then aside all state and that due respect which in public he would expect."[1]

---

[1] Strafford's Letters and Despatches, ii. 433.

CHAPTER VIII.

THE IRISH MASSACRE—THE GRAND REMONSTRANCE—IMPEACH-MENT OF LORD KIMBOLTON AND THE FIVE MEMBERS OF THE HOUSE OF COMMONS.

A RECESS having been agreed on from the 9th of September to the 20th of October, since the Scots army was now gone out of the kingdom, the English army almost disbanded, and the plague increasing in the cities of London and Westminster, and parts adjoining,[1] both Houses appointed committees to act during the recess.[2] They also appointed commissioners to attend the King in his journey to Scotland, for which he set out on the 10th of August.[3] The commissioners appointed for this purpose were William, Earl of Bedford, Edward Lord Howard, Sir William Armyne, Sir Philip Stapleton, Mr. Fiennes, and Mr. Hampden.[4] Hume says that these commissioners were sent, "as was pretended, to see that the articles of pacification were executed; but really to be spies upon him, and extend still farther the ideas of parliamentary authority, as well as eclipse the majesty of the King." I doubt much whether the Parliament thought about "eclipsing the majesty of the King," but they having among them one or two men with some brains under their steeple-crowned hats, saw that their King was a man who, having lied to them times out of number, was not to be trusted; whom, indeed, it was

---

[1] Parl. Hist. ii. 904.
[2] Ibid., 910, 911.
[3] Ibid., 900.
[4] Ibid., 902.

safer to meet as an enemy on a field of battle than as a friend in a Parliament House, a council chamber, or a drawing-room.

It was natural enough that Charles should seek to avoid the consequences of the concessions he had made, however constitutional they might be; and there is evidence enough now that he did seek to avoid them. The means by which he sought to accomplish this end were not at first open war against the Parliament, but belonged to that species of proceedings which, in the French language, are called "*coups d'état*," and for which, very happily, the English language furnishes no synonym. The history of the next ten months is, in fact, a history of a series of *coups d'état* by the King to crush his opponents. That they were unsuccessful is not surprising when the character of Charles and the qualities requisite for success in that branch of political business are considered. Whatever other qualities for success in such enterprises may be desirable, it may be safely laid down that, together with thorough unscrupulousness, unbounded daring, and at least a considerable degree of a certain kind of talent, are indispensable. Charles may have had unscrupulousness enough, but neither of courage nor of dexterity had he the amount required. There may be instruction derived from an account of plots against the liberties of mankind devised and executed with ability and courage. But Charles's plots were all so ill devised and so clumsily and feebly executed, that it would be a waste of time to enter into minute details of them.

The difficulty of getting at the truth under a government which considers its safety to consist in enveloping its deeds in darkness, I have shown in my Essays on Historical Truth, in reference to the immediate predecessor of the

King now on the throne of England; and even the Long Parliament was not much more favourable to the publication of its proceedings than the Stuart kings were of theirs. Sir Simonds D'Ewes wrote those notes, of which Mr. Forster has made such excellent use in his work on the Debates on the Grand Remonstrance, "with note-book on his knee and ink-bottle hanging at his breast,"[1]—a circumstance presenting a strange contrast to the accommodation now afforded for reporting debates. But at that time note-taking, even under such difficulties as those abovementioned, was strongly opposed by some members of the House.[2] If we possessed the letters written by the Parliamentary Commissioners appointed to proceed to Edinburgh with the King to the committees of both Houses appointed to sit during the recess, we should know more than we do of the affair called "The Incident." Even with all the assistance Mr. Forster has been able to derive from his careful study of D'Ewes's manuscript, I do not find anything specific added to what was before known. On the 20th of October, when both Houses met after the recess, Pym, in the course of his report to the House of what had happened in that interval, said: "For the letters last received out of Scotland from the committee, they speak of something intended to be done there upon the persons of divers lords of Scotland."[3] This, it will be seen, is very vague, nor does Mr. Forster's statement that "the letters now handed in from the member for Bucks [Hampden], which had reached the committee by an express, detailed the scheme just discovered at Edinburgh for the assassination of the leaders of the Covenant," add any details to

---

[1] Forster, The Debates on the Grand Remonstrance, p. 123. London, John Murray, Albemarle Street, 1860.

[2] Ibid., p. 124, note.   [3] Parl. Hist., ii. 914, 915.

remove the vagueness, since, he adds, "the entire contents of these letters," and consequently the details of the scheme of assassination, "were not divulged."[1]

Sir Walter Scott, who will not be supposed to have entertained any prejudices against Charles and his cause, says: "There can be little doubt that Montrose's disclosures to the King concerned the private correspondence which passed between the Scottish Covenanters and the opposition party in the Parliament of England, and which Charles might hope to convert into an accusation of high treason against both."[2] The *Incident*, therefore, may be considered as having some obscure connection with the attempt to arrest the five members, and consequently as a part of one of Charles's unsuccessful *coups-d'état*.

Notwithstanding the admission even by Mr. Brodie, after a most full and searching examination of the evidence, that the authenticity is doubtful[3] of the commission alleged to have been granted by Charles to the Irish rebels, I think there is sufficient evidence to class the Irish insurrection as another of those unsuccessful *coups-d'état* attempted by Charles to establish his absolute authority.[4] But whether or not Charles sanctioned and encouraged a rising in Ireland against the dominant power,—that of the Protestants, which was not at that time *his* power,—it is certain that Charles and his courtiers, instead of exerting themselves to punish the leaders of the insurrection and massacre in Ireland, gave, as Pym declared, the English

[1] Forster, Debates on The Grand Remonstrance, pp. 165, 166.
[2] History of Scotland, contained in "Tales of a Grandfather," i. 422. Edinburgh, 1846.
[3] Hist. of Brit. Emp., iii. 190.
[4] This view is corroborated by some passages in a letter printed by Mr. Forster from the MS. in the State Paper Office in his "Arrest of the Five Members," p. 299, which work I had not seen when the passage in the text was written.

Parliament too much reason to suppose that they were favourably disposed towards them.[1]

To enter into the revolting details of this insurrection and massacre is foreign to the plan of this history. Any one who wishes to read the particulars of women and children butchered with every circumstance of atrocity by armed men, may have recourse to the examinations of eye-witnesses of these revolting atrocities attested upon oath, which are published in Sir John Temple's history of this disgusting massacre, called the Irish Rebellion of 1641. King James, departing from the policy of Queen Elizabeth, had permitted and encouraged Irish regiments under Irish officers to enter the Spanish service. Those regiments were therefore ready to return to their native country with all the advantages of military discipline, and with all the arts of Spanish cruelty added to their own, whenever it suited the policy of the King of Spain to disturb the British Government, or the policy of the House of Stuart to employ them for the destruction of the English Constitution and the establishment of a pure despotism in its place. King Charles went much further than King James had gone. He not only allowed such levies, but he granted a commission to the Earl of Antrim[2] to raise an army of

---

[1] "The ill-affected party," says Captain Slingsby, "which are those that follow the Court, do now speak very favourably of the Irish; as those whose grievances were great, their demands moderate, and may stand the King in much stead."—Slingsby to Pennington, 6th January 164½ printed from the MS. in the State Paper Office in Mr. Forster's "Arrest of the Five Members," pp. 298, 299.

[2] There is reason to believe that his Queen, Henrietta Maria, was the promoter of this as of much which gave to this struggle its worst and most sanguinary character—that she had nearly as much to do with the Irish massacre as her relative Catharine de' Medici had with that of St. Bartholomew. There is a letter from her to Strafford in 1638 which shows that she was in confidential communication with the Earl of Antrim two or three years before the massacre. See Strafford's Letters and Despatches, ii. 221. And the English

native Irish to be employed against Scotland, from the wildest portion of the natives; "as many Oe's and Macs" —wrote Strafford, who had sense enough at least to remonstrate against this—"as would startle a whole council-board on this side to hear of."[1] But though Strafford remonstrated against the commission to Antrim, the army which he himself had levied for the same service, amounting to 8000 foot and 1000 horse, were all Papists; while the severe restrictions upon saltpetre and gunpowder disarmed the Protestants. At the same time Strafford's government had excited general discontent and disgust both in Protestants and Catholics of all ranks; while the ecclesiastical innovations introduced by him in accordance

House of Commons in one of their declarations concerning Ireland, charge the King, "That although the rebels had most impudently styled themselves *The Queen's Army*, and professed that the cause of their rising was 'To maintain the King's prerogative and the Queen's religion against the Puritan Parliament of England;' and therefore both Houses of Parliament did humbly and earnestly advise His Majesty to wipe away the dangerous scandal, by proclaiming them rebels and traitors to His Majesty and the crown of England, which thus would have mated and weakened the conspirators in the beginning, and have encouraged both the Parliament here, and good people there, the more vigorously to have opposed their proceedings: yet such was the power of evil counsel about him, that no proclamation was set forth to that purpose till almost three months after the breaking out of this rebellion; and then command given that but forty should be printed, nor they published till further directions should be given by His Majesty." See May, Hist. of the Parlt., bk. ii. ch. ii. *sub fin.* Mrs. Hutchinson says, speaking of Nottinghamshire: "All the Popish gentry were wholly for the King, whereof one Mr. Golding, next neighbour to Mr. Hutchinson, had been a private collector of the Catholics' contributions to the Irish Rebellion, and for that was, by the Queen's procurement, made a knight and baronet."—Memoirs of Col. Hutchinson, p. 117, Bohn's edition. London, 1854.

[1] The Lord-Deputy to Mr. Secretary Windebank, March 20, 163⅜. Strafford's Letters and Despatches, ii. 300. Antrim's propositions, nineteen in number, will be found pp. 305, 306. They conclude with "names of my friends," among which are the names of some very active in the subsequent massacre,—Macgennis, Macguire, Phelim O'Neale and his brother, Hugh McMahon;—so that the ringleaders of this massacre were literally the same persons to whom Charles had granted a commission to commit their butcheries in Scotland, which some of them afterwards carried out under Montrose.

with the pressing demands of Laud disgusted the Protestants by its approach to Romanism, without gaining the Romish party, whom an English Pope did not satisfy, and whose clergy perceived themselves still hopelessly excluded from all participation in church livings.

On the reassembling of the English Parliament on the 20th of October, the question which occupied the attention of the Commons was the Remonstrance or declaration on the state of the kingdom, which contained a full recapitulation of all the grievances and acts of misgovernment that had been inflicted on the nation from the commencement of the reign.[1] The Bill for preventing the dissolution of Parliament without their own consent, though a more decidedly revolutionary measure, had passed almost without opposition; but the Remonstrance formed the subject of the most violent party contest that had yet taken place. The idea of a remonstrance, which should set forth the many illegal practices of the Government, had been entertained from the first sitting of this Parliament,[2] and on the reassembling of Parliament in October 1641, it was vigorously urged forward by one of the two great parties into which the Parliament appeared to have suddenly divided itself almost immediately after the execution of Strafford. Respecting the nature of these two parties and their relation to the two great parties which have appeared in Parlia-

[1] Parl. Hist., ii. 946-964. May, Hist. of the Parlt., bk. ii. ch. 2, pp. 88, 89. Ed. Maseres, London, 1812. Forster, The Grand Remonstrance. See pp. 215-273 for Mr. Forster's Abstract of the Grand Remonstrance. Of the difficulty of reproducing it in modern history Mr. Forster says: "It is not merely that it occupies fifteen of Rushworth's closely-printed folio pages, but that, in special portions of its argument, it passes with warmth and rapidity through an extraordinary variety of subjects of which the connection has ceased to be always immediately apparent."—Ibid, p. 116. There appears to be some slight verbal differences between the copy of the Remonstrance in Rushworth and that in the Parliamentary History.

[2] Commons' Journals, ii. 25, 32, 42, 234.

ment since the beginning of the eighteenth century some misconception appears to have prevailed.

To say that "the corporate existence of the two great parties which have ever since alternately governed the country,"[1] which "during some years were designated as Cavaliers and Roundheads, and were subsequently called Tories and Whigs,"[2] dates from the day on which the Houses met again after their recess of six weeks, from 9th September to 20th October 1641, appears to be a misconception. In point of fact, the conflict at that time in England was between the King, who sought to destroy the English Constitution, and that portion of the English nation who sought to preserve that Constitution. To call that portion of the nation who were now willing to be the abettors of the King in his design against the Constitution, and who can only be correctly designated as a band of courtiers, a great constitutional party, leads to confusion of ideas respecting the very foundation of the English Constitution, and of the nature of the great struggle in which the English people were now about to engage. There is evidence enough to show that this King was willing to engage in schemes for the accomplishment of his object,—the enslaving of the English nation,—as unconstitutional, as inhuman, as sanguinary, as those which the tyrants of France and Spain had recently employed for the destruction of all civil and religious liberty in France, Holland, and the Netherlands. To constitute a great political party there needs something more than to be the creatures of such a King as this. Such persons partook more of the nature of that species of politicians known by the designation of "the King's friends" during

[1] Macaulay's History of England, i. 47. London, 1864.
[2] Ibid., p. 48.

the first ten years of the reign of George III., than of the nature of a great political party, which to merit such a designation must have at least some great public objects, extending somewhat beyond the royal family and the royal household.

Further, in speaking of the two great parties which appeared in the English Parliament when the Houses met again on the 20th October after the six weeks' recess, Lord Macaulay says: "Of both the best specimens will be found not far from the common frontier. The extreme section of one class consisted of bigoted dotards: the extreme section of the other consisted of shallow and reckless empirics."[1] If, by these words, Lord Macaulay means that the constitutional liberty of the English people could have been secured by any amount of concession and compromise in dealing with such a king or such a man as Charles I., I dissent from his opinion on this matter, so far as to say that to those who think that such questions as that which was at issue between Charles I. and the Long Parliament were to be solved by parliamentary harangues and resolutions, or by any other argument than the sword, belong the hard names which Lord Macaulay has so liberally bestowed in the sentence I have just quoted from his History.

Moreover, there is an aspect of this question to which neither Lord Macaulay nor Mr. Forster has, in my judgment, given the importance that belongs to it—an aspect, without the study of which, the true nature of the question at issue cannot be thoroughly understood. For the character of King James and his court had so much to do in engendering the spirit that produced the great

[1] History of England, i. 47, 48. London, 1864.

Puritan rebellion upon which we are now entering, that without taking into account the true character of that tyrant, his vices and his crimes, it is impossible to place before our minds the intense hatred borne towards him and his by the warlike religious enthusiasts who considered him and his race as much accursed of God as the men of ancient days who, as their Bible told them, were destroyed for their vices by fire from heaven.

It is hardly necessary to go into a long digression to attempt to account for the appearance of two hostile parties in the English Parliament soon after the execution of Strafford. The unanimity that had appeared when the Long Parliament first met disappeared when "the one formidable obstacle had been removed, by Strafford's death, to their own entry into Charles's counsels; and without further guarantees for the security of any one concession they had wrested from the crown, Hyde and his associates were prepared to halt where they stood, or even (as in the case of the Episcopacy Bill) to recede from ground they had taken up."[1] When the bill to take away the bishops' votes in the House of Lords was reproduced, Lord Falkland said that he had changed his opinion on that as well as many other subjects, and declared his determination to vote against it. "This," observes Mr. Forster, "was the first frank, bold announcement of the rupture in the parliamentary party."[2]

While to Hyde and others the royal favour and consequent official employment might be inducements, Lord Falkland was too rich already to care for the emoluments of office, and his mind also was of a different nature from Hyde's. I have said that the character of King James and his court had much to do in raising up the spirit of

[1] Forster, The Grand Remonstrance, p. 153.   [2] Ibid., p. 168.

hatred to monarchy that produced the great rebellion. Now, a curious phenomenon is here observable. Some of the English nobility, who, from their own or their ancestors' position at the court of the first Stuart, possessed the most intimate and accurate knowledge of the qualities of kingship, were members of the government called the Commonwealth. Thus, William Cecil, Earl of Salisbury (the son of Robert Cecil, created Earl of Salisbury by King James in 1605), and Philip Herbert, created Earl of Montgomery by King James, also in 1605, and who succeeded his brother as Earl of Pembroke in 1630, were both members of the Rump and also of the first Council of State; and this Earl of Salisbury was one of the members present at the last meeting recorded in the order-book of the Council of State, on Friday, the 15th of April 1653, preceding that Wednesday, the 20th of April, when Cromwell destroyed them and their cause. Basil Fielding, Earl of Denbigh, another member of the Council of State, also owed his peerage to James I.; his father William Fielding, having been created Earl of Denbigh in 1622, through the influence of George Villiers, Duke of Buckingham, whose sister, Susan Villiers, he had married. Thus the men who knew most respecting the court of the Stuarts enrolled themselves among those who pronounced "the office of king in this nation to be unnecessary, burdensome, and dangerous."

Now, Lord Falkland also owed his peerage—a Scotch peerage which did not give him a seat in the House of Lords—to James I.; his father having been by James not only created Viscount Falkland in 1620, but appointed Lord Deputy of Ireland in 1622, in which office he continued till 1629. This first Lord Falkland is said to have possessed abilities, on which point I do not presume to

offer any opinion further than that I should infer from
the title of the only work of his which was published, but
which I have never seen, "History of the Most Unfortunate Prince Edward II.," that his abilities were considerable, since they enabled him to follow the example of
those ingenious Greek sophists who wrote panegyrics on
characters remarkable for depravity. In this species of
ingenuity his son, the Lord Falkland of the Long Parliament, bore some resemblance to him, at least to judge
from some specimens of his writing printed by Mr.
Forster, in a note to his section on Lord Falkland. As
the first Lord Falkland discovered that Edward II., who
is supposed in some points of character to have borne a
resemblance to James I., possessed certain qualities that
rendered him an eligible subject for a history; so the
second Lord Falkland discovered that Ben Jonson's
comedies were "ethick lectures," which "purged and
amended" the "thoughts and wills" of all his spectators,
not one of whom could call Jonson's "chaste stage the
cause of any crime of his." Whatever merit belonged to
Ben as a writer, one would hardly have thought of
"chaste" as the precise word applicable to his "stage."
Sir Walter Scott was well read in Ben Jonson, and was
much indebted to his works for assistance in delineating
many of the characters and scenes in his "Fortunes of
Nigel;" but Scott seems to have taken a totally different
view from Falkland's of the moral tendencies of Ben's
"stage." Mr. Gifford, in his Memoir of Ben Jonson,[1]
prefixed to his edition of that writer's works, having expressed some indignation at the charge brought by Sir
Walter Scott in his "Life of Dryden[2]" against Ben
Jonson of brutal coarseness of conversation, and of

[1] P. 180.   [2] P. 264.

vulgar and intemperate pleasures, Scott, in the second edition of that work, noticed the remarks of Mr. Gifford, and signified his adherence to the opinion he had before given. "Few men," he says, "have more sincere admiration for Jonson's talents than the present writer. But surely that coarseness of taste, which tainted his powerful mind, is proved from his writings. Many authors of that age are indecent, but Jonson is filthy and gross in his pleasantry, and indulges himself in using the language of scavengers and nightmen. His 'Bartholomew Fair' furnishes many examples of this unhappy predilection." This is precisely what might be expected in the court poet of James I. But we are here only concerned with the characteristics of Ben Jonson's manner of writing, in so far as they may throw light on the character of Lord Falkland. We know a good deal of the character of Sir Walter Scott, and we know that whether or not Ben Jonson's writings furnished sound moral lessons, Scott's did furnish such lessons; and we see that Scott charged Jonson with writing in language not calculated to form the "ethick lectures" which Lord Falkland attributed to him. Now, while we know so much of Scott who censures Ben Jonson, we know almost nothing of Falkland, who praises him, but what Clarendon, his friend and panegyrist, has told us; and we know enough of Clarendon's unscrupulous advocacy to refuse to accept either his praise or his blame of any man, unless confirmed by independent unexceptionable testimony. The conclusion would seem to be that Hyde and Falkland, though they objected to the tyranny and insolence of Strafford, having got rid of Strafford, had now no objection to the tyranny and other vices of the Stuarts, provided one of them stepped into the place left vacant by the death of Strafford. Whether or not they

knew as much of the darker vices of the court of James
I. as those peers who, as we have seen, went all the way
with the Commonwealth-men, they were not willing to act
any longer with Pym and Hampden. Those who agree
with Lord Macaulay's assertion that the Puritan austerity
drew to the King's faction all who made pleasure their
business, who affected gallantry, splendour of dress, or
taste in the lighter arts, may account for their defection
from the party of Pym and Hampden on this ground.
But this is one of the sweeping assertions of Lord Macaulay that is by no means strictly true; since the Council of
State of the Commonwealth contained many men well
described in the words applied by Aubrey to Challoner,
" He was as far from a Puritan as the east from the west.
He was of the natural religion, and of Henry Martyn's
gang, and one who loved to enjoy the pleasures of this
life."[1] This does not prove that the general character of
the insurrection against Charles was not Puritan, but only
that it is not strictly accurate to say that the Puritan
austerity drove to the King's faction *all* who were not
Puritans. The strength of the party of the Parliament,
still more of the army of the Parliament, lay in the intense
religious enthusiasm which emphatically characterised the
English Puritans of the seventeenth century.

King Charles had passed the Petition of Right, and had
acted in direct violation of its provisions; nevertheless
Hyde and Falkland said that the King, having now consented to a law that a Parliament should be held at least
once in three years, to the abolition of the Star Chamber,
the High Commission, the Council of York, and to the
execution of Strafford, should be trusted in future as no
longer seeking to encroach on the ancient rights of the

[1] Aubrey's Lives, ii. 282. London, 1813.

English people. On the other side, Pym and Hampden were not unmindful of the fact that, not only had Charles disregarded the Petition of Right which he had passed himself, but that Magna Charta had been violated repeatedly by successive kings; that in truth the very same nature which made men tyrants made them without faith and without mercy; and that such men were to be watched as dangerous beasts of prey were to be watched, with an unsleeping and armed vigilance. Such is the substance of many parliamentary harangues and resolutions, divested of the formal hypocrisy with which men speak of a tyrant whom they know to be using every means he can devise to destroy them,—as full of grace and goodness,—as most gracious, most excellent, and even most sacred. If there had been good ground for imputing to Charles any portion of these qualities of grace and goodness which the modern phraseology ascribes to kings and royal and imperial persons, it might indeed be said that it was offering an insult to the King to enumerate grievances and miscarriages which had already been redressed, as the Remonstrance—the Grand Remonstrance—had for its avowed purpose to do. And this probably caused the defection from the party of Pym and Hampden of many who may have sincerely believed the King to be a better and more truthful man than he was.

After many debates upon separate clauses, the Grand Remonstrance was settled and brought in engrossed on Saturday, the 20th of November 1641. Clarendon says that the popular party urged its passing on the same day, and that a postponement until the next day of sitting was obtained with difficulty. As they left the House, Cromwell asked Lord Falkland, "Why he would have it put off, for that day would quickly have determined it?" Falkland answered, "There would not have been time enough; for sure it would take some debate." Cromwell replied, "A very sorry one."[1] Cromwell, however, was mistaken, for the debate which took place on Monday the 22d of November, and during which there were two several divisions on particular clauses, lasted from twelve at noon to the then unprecedented hour of twelve at night.[2] And then another debate arose on the question of publishing, which lasted till three in the morning.[3] The division by which the Remonstrance was finally adopted was—yeas 159, noes 148. It was then moved by Hampden that the Remonstrance should not be printed without the particular order of the House; and as this implied an intention of printing it, the court party proposed that the word "published" should be substituted for "printed," but the amendment was lost by 101 to 124. After this last division Mr. Hyde, according to a plan agreed on by him and his friends, proposed a protestation. A scene of the wildest uproar ensued, which lasted till three in the morning. Warwick, who was present, says: "We had sheathed our swords in each other's bowels, had not the sagacity and great calmness of Mr. Hampden, by a short speech, prevented it."[4] In the end, the printing of the Remonstrance was postponed until further orders, but the House refused to restrain its publication by a majority of 124 to 101.[5] As the members left the House, Lord Falkland asked Cromwell "whether there had been a debate?" to

---

[1] Clar. Hist. ii. 42.   [2] Commons' Journals, ii. 321.
[3] Of this debate the speech of Sir Edward Dering, published by himself at the time, was supposed to be the only fragment in existence till the appearance of Sir Ralph Verney's Notes. And now a more complete report has been published by Mr. Forster from a careful comparison of the notes of Verney and D'Ewes.—Forster, The Grand Remonstrance, p. 290, and note.
[4] Warwick's Mem., 202.   [5] Commons' Journals, ii. 322.

which he answered, that " he would take his word another time," and whispered in his ear, with some asseveration, that "if the Remonstrance had been rejected he would have sold all he had the next morning, and never have seen England more, and he knew there were many other honest men of the same resolution."[1]

The strong objections entertained by the majority to the liberty of protesting exercised by the Lords being extended to the Commons were manifested by an attempt to punish some one of the protesters. Clarendon says they would have selected him, but for the protection afforded him by Sir John Hotham, Stapleton, and others of the northern men, who were grateful to him for having aided to free them from the thraldom of the Council of York. Jeffrey Palmer, a lawyer, and a friend of Hyde's, was the victim substituted for Hyde. Palmer was compelled to answer by a majority of 48, and sent to the Tower by a majority of 41; but the House refused to sanction his expulsion, to which extent of punishment Pym and Hampden and the other Puritan leaders did not go, by a majority of 32.[2] The question as to the exercise by the Commons of that liberty of protesting, which is an ancient right of the Lords, was, on the 20th of December, brought before the House for determination, when it was resolved "that in no case a protestation ought to be desired by any member of this House, or admitted by this House, being desired."[3] There is in Sir Ralph Verney's Notes[4] a short report of three speeches on this subject by Hyde, Holborne, and Sir Henry Vane the elder. "Old Sir Henry Vane" said,

---

[1] Clar. Hist., ii. 312.
[2] Commons' Journals, ii. 324.; Sir Ralph Verney's Notes, pp. 126-128.
[3] Commons' Journals, ii. 350. [4] P. 136.

"The liberty of protesting used in all foreign diets and councils is no more to be urged here than the use of the common law there, where they are governed by the civil law; and till Sir Edward Cook's time, *nemine contradicente*, was never put into any of our votes and orders." This argument being founded only on precedent does not touch the rationale of the question, but if good for nothing else the argument of "Old Sir Henry Vane" may serve as an instructive specimen of the tyranny of majorities.[1]

The Remonstrance was voted on the 22d of November, and the King arrived from Scotland on the 25th. On the 1st of December the Remonstrance was presented to the King at Hampton Court by a committee of the Commons, and along with it a petition, in which, among other things, they prayed that the bishops should be deprived of their vote in Parliament. Mr. Forster gives an interesting account from the MS. notes of Sir Simonds D'Ewes, who was present as one of the committee of the Commons, of the unusually gracious reception given them by the King. On their arrival at the palace, they had to wait only a quarter of an hour before being ushered into the King's presence; and when they sank upon the knee, Charles desired them to rise, and listened attentively as Sir Ralph Hopton read the petition. When the reading was finished the King said, "Doth the Houses intend to *publish* this declaration?" to which they replied that they could give no answer to the question." "Well, then," said the King, "I suppose you do not expect *me* to answer now to so long a petition;" adding some words to the effect that in Scotland they were satisfied with him, and he with them.

---

[1] See the representation of minorities discussed in the seventh chapter of J. S. Mill's "Considerations on Representative Government."

He then gave them his hand to kiss; "committing them to the entertainment of his comptroller, and the lodgement of his harbinger; both being of the worthiest."[1] Just as they were about to leave the palace, a message was brought to them from the King with request for its immediate delivery to the House of Commons, "that there might be no publishing of the Declaration till the House had received His Majesty's answer."[2] "The reader will now judge," observes Mr. Forster, "to what extent the facts justify Clarendon in stating that, when it was finally resolved to publish the Remonstrance, this was done in violation of a compact or understanding against any such step until the King's answer was received. On the one side there was a strong wish expressed undoubtedly, but on the other this wish was met by neither compact nor understanding."[3]

On the 15th of December the printing of the Remonstrance, concerning the state of the kingdom, the Great or Grand Remonstrance as it came to be called, to distinguish it from the many similar State Papers of less importance issued during the war, was moved in the House of Commons, and after a vehement debate was carried by 135 to 83. The order was then given for immediate printing.[4] The effect of this appeal to the people of England may be partly known from the admission of Clarendon,[5] who may be believed here if nowhere else, that it was like a trumpet-blast calling them to battle in a cause which was thoroughly their own.

"It may be true, or it may be false," observes Mr. Forster, "that Cromwell would have sold all he had the next morning if the Remonstrance had been rejected, and would

---

[1] Forster, The Grand Remonstrance, pp. 368-370. [2] Ibid.
[3] Ibid.   [4] Ibid., pp. 406, 407.   [5] Ibid., p. 418.

never have seen England more; but that Falkland heard him say so would seem to be undoubted, and the fact is a singular proof of the gravity of the conjuncture which had arisen."[1] If this story appears improbable as being inconsistent with Cromwell's strength of character, which would arm him against despair, it may be observed that Cromwell might see, with the quick glance of genius, more clearly than others,—as he afterwards saw, what Essex, what even Hampden did not see, where the military strength of the Royalists lay, and by what means that strength could be overpowered,—that if the Remonstrance had been rejected, such a fact proving the party of the court to be stronger in the House of Commons than the party opposed to them, seemed to forebode another ten years or more of civil and religious tyranny, such as those dark years in which had passed the prime of his manhood, and during which Englishmen were forbidden by their tyrants to mention so much as the very word "Parliament," and were even forbidden to "presume to talk of religion at their tables and in their families." A man like Cromwell had naturally no inclination to go on living another ten years of such a life as that; and would, on the other hand, rather seek refuge from it in the wilds of America, for the fact of such a parliamentary majority on the side of the court would imply a hopelessness of an armed resistance. And as to the plea that all the "capital grievances had no longer any existence," it is to be remembered that the abolition of the Star-Chamber, of the High Commission and the Council of York, and the execution of Strafford altogether, hardly exceeded or even equalled in importance the passing of the *Petition of Right;* and, nevertheless, Charles had trampled under foot

[1] Forster, The Grand Remonstrance, p. 417.

the provisions of that second Great Charter for a period of more than ten years. But happily the result was different, and kings were to learn a lesson from Cromwell which they will remember as long as this world lasts.

On the 3d of January the King sent the Attorney-General to impeach Lord Kimbolton and five members of the House of Commons—Hampden, Pym, Holles, Haselrig, and Strode—at the bar of the Lords, on a charge of high treason. The King also sent persons to seal up the trunks, studies, and chambers of the accused members. The Commons having received notice of this, desired a conference with the Lords upon this breach of privilege. They also again expressed their wish that their Lordships would concur in asking a guard which should be approved of by both Houses, or if a guard could not be obtained, they desired their Lordships to take it into consideration to adjourn to another place, where they may sit in security. The Lords ordered "that all the chambers, studies, and trunks that were sealed or locked, belonging to Mr. Holles, Mr. Pym, Mr. Hampden, or to any member of Parliament, should be forthwith unsealed and unlocked," and agreed to join with the Commons in a petition for a guard. While these things were going on, a sergeant-at-arms came to the House of Commons and demanded the five members. The Commons having commanded the sergeant to withdraw, appointed a committee to acquaint His Majesty that, as the message was a matter of such consequence as to concern the privileges of all the Commons of England, they will take it into serious consideration, and will attend His Majesty with an answer in all humility and duty, and with as much speed as the greatness of the business will permit, and in the meantime will take care that those gentlemen mentioned in the message shall be ready to answer any legal charge laid against them. The Speaker then, by command of the House, enjoined the accused members to give regular attendance until further order.[1]

On the morning of Tuesday, the 4th of January, information having been received that the five accused members were to be taken away by force, the House adjourned till one o'clock. As soon as the House met again, it was moved that, since there was an intention to take these five members by force, they should, to avoid all tumults, be commanded to absent themselves. Upon this, the House gave them leave to absent themselves, but entered no order for it, and then the five gentlemen went out of the House. A little after, the King came, with all his guard and all his pensioners, and two or three hundred soldiers and gentlemen. The King commanded the soldiers to stay in the hall, and sent in word to the Commons that he was at the door. The Speaker was commanded to sit still, with the mace lying before him; and then the King entered the House, taking the palsgrave with him, and commanded all the rest upon their lives not to come in. The door was then kept open, and the Earl of Roxburghe stood within the door, leaning upon it. The King then went up towards the chair, with his hat off, and the Speaker stepped out to meet him. Then the King stepped up to his place, and stood upon the step, but sate not down in the chair. And after he had looked a great while, he said he would not break their privileges, but treason had no privilege; he came for those five gentlemen, for he expected obedience yesterday, and not an answer. Then he called Mr. Pym and Mr. Holles by name, but no answer was made. Then he asked the Speaker if they were there, or where

[1] Parl. Hist., ii. 1006–1008; Sir Ralph Verney's Notes, pp. 137, 138.

they were. Upon that the Speaker fell on his knees, and desired his excuse, for he was a servant to the House, and had neither eyes nor tongue to see or say anything but what they commanded him. Then the King told him he thought his own eyes were as good as his, and then said, "Well, since I see all the[1] birds are flown, I do expect from you that you will send them unto me as soon as they return hither," adding that otherwise he must take his own course to find them, for their treason was foul, and such a one as they would all thank him to discover. Then he assured the House they should have a fair trial, and so went out, with his hat off till he came to the door. The House then instantly resolved to adjourn till to-morrow at one of the clock, that in the interim they might consider what to do.[2] Rushworth, in his account, says : "The King having concluded his speech, went out of the House again, which was in great disorder, and many members cried out aloud, so as he might hear them, '*Privilege! Privilege!*' and forthwith adjourned till the next day at one o'clock."[3]

It is stated by several contemporary writers, by Bates,[4] and Sir Philip Warwick,[5] two Royalist writers, as well as

---

[1] In the original copy of Rushworth's report of what was said by the King, preserved in the State Paper Office, the King, among other corrections, has altered "my birds" to "the birds." See a copy of the portions in which the material corrections occur, with the latter printed in fac-simile, in Forster's Arrest of the Five Members, pp. 188, 189.

[2] Sir Ralph Verney's Notes, pp. 138, 139.

[3] Rushworth, iv. 473, *et seq.* The King having observed Rushworth "taking his speech in characters, sent for him the same evening and commanded him to give him a copy of his speech. Rushworth "transcribed His Majesty's speech out of his characters, His Majesty staying in the room all the while, and then and there presented the same to the King, which His Majesty was pleased to command to be sent speedily to the press, and the next morning it came forth in print."—Sir Ralph Verney's Notes, pp. 138, 139.

[4] Elenchus Parl., i. 24. [5] Memoirs, p. 204.

by Rushworth, that Mr. Pym had received private information of the King's design to take away by force the five accused members of the House of Commons, from the Countess of Carlisle, sister to the Earl of Northumberland, "who," says Sir Philip Warwick, " had now changed her gallant from Strafford to Mr. Pym, and was become such a she-saint, that she frequented their sermons and took notes." Mr. Forster[1] thinks there is no ground for Sir P. Warwick's assertion that the Countess of Carlisle "had now changed her gallant from Strafford to Mr. Pym;" and that this imputation was one of the many Royalist libels against Pym. But as Pym had no Boswell, we have too little trustworthy information as to his private life to entitle us to pronounce Warwick's statement to be absolutely false. However that might be, it was the opinion at the time that the warning had prevented bloodshed and many momentous consequences. Sixteen years after that day, in one of the Parliaments of Cromwell, Sir Arthur Haselrig, one of the accused members, said: "On the King's return the Queen raged and gave him an unhandsome name (poltroon), for that he did not take others out; and certain, if he had, they would have been killed at the door."[2] The account in a MS. cited by Mr. Forster,[3] is much to the same purport, namely, that the Queen exclaimed, "*Allez, poltron!* go, pull these rogues out by the ears, *ou ne me revoyez jamais!*" It is easy for women and boys[4] to talk of pulling "these rogues out

[1] Arrest of the Five Members, pp. 135, 136, and note.
[2] Burton's Diary of the Parliaments of Cromwell, iii. 93.
[3] Arrest of the Five Members, p. 138.
[4] Ludlow mentions a somewhat similar expression used by a young gentleman of the Inns of Court—" What! shall we suffer these fellows at Westminster to domineer thus? Let us go into the country, and bring up our tenants to pull them out."—Ludlow's Memoirs, i. 22. 2d edition. London, 1721.

by the ears;" but the only men who have played that game with any considerable success have been Cromwell and Bonaparte. Washington might also have played it successfully; but he was a man of another mould, and he refused "with great and sorrowful surprise" (such were his words) the supreme power and the crown which certain discontented officers offered him.

On Wednesday, the 5th of January, the House ordered a committee to sit at Guildhall. This was to consider and advise how to right the House in point of privilege, broken by the King's coming the day before, with an armed force, to take members out of their House. They allowed the Committee on Irish Affairs to sit, but would meddle with no other business till this should be ended. They acquainted the Lords in a message with what they had done, and then they adjourned the House till Tuesday next.[1] On the same day the King went into the City with his usual attendants, and in his passage thither some people cried aloud, "Privilege of Parliament!" "Privilege of Parliament!" and one Henry Walker, an ironmonger and pamphlet-writer, threw into His Majesty's coach a paper, wherein was written, "To your tents, O Israel!" for which he was committed, and afterwards proceeded against at the sessions.[2]

On the 7th, Guildhall being occupied, the Committee adjourned to Grocers' Hall, situated between Guildhall

[1] Sir Ralph Verney's Notes, pp. 139, 140.
[2] Rush., iv. 479. This account of the conduct of the mob is corroborated by a letter from Captain Slingsby to Admiral Pennington, dated 6th January 1641-42, quoted in Mr. Forster's Arrest of the Five Members, p. 260, from the MS. in the State Paper Office. Clarendon says that Walker cried with a loud voice, "To your tents, O Israel!" and is followed by Hume, who cites Rushworth and Clarendon as his authorities. If he had cited Clarendon only, he might have used the words he has used, but how he could bring Rushworth as an authority for using them is indeed a mystery.

and the present Bank of England; the five members being at the time concealed in Coleman Street, where, Whitelocke says, "they wanted nothing." At this meeting of the Committee, it was "resolved upon question, that it is sufficiently proved that the coming of the soldiers, papists and others, with His Majesty to the House of Commons on Tuesday, to take away some members of the House, and, if that had been denied or opposed, then to fall upon the House of Commons in an hostile manner, was a traitorous design against the King and Parliament." It was also resolved upon the question, "That these five gentlemen may, and ought to come to attend this Committee, notwithstanding any warrant issued out, or other matter or accusation against them."[1]

It is to be borne in mind that such was the military organisation of the city of London that there were at that time in the city and suburbs 40,000 men in complete arms, and near 100,000 men with halberds, swords, clubs, and the like.[2]

On the 8th, at the same place of meeting, it was further resolved, "That a printed paper in the form of a proclamation lately issued out for the apprehending of these five gentlemen is false, scandalous, and illegal,[3] and that all acts of the citizens of London, or any other person whatsoever, for the defence of the Parliament, and the privileges thereof, are according to their duty, and the late Protestation, and the laws of the kingdom, and that if any person at all arrest or trouble them for so doing, he is declared an enemy of the Commonwealth."[4]

---

[1] Sir Ralph Verney's Notes, p. 140.
[2] D'Ewes—cited Forster's Arrest of the Five Members, p. 323. "The general cry of the city," says D'Ewes, "was Arm! Arm! with much vehemence, and knocking at men's doors with much violence."
[3] The proclamation was issued on that day, the 8th.
[4] Sir Ralph Verney's Notes, pp. 140, 141.

On the 10th of January, it was resolved upon question, "That the publishing of several articles, purporting a form of a charge of high treason against Lord Kimbolton and the five gentlemen, by Sir William Killegrew, Sir William Fleming, and others, was a high breach of the privileges of Parliament, a great scandal to the King and his Government, a seditious act maliciously tending to the subversion of the peace of the kingdom, and an injury and dishonour to the said members, there being no legal charge or accusation against them. That the privilege of Parliament and liberties of the subject, so broken, cannot be fully vindicated unless the King will discover who advised him to seal up the trunks and apprehend those members, and to come in his person to the Parliament, that such persons may have exemplary punishment."[1]

On that same day, the 10th of January, the King left London, to which he never returned till he was brought thither as a prisoner.[2]

Parliament resumed its sittings at Westminster on Tuesday the 11th of January 1641-42. The Committee of the Commons called upon the Sheriffs of London and Middlesex to raise the *posse comitatus* as a guard. On this occasion, likewise, many captains of vessels and mariners made an offer of their services, and their offer having been accepted, they carried their guns from their ships to Westminster. On the same day, the City Committee of the Commons, together with Lord Kimbolton and the five members, went at about one o'clock to the Three Cranes, a wharf in the Vintry, and there took water, accompanied by from thirty to forty long boats, armed with guns, and carrying flags, besides a great number of smaller vessels filled with citizens and mariners. Skippon, appointed by

---

[1] Sir Ralph Verney's Notes, p. 141.   [2] Rushworth, iv. 482-484.

the City commander of the trained bands, marched at the same time by land to form a guard around the two Houses.[1]

On the same day, many knights, gentlemen, and freeholders from Buckinghamshire, to the number, says Rushworth, of about 4000, riding every one with a printed copy of the Protestation, lately taken for the defence of the King and Parliament, in his hat, came to the Parliament, with a petition from the County to the Lords and another to the Commons.[2]

---

[1] Rushworth, iv. 484. Whitelocke, p. 54. Sir Ralph Verney's Notes, pp. 142, 143.
[2] Rushworth, iv. 486. Whitelocke, p. 54. Parl. Hist., ii. 1029, 1030.

CHAPTER IX.

PREPARATIONS FOR WAR BETWEEN THE KING AND PARLIAMENT.

MATTERS had now reached that point when all men saw that war between the King and Parliament, or at least between the King and the Puritan leaders of the majority of the Commons, was inevitable. The first object therefore with each party was to obtain the command of the military force of the kingdom.

It is perfectly clear, from an examination of the best legal authorities, that the power of the militia was not, in a strictly legal sense, in the Parliament without the King, one of the limbs of the Parliament, and still less in the King without the other two limbs of the Parliament, the Houses of Lords and Commons. And this was the view taken of the matter by Whitelocke, in an able speech which he delivered during the debate in the House of Commons concerning the militia, on the 7th of February 1641–42.[1] But in times like these the strict letter of the law is not much attended to by either party; and while the Parliament issued an ordinance[2] and took measures for securing the militia throughout the kingdom, the King issued the obsolete commissions of array.[3]

On the 9th of February the Parliament passed their ordinance concerning the militia.[4] On the 28th of February

---

[1] Parl. Hist., ii. 1078, 1079.
[2] Ibid., pp. 1083–85.
[3] Ibid., pp. 1380, 1382, 1405.
[4] Ibid., p. 1083.

the Commons passed a series of eleven resolutions respecting the government of the militia, the first of which was "that the King's answer is a denial to the desires of both Houses of Parliament concerning the militia;" and the ninth, "that no charter can be granted by the King to create a power in any corporation over the militia of that place without consent of Parliament."[1] And on the 5th of March 1641–42 the Commons resolved upon question, "That all commissions of lieutenancy granted under the great seal are illegal. That all those commissions be forthwith brought in to be cancelled. That whosoever shall execute any power over the militia of this kingdom, or Wales, by colour of any commission of lieutenancy, shall be accounted a disturber of the peace of the kingdom. That the Lords be moved to join with us in these votes."[2]

The King, however, sent out commissions of array, which were now unsupported by any statute, and were therefore illegal; while the Parliament sent out commissions under their ordinance concerning the militia, which was equally illegal, into all the counties. Mrs. Hutchinson informs us that between those appointed to put these commissions in execution "there were fierce contests and disputes, almost to blood."[3] That these disputes went farther than "almost"—sometimes altogether to blood—appears from a story respecting the death of Blake's brother Samuel, who of all his brothers resembled the great admiral most in the fearlessness of his nature, and to whose son Robert, one of his most gallant sea-captains, the admiral left by his will the gold-chain given him by the Parliament. Samuel Blake, hearing at a small village

[1] Sir Ralph Verney's Notes, pp. 158, 159.   [2] Ibid., p. 161.
[3] Memoirs of Colonel Hutchinson, p. 116. London, 1854.

ale-house at Pawlet, about four miles down the river from Bridgewater, that a captain of array and one of his followers were crossing the river to beat up recruits for the King's service, instead of carrying the intelligence to his brother, who was his commanding-officer, mounted his horse and rode after the two officers. When he came up with them a quarrel ensued, and he was killed. When the news came to Bridgewater, the officers of the regiment were seen to talk very seriously together in small groups, none of them liking to tell Colonel Blake what they were talking about. At last he asked one of them very earnestly, and the gentleman replied, with some emotion, "Your brother Sam is killed," explaining how it happened. The Colonel, having heard him out, said, "Sam had no business there;" and as if he took no further notice of it, turned from the Cornhill or market-place into the Swan Inn, and, shutting himself in a room, gave way to his sorrow for his brother's untimely death, saying, "Died Abner as a fool dieth!"[1]

In the meantime the Queen had gone to Holland, where she purchased arms and ammunition by disposing of the crown jewels. A few days after the King's removal from Whitehall it had been resolved, in a Cabinet Council at Windsor, that the Queen, who was about to depart with her daughter for Holland, should carry the crown jewels thither to pledge for money, ammunition, and arms, and to procure, by the intervention of the Pope's nuncio, 4000 soldiers from France and 4000 from Spain. As these statements are in direct opposition to the solemn declarations made by King Charles at this time, it becomes necessary

[1] The History and Life of Robert Blake, Esq. of Bridgewater, General and Admiral of the Fleets and Naval Forces of England, written by a gentleman who was bred in his family, cited in Dixon's Robert Blake, p. 51. London, 1852.

to cite the authorities for them with as much precision as possible. The statement as to the jewels is made on the authority of Ludlow,[1] Mrs. Hutchinson,[2] May,[3] and Whitelocke.[4] The authority for the resolution formed in the Cabinet Council at Windsor is Father Orleans,[5] who is cited to that effect in Neal's History of the Puritans. With regard to the statement respecting troops from foreign powers, Ludlow expressly says that the Parliament had "discovered that the King had sent abroad to procure what assistance he could against his people;"[6] and in the State Papers of the time, the charge is made by the Parliament, and denied by the King.

When the Parliament understood how busy the Queen was in raising money upon the crown jewels, and perceived from unmistakable signs what course the King had resolved to pursue, they entered into a resolution, which they published, that the King intended to levy war against the Parliament; and passed an ordinance that whoever assisted in selling or pawning any of the crown jewels, or lent money upon them, should be held a promoter of the present war, and an enemy to the State, and ought to give satisfaction out of his own estate to the public.[7]

Charles complained much of the vote asserting his intention of making war, declaring that God knew his heart

---

[1] Vol. i. 26.
[2] P. 97. Bohn's edition.
[3] Lib. ii. 42.
[4] P. 55.
[5] Tome iii. 72, *et seq.* The following not unimportant remark is made by Mr. Brodie as to the relative value of manuscript and published authorities. "Mr. Laing says that he could not discover Neal's authority, but justly remarks that his statement coincides with the inadvertent discoveries of Clarendon. I should be surprised at this, had I not early perceived that Laing, while he had looked through a number of manuscripts, had not sifted the numerous publications—including Neal himself. . . . Had Laing looked through Neal, he would have found his authority within a few pages of that quoted by him, p. 605."—Brodie's History, iii. 336, note.
[6] Ludlow's Memoirs, i. 38.
[7] Parl. Hist., ii. 1323, 1324.

abhorred it.[1] To such a height did·he and his confidential advisers carry their false assertions that even on the 15th of June, when the arms had been purchased and sent from Holland, and the warlike preparations were far advanced, he mentioned in Council, "the rumours spread, and informations given, which might induce many to believe that His Majesty intended to make war against his Parliament; professed before God,[2] and said he declared to all the world, that he always had and did abhor all such designs, and desired his nobility and council, who were there, upon the place, to declare whether they had not been witnesses of his frequent and earnest professions to that purpose whether they saw any colour of preparations, or counsels that might reasonably beget a belief of any such design; and whether they were not fully persuaded that His Majesty had no such intention: but that all his endeavours, according to his many professions, tended to the firm and consistent settlement of the true Protestant religion, the just privileges of Parliament, the liberty, the law, peace, and prosperity of the kingdom." Whereupon all the lords and councillors present signed a paper in these words:: "We, whose names are underwritten, in obedience to His Majesty's desire, and out of the duty which we owe to His Majesty's honour and to truth, being here upon the place, and witnesses to His Majesty's frequent and earnest declarations and professions of his abhorring all designs of making war upon his Parliament,

[1] Charles's free use of the invocation of God was quite a characteristic of his predecessors, James I. and James's mother.

[2] In the King's declaration of 15th June, which was published, he says: "We have upon all occasions, with all possible expressions, professed our full and unshaken resolutions for; peace; and we do again, in the presence of Almighty God, our Father and Redeemer, assure the world, that we have no more thought of making war against our Parliament than against our own children."—Parl. Hist., ii. 1377.

and not seeing any colour of preparations or counsels that might reasonably beget the belief of any such designs, do profess before God, and testify to all the world, that we are fully persuaded that His Majesty hath no such intention; but that all his endeavours tend to the firm and constant settlement of the true Protestant religion, the just privileges of Parliament, the liberty of the subject, the law, peace, and prosperity of this kingdom."[1]

The Parliament now prepared vigorously for war. They borrowed £100,000 from the citizens of London, and passed an ordinance for exercising the militia.[2] They also issued many orders concerning raising men, and buying horses and armour.[3] On the 16th of June the Lords received intelligence from their lord-lieutenants in several counties in England of their great success in executing the Parliament's orders concerning the militia; and the great cheerfulness the country expressed in submitting to their commands.[4] While in some counties, and in almost all the towns, the Parliament prevailed in the raising of forces; in other counties the King was successful. The King nominated Sir John Pennington, and the Parliament the Earl of Warwick, to the command of the fleet. The sailors were all devoted to the Parliament, and when their officers endeavoured to preserve authority over them for the King, they immediately seized those officers as enemies to the State, and sent them to London. Thus the Earl of Warwick obtained the command of the fleet for the Parliament.[5] The Parliament appointed the Earl of Essex Captain-General of

---

[1] Clar., ii. 654, *et. seq.* [2] Parl. Hist., ii. 1328.
[3] Parl. Hist., ii. 1373. [4] Ibid. p. 1373.
[5] Clar., ii. 674, *et. seq.* Rush., iv. 502, 530, 572. May, lib. ii. 94.

the Forces;[1] and they passed an ordinance for the levying of tonnage and poundage.[2]

On the 23d April 1642, when the late army was disbanded, all the artillery, ammunition, and arms, of which there were 16,000 stand, had been deposited in Hull; and the Parliament, by the appointment of the Hothams as governors of Hull, and other measures, had defeated a scheme undertaken by the Earl of Newcastle and Captain William Legge (the latter a great favourite of Charles and deeply concerned in the army plot) for taking possession for the King of the town and magazine.[3] The Parliament ordered the magazine to be removed to the Tower; but this had not yet been done, and Charles resolved to attempt to obtain possession of those military stores. Sir John Hotham being suspected of an inclination to the Royalist party, the Parliament, while from his influence in the neighbourhood they had deemed it advisable to trust him, joined with him in the same commission his son, in whom they had greater confidence.[4] Charles, probably expecting to gain over Sir John Hotham, advanced towards Hull with three hundred horse.[5] He sent a messenger with a letter to the Governor, Sir John Hotham, purporting that he intended to visit his town of Hull and his magazine there, and commanding that the governor should provide for the reception of him and his train. A message declining the visit was returned, but as the King nevertheless continued to advance, the gates were shut, the drawbridge drawn up, and the garrison

---

[1] Parl. Hist., ii. 1414. [2] Parl. Hist., pp. 1429-1433.
[3] Ibid., ii. 1195. [4] Clar., ii. 309.
[5] The Declaration of the Parliament says "400 horse" (Parl. Hist., ii. 1195); but Sir John Hotham's letter to the Speaker says, "His Majesty had in his train, to the best of all our judgments, 300 horse. I was advertised (but the certainty I knew not) that 400 horse lay farther off."—Ibid., p. 1198.

Preparations for War.

was ordered to act on the defensive. Charles having tried in vain menaces and persuasion in order to effect an entrance into the place with his followers,[1] proclaimed Hotham a traitor, and demanded his punishment of the Parliament. To the King's declaration the Parliament published an answer, in which they justified the act of Hotham, as done by their authority, and on the ground that the fortresses of the kingdom were merely intrusted to him for the general good, and were not to be viewed as his private property.

Towards the end of May the Lord Keeper Littleton deserted the Parliament and joined the King at York, having previously delivered the great seal to a person sent with a letter from the King to receive and carry it to the King's quarters.[2]

The most zealous supporters of Charles were the Papists and the High Church party, whose principles were not far removed from Popery. Besides that portion of the nobility and gentry included in the above denominations, there were also many courtiers who were prepared to carry matters to any extremity in behalf of the Crown in order to obtain the rewards promised for so doing;

[1] Sir John Hotham, in his letter to the Speaker, says, "Then he retired to a little house without the walls, and, after one hour's stay, returned and demanded again my resolution. I made the same answer as before; and I think then (but I don't well remember it) he demanded entrance for himself and twenty horse; but in my judgment (as I well saw how the state of affairs stood) being fully satisfied that, if his person were in with but half that number, I was in no ways master of the town."—Parl. Hist., ii. 1199. Yet Mr. Brodie says that "Hotham proposed to admit the King with the Prince and twelve followers," and that the statement that the King proposed to enter with twenty followers appears to have been quite unfounded.—Hist. Brit. Emp., iii. 330, and note. At the end of his letter Hotham has this sentence with reference to the composition of Charles's train, "I am sorry to write who were the men, for there were many of those who were at the Parliament door when the King came to the House."

[2] Rush., ii. 1273 and note. Parl. Hist., ii. 1270-1274.

but there were also not a few who had joined the King, not so much from a conviction of the justness of his cause, or any desire for its success, as from some disgust they had taken up from the cause of the Parliament and its leaders, and some fear of a diminution or subversion of their own privileges. These men dreaded the success of either party if it were to be obtained by success in war. This was the cause of Lord Falkland's marked uneasiness and anxious desire for peace. There are some passages in the letters of Robert Lord Spencer to his wife, a daughter of the Earl of Leicester, which sufficiently explain the causes of the uneasiness of Lord Falkland and many others who had joined the same side. In a letter dated Shrewsbury, 21st September 1642, Lord Spencer says, "The King's condition is much improved of late; his force increaseth daily, which increases the insolency of the Papists. How much I am unsatisfied with the proceedings here, I have at large expressed in several letters. Neither is there wanting daily handsome occasion to retire, were it not for grinning honour. For let occasion be never so handsome, unless a man were resolved to fight on the Parliament side, which, for my part, I had rather be hanged, it will be said without doubt, that a man is afraid to fight. If there could be an expedient found to solve the punctilio of honour, I would not continue here an hour. The discontent that I, and many other honest men receive daily, is beyond expression. . . . The King is of late very much averse to peace by the persuasions of 202 and 111. I fear 243 (Papists) threats have a much greater influence upon 83 (King) than upon 343." In the next letter, undated, but shortly after the preceding, he says, "If the King, or rather 243 (Papists), prevail, we are in sad condition, for they will be insupportable to all, but most to us who have opposed them, so that if the King prevail by force, I must not live at home, which is grievous to me, but more to you."[1]

These remarks of Lord Spencer may enable us in some measure to understand, what otherwise might be unintelligible, why so large and important a portion of the English people were now willing to risk their lives in defence of a king who had governed so ill as Charles had done since he had succeeded to the throne. And if, further, we consider that Charles, by adopting James's minion Buckingham as his chief minister, proved that he also adopted the code of morals of James and his Court; and that that code of morals was one that had spread corruption of the most foul and deadly kind throughout all classes that came into contact with that Court, we may see clearly enough that the war which was now breaking out would be a war to the death; inasmuch as it would be a war between those who really sought, as far as in them lay, to obey the precepts of the Christian religion, and whom their enemies in derision called Puritans, and those who, whether they styled themselves Papists or Arminians, really selected for their approval the conduct of those whose life, as far as it squared with any religion, was more conformable to the Greek than either to the Hebrew or Christian religion.

On the other side, again, although the support of the towns of trade, as well as of the Presbyterians and of those who were called Puritans, gave much of a popular and even democratical colour to the party of the Parliament, that Parliament distinctly announced itself as belonging to the gentry, and not to the commonalty of the kingdom. And to whatever degree it may be considered as for

[1] Sidney Papers, ii. 667, 668.

a time at least representing popular interests (the republican spirit which appeared during the course of the struggle must be regarded as confined to the Parliamentary army and not extending to the general body of the population), in its origin, as in its end, the party of the Parliament was aristocratical or oligarchial rather than democratical. It is not to be inferred from this that the Parliament in substituting their divine right for the divine right of kings did no good. It was a step in the right direction, at that time and in that place, towards the only divine right that man may safely own,—the divine right of Justice and of Truth. And the answer of the Parliament to the charge in one of the King's declarations, "That they have endeavoured to raise an implacable hatred between the gentry and commonalty of the kingdom," while it throws light on the nature of the struggle, appears to draw a just distinction between the portion of the gentry which formed the Parliament and that which followed the King. "They conceive it," they say, "a charge of a strange nature, that they should endeavour to raise the hatred of the commonalty against themselves. For so it must follow, unless the contrivers of that declaration will deny the Parliament to be gentlemen. But though we know (say they) well, there are too many of the gentry of this kingdom, who, to satisfy the lusts of their own ambition, are content to sell their birthrights, to render themselves and their posterity to perpetual slavery, and to submit themselves to any arbitrary and unlimited power of government, so they may for their own time partake of that power, to trample and insult over others; yet we are certain that there are many true-hearted gentlemen who are ready to lay down their lives and fortunes (and of late have given ample testimony thereof) for maintenance of their laws, liberties, and religion, with whom, and others of their resolution, we shall be ready to live and die."[1]

On the 1st of June a petition was agreed on by both Houses to be sent to their committee at York, to be there presented to the King, with nineteen propositions annexed, which were to this effect: That the Privy Councillors and the Great Officers and Ministers of State should only be appointed with the approbation of both Houses of Parliament: That the great affairs of the kingdom should not be concluded by private men, or by unknown or unsworn councillors; but that such matters as concern the public, and are proper for the high court of Parliament, may be debated and transacted only in Parliament; and such other matters of State as are proper for the Privy Council should be there concluded, by the advice of the major part of the Council, attested under their hands: That the Council should be limited to a certain number, not exceeding twenty-five, nor under fifteen; and if any place in the Council happen to be void in the intervals of Parliament, it should not be supplied without the assent of the major part of the Council, and the choice should be confirmed at the next sitting of the Parliament, or else be void: That no marriage should be concluded for any of the King's children, with any foreign prince or other person whatsoever abroad or at home, without the consent of Parliament; and that their governors should be appointed with the approbation of both Houses: That the laws in force against Popish recusants be strictly put in execution: That such

---

[1] May's History of the Parliament, bk. iii. c. i. p. 28, or bk. iii. c. i. p. 175 of Maseres' edition. London, 1812. Ludlow says: "What vast numbers depended upon the King for preferment or subsistence; how many of the nobility and gentry were contented to serve his arbitrary designs, if they might have leave to insult over such as were of a lower order."—Ludlow's Memoirs, i. 120, 121. 2d ed. London, 1721.

a reformation should be made of the Church-government and Liturgy as both Houses of Parliament should advise: That all Privy Councillors and judges should take an oath, the form whereof to be settled by Act of Parliament, for the maintaining of the Petition of Right, and of certain statutes made by the Parliament, which should be mentioned by both Houses of Parliament: That all the judges and all officers placed by approbation of both Houses of Parliament, should hold their places, *quamdiu se bene gesserint*: That His Majesty should rest satisfied with the course the Lords and Commons had appointed for ordering the militia, until the same should be further settled by a bill: That the justice of Parliament should pass upon all delinquents: That a general pardon be granted with such exceptions as should be advised by Parliament: That the forts and castles be disposed of with the approbation of Parliament: That Peers made hereafter be restrained from sitting and voting in Parliament, unless they be admitted thereunto with the consent of both Houses of Parliament.

"Should I grant these demands," said the King, "I may be waited on bareheaded; I may have my hand kissed; the title of majesty may be continued to me; and the King's authority signified by both Houses, may still be the style of your commands; I may have swords and maces carried before me, and please myself with the sight of a crown and a sceptre (though even these would not long flourish, where the stock upon which they grew was dead); but as to true and real power, I should remain but the outside, but the picture, but the sign of a king."[1]

On the 25th of August 1642, Charles erected his stan-

---

[1] Parl. Hist., ii. 1324, *et seq.* Rushworth, iv. 722, *et seq.* May, lib. ii. 74, *et seq.* Ludlow, i. 31, *et seq.*

dard at Nottingham. " The likeness of the standard," says Rushworth, " was much of the fashion of the city streamers used at the Lord Mayor's show, having about twenty supporters, and was carried after the same way; on the top of it hung a flag, the King's arms quartered, with a hand pointing to the crown, which stood above with this motto, 'Give Cæsar his due.'"[1]

[1] Rushworth, iv. 728.

CHAPTER X.

COMMENCEMENT OF THE WAR—BATTLE OF EDGEHILL—KING'S ATTACK ON BRENTFORD.

IN the second chapter of this History I have cited from an ancient roll of Parliament, furnished by Sir Robert Cotton from his valuable collection of records to Sir John Eliot, the precedent of the misgovernment of King John and Henry III. as a parallel to the misgovernment of King James and Charles I. Hume justly remarks that the power of the Norman princes in England had become so great that it required a very great amount of misgovernment on the part of even so weak and vicious a king as John, before his barons could entertain the view of conspiring against him, in order to retrench his prerogative. The parallel between the times of John and Henry III. and those of James and Charles I., holds here also as well as in other points. The power of the crown had become so great in England after the Wars of the Roses that foreign ambassadors in England express their astonishment at the patience of the English people under the misgovernment of James, calling it cowardice,[1] some of them going so far as to say that there were no men in England. And yet Mr. Hallam affirms of the Parliament that " scarce two or three public acts of justice,

---

[1] See the despatches of the French ambassador Tillierès, cited in Chap. I. of this History, and published from the French archives in Raumer, ii. 263-265, 270, 271.

humanity, or generosity, and very few of political wisdom or courage, are recorded of them, from their quarrel with the King to their expulsion by Cromwell." It seems as strange to talk of the Parliament's quarrel with the King as it would be to talk of a traveller having a quarrel with a highwayman because the highwayman wanted to rob him. The barons had a quarrel with King John, and made him pass Magna Charta, which of course he and his son violated whenever they could; and then, again, the barons had another quarrel with Henry III., and conquered him and made him a prisoner. But here the parallel stops, for Henry III. and his son Edward I. escaped from imprisonment; but Charles I. had got into the gripe of men who were resolved he should be made an example, to show to all succeeding ages that kings were not to commit crimes with impunity.

Upon the raising of the royal standard, on the 25th of August 1642, the war broke out over almost all England. In the battles and skirmishes which then took place it it appeared that, for the first year, at least, the advantage was, for the most part, with the royal cause. So that the balance which at the commencement of the war was in favour of the Parliament, from their being in possession of most of the fortified places in England, with the magazines of arms and ammunition which they contained, and from having also great numbers of men at their disposal, with power to raise large sums of money to pay them, was after a little time turned in favour of the King. This appears to have arisen chiefly from the fact, to which I have adverted before, of the superior skill, the result of long practice, in the use of arms, of the nobility and gentry, a much larger number of whom joined the army of the King than that of the Parliament. The servants of these gentlemen, too, particularly their grooms and gamekeepers, as well as their tenants, would be likely to possess both more skill in the use of arms, and, from their open-air occupations, more power to endure the fatigues and hardships of war, than the citizens, accustomed to indoor occupations and a town life, who would form the bulk of the troops of the Parliament. In some respects the intelligence of the Parliamentary troops might be superior. However, under ordinary circumstances, a capability of enduring fatigue, privations, and all the varieties of weather, wet, heat, and cold, coupled with obedience to orders, may be found more useful than superior intelligence in the soldier. But the circumstances of this war were extraordinary, inasmuch as the element of religious enthusiasm entered strongly into it; and there only needed a man of genius who could see how to avail himself of this element in order to render his troops by means of it, joined to discipline in them and skill and daring in their leaders, even though in a considerable part composed of tradesmen accustomed to indoor occupations, able to face with advantage in the field country-gentlemen and their tenants and servants.

It is but justice to add, that the success of the King's cause in the beginning of this war was also in a great degree owing to the royal cavalry, a body of men conspicuous for their gallantry, and chiefly composed of the sons and kinsmen of the English nobility and gentry, and to the spirit of their commander, Prince Rupert, the King's nephew, who, though not possessed of prudence corresponding to his bravery and activity, must be reckoned a very active and enterprising cavalry officer. Whatever may be the opinion of the cause for which they fought, it must be admitted, on the testimony of no less an authority than Cromwell himself, that those partisans of the Stuarts in the middle of the seventeenth century fought well and strongly for a race of kings who brought nothing but dishonour and disaster upon them and theirs.

Having mentioned the activity of Prince Rupert, I must also notice some other qualities which belonged to him, and which gave a sanguinary character to the struggle at its very commencement.

Prince Rupert, the second son of the Elector Palatine by the Princess Elizabeth, the sister of King Charles, and Prince Maurice, his younger brother, had arrived in England in September 1642, and were soon put by the King their uncle into employment and command; "in which they showed themselves," says May, "very forward and active: and if they were more hot and furious than the tender beginnings of a civil war would seem to require, it may be imputed to the fervour of their youth, and the great desire which they had to ingratiate themselves with the King, upon whom, as being no more than soldiers of fortune, their hopes of advancement wholly depended." Prince Rupert, the elder and the more furious of the two, within a fortnight after his arrival, at the head of a small party, made a rapid march through several counties, "not inviting the people," says May, "so much by fair demeanour as compelling them by extreme rigour to follow that side which he had taken. Many towns and villages he plundered, that is to say, robbed (for at that time first was the word *plunder* used in England, being born in Germany, when that stately country was so miserably wasted and pillaged by foreign armies), and committed other outrages upon those who stood affected to the Parliament, executing some, and hanging up servants at their masters' doors for not discovering of their masters."[1]

Besides the difference between the qualities of the royal and those of the Parliamentary troops already noticed, there were other circumstances unfavourable to the cause of the Parliament at the beginning of the war. So many of the members of the House of Lords had, when actual war broke out, gone over to the King, that it was deemed necessary to gratify those that remained by conferring on them the chief commands both in the army and the fleet. The advantage, therefore, of making ability the only test of a commander was at first entirely lost. Thus the Earl of Essex was appointed to the command of the army of the Parliament.

Robert Devereux, Earl of Essex, had served in the Low Countries, and it seems to have been thence inferred, somewhat rashly, that he was competent to command the army. Whether the ill-usage he had formerly sustained from the Court tended to give him some degree of popularity, or his own character, like that of his father, was calculated to gain him friends, or his rank as the representative, or at least the bearer, of an ancient title determined the Parliament in his favour, they certainly committed a very grave error in committing to him the command of their army; as they did generally in concluding that the peerage of their time, because they bore many of the titles, were the representatives either of the military power or the military qualities of the ancient nobility. While Humphrey de Bohun, the Earl of Essex and Hereford of the thirteenth century, who married Elizabeth Plantagenet, daughter of Edward I., could bid open defiance to the most vigorous

[1] May, History of the Parliament, bk. iii. ch. i. pp. 159, 160. Maseres' edition. London, 1812.

and warlike of the Plantagenet kings, Robert Devereux, the Earl of Essex of the seventeenth century could be insulted with impunity by the worst and basest of the Stuarts. The difference between the nobility before the change and the nobility existing then is expressed in a few words by Sir Walter Raleigh: "The lords in former times were far stronger, more warlike, better followed, than they now are. Your Lordship may remember in your reading that there were many earls could bring into the field a thousand barbed horses, many a baron five or six hundred barbed horses, whereas now very few of them can furnish twenty fit to serve the King."[1]

The truth of Raleigh's observation as to the power of the nobility in that age is remarkably proved by the subscription-list of money and horses to be brought in by the Lords for the service of the Parliament:

		Horses.
The Lord-Admiral, Earl of Northumberland	£2000	...
Earl of Essex	1000	20
Earl of Holland	...	30
Earl of Pembroke	1000	40
Earl of Bedford	800	...
Earl of Bolingbroke	500	20
Earl of Lincoln	...	20
Lord Say and Sele	1000	...
Lord Paget	...	10
Lord Kimbolton	...	10
Lord Roberts	1000	...
Lord Brooke	1000	20
Lord Grey de Werke	1000	...
Lord Fielding	500	...
Lord North	200	...
Lord St. John	...	10
Lord Rochfort	...	10
Lord Wharton	300	6

---

[1] The Prerogative of Parliaments, i. 206, of Birch's edition of Raleigh's Works.

The horsemen were all to be completely armed, and many of the Lords engaged to serve in person.[1]

Hampden, Holles, and other leading members of Parliament served as colonels of the regiments which they had in part raised. These regiments were at first distinguished by the different colours of their dress, probably after the old feudal fashion, adopting the colours of their leaders. Thus Hampden's regiment was known as Colonel Hampden's regiment of green coats; and Holles's as Colonel Holles's regiment of red coats. But after the battle of Marston Moor all the Parliament's forces, horse and foot, adopted red coats, which, it would appear, had been worn from the first by the forces of the Eastern Counties Association. This measure of uniformity of colour, that colour being red, was found to be necessary to distinguish the Parliament's troops from the King's, and to prevent the slaughter by mistake of friends by friends.

Denzil Holles was the second son of John first Earl of Clare, and may therefore be considered as belonging to the new nobility rather than to the ancient gentry of England. He may, indeed, also have belonged to the ancient gentry, but the scurrility of his criticism on the composition of the Parliamentary army suggests the question, What were the public or private services to the State for which Denzil Holles's father was, by King James I., created Baron Houghton in the county of Nottingham on the 9th of July 1616, and Earl of Clare[2] in the county of Sussex on the 2d of November 1624? There was not one of those Parliamentary colonels and other officers

---

[1] Parl. Hist., ii. 1362.

[2] Of Denzil Holles's brother, John Holles, second Earl of Clare, of this family, Mrs. Hutchinson says, "The Earl of Clare was very often of both parties, and, I think, never advantaged either."—Memoirs of Colonel Hutchinson, p. 117. Bohn's edition. London, 1854.

who could not clearly and promptly point out the deeds for which he had received his rank, deeds for which neither he nor any of his descendants would have cause to blush. It was, it must be allowed, provoking to a leading Parliament man to find his merits quite overshadowed in the field by those of men who made no figure in Parliament and in the war of words; but Denzil's anger must have greatly overmastered his judgment when he forgot what sort of a question he invited men to open when he penned the greater part of the book which he denominated his " Memoirs," from 1641 to 1648. The conduct of Denzil Holles becomes more open to condemnation when compared with that of some of those whom he designates "a notable dunghill," and who died, as they had lived, with unswerving fidelity to what they termed the Good Old Cause.

Although the English nobility who attended Charles, dreading the power which they foresaw that the King's success in the struggle would give to the Roman Catholic party, advised moderation, Charles, besides having given a promise to the Queen not to make any concessions, persisted because he thought that in any event he could not be a loser. The result which the Independents finally brought about never entered into his calculations. Whatever others might suffer, he considered himself personally safe. Accordingly, he vigorously carried on his levies.[1] He not only "permitted but commanded" the Earl[2] of

---

[1] " Newcastle, this is to tell you that this rebellion is grown to that height that I must not look what opinion men are who at this time are willing and able to serve me; therefore I do not only permit but command you to make use of all my loving subjects' services without examining their consciences (more than their loyalty to me), as you shall find most to conduce to the upholding of my just royal power.—Your most assured faithful friend, CHARLES R. Shrewsbury, 23d September 1642."—Ayse. MSS. British Museum, 4161, vol. 69.

[2] Created Marquis of Newcastle, 27th October 1643.

Newcastle to levy a great number of Roman Catholics, though with the most solemn oaths he denied the fact, and in one of his declarations told the Parliament that in their army there were more Papists than in his.[1] He obtained arms by taking them from the trained bands, and ransacking the armouries of noblemen. Men of rank in Derbyshire, Staffordshire, and Shropshire supplied him with plate and money. He established a mint and issued coin. The waggons and carriage-horses prepared for Ireland were seized by his orders at Chester as they were ready for embarkation. On his march to Shrewsbury he made a speech between Stafford and Wellington on the 19th of September, and caused his protestation to be then also read at the head of his army, wherein, among other things, he told them that they would meet no enemies but traitors, most of them Brownists, Anabaptists, and Atheists, who would destroy both Church and Commonwealth. In this protestation, with deep vows and imprecations upon himself and his posterity, he declared his whole care and intentions to be for the maintenance of the Protestant religion, the laws of the land, and the liberty and property of the subject, together with the privilege of Parliament, as he was accustomed to do in his former speeches.[2]

The term Brownist, used as a name of reproach by the Court party for those who were also called Puritans, another name of reproach, was derived from Robert Brown, a clergyman of the reign of Elizabeth, who is generally reputed to have been the first person in England who

---

[1] May, Hist. of the Parl., bk. iii. ch. i. p. 173. London, 1812. Maseres' edition. In this declaration, after a strong protestation of his care for the extirpation of Popery, he admits that "some eminent men of that religion are armed in his service."

[2] May, Hist. of the Parl., bk. iii. ch. i.

publicly avowed the principles of English Independency. Shakspeare has favoured us with some excellent jokes on Brownists and Puritans. He, as a Court poet following the Court fashion, makes one of his characters say, "I had as lief be a Brownist as a politician;" and "If I thought he was a Puritan, I'd beat him like a dog." It turned out to be not quite so easy a feat to beat a Puritan as Shakspeare's Aguecheek imagined. Some of these jokes of Shakspeare, put into the mouth of Falstaff, as well as of Aguecheek, remind one of some of the excellent jokes of Aristophanes against men whose opinions he disliked.

When the King left Birmingham, the townsmen seized his plate and furniture, and conveyed them to Warwick castle. They also refused to manufacture swords for the Royalists, while they largely supplied the army of the Parliament. For this they suffered when in April of the following year Prince Rupert burned a part of the town; according to the following statement of a contemporary paper:—"By two several letters this day from Birmingham in Warwickshire the cruelty of Prince Rupert in burning and plundering the town is confirmed; that there were more than eighty dwelling-houses burnt to ashes, and all the goods that were in them; fifteen men and two women burnt by the fire."[1]

The King marched towards London, and Essex followed him. But such was the generalship on both sides, that the two armies continued their march for ten days within twenty miles of each other, without intelligence of each other's motions. At midnight on the 22d of October Charles, while he was preparing to besiege Banbury Castle,

[1] Perfect Diurnall, Tuesday, 11th April 1643. There is an old tract bearing the following title—"Prince Rupert's burning love to England discovered in Birmingham's flames."

was surprised by information that Essex was in the neighbourhood. The royal army had been living at free quarters, and the country was for this as well as other reasons hostile to them. A great portion of the Parliamentary army was about a day's march behind the main body. It was, moreover, expected that many of the Parliamentary officers would desert to the King. For these reasons Charles resolved upon an immediate battle. The army under Essex did not much exceed 10,000.[1] According to some accounts the King's army was 18,000[2] strong. This is probably an exaggeration, but it was undoubtedly not less than 12,000. A battle that is not directed by some commanding mind has little, if any, more interest than a riot, or street fight, or than a fight between game-cocks or dogs, or any other pugnacious animals. If there was any commanding mind here, it was not in a commanding situation, and that being the case it is a matter of indifference whether Charles or Essex was the stupider man. There was, indeed, a captain of a troop of horse in Essex's regiment on the right wing of the army of the Parliament, by name Oliver Cromwell,[3] whose genius was des-

[1] May says twelve regiments of foot and about forty troops of horse, little in all exceeding the number of 10,000 men.—Hist., bk. iii. ch. i. The Lord Wharton, in his relation of the battle to the City of London, says eleven regiments of foot and about thirty-five or forty troops of horse.—Parl. Hist., ii. 1496.

[2] May says the King's army consisted of about 14,000 foot and about 4000 horse and dragoons.—Hist. bk. iii. ch. i. The Royalists declined to specify their numbers.

[3] Sanford's Studies and Illustrations of the Great Rebellion, p. 521. Among his other contemporary authorities Mr. Sanford cites from the King's Pamphlets in the British Museum Nath. Fiennes' True and Exact Relation to his Father. Mr. Sanford says :—"Nath. Fiennes adds to his account, 'These persons under-written were all of the right wing, and never stirred from their troops, but they and their troops fought till the last minute.' Among these we find *Captain Cromwell*," p. 526, note. This disposes of the statements of Denzil Holles as far as regards Cromwell and the battle of Edgehill: though it may seem superfluous and almost ridiculous to defend Oliver Cromwell against the charge of cowardice.

tined to create and lead for the Parliament of England an army which for all the qualities of men and officers that ensure victory had never been equalled upon earth. But the genius of Oliver Cromwell was not now in its proper place, any more than the stupidity or dull mediocrity of Essex was in its proper place.

The battle, called by some the battle of Edgehill, by others the battle of Keynton or Kineton,[1] as it is now written—a small town in Warwickshire, about midway between Stratford-upon-Avon and Banbury—was fought on Sunday the 23d October 1642. Essex had intended to rest Sunday in Kineton to await for the remainder of his forces; but on Sunday morning the enemy was discovered not far off, occupying a high and steep ridge of hill called Edgehill. Not far from the foot of that hill was a broad plain called *The Vale of the Red Horse*,—"a name," observes May, "suitable to the colour which that day was to bestow upon it; for there happened the greatest part of the encounter." The Vale of the Red Horse does not,[2] however, derive its name from any deeds of blood, but from a colossal figure of a horse carved in the ferruginous sands of the slope of Edgehill, now obliterated by the progress of enclosures, and replaced by one of much smaller dimensions.

[1] Kineton is twelve miles north-west of Banbury. Edgehill is four miles on the Banbury side of Kineton.

[2] Washington Irving, after describing his walk from Stratford-on-Avon to Charlecot, the old mansion of the Lucy family, adds—"This beautiful bosom of country is called the Vale of the Red Horse." (The Sketch Book, by Washington Irving. Stratford-on-Avon.) This seems to be a mistake. The plain or vale called the Vale of the Red Horse is separated from the valley of the Avon at Stratford-on-Avon by some rising ground scarcely worth the name of hills, and is nearly parallel to it. This Vale of the Red Horse appears really, though perhaps not in name, to open into the valley of the Avon at Charlecot, about four miles above and nearly east of Stratford-on-Avon, as a stream, the branches of which rise about the foot of Edgehill, joins the Avon there, after a somewhat winding course of about ten miles.

Into this plain or valley Essex marched and drew up his army in line of battle at the distance of about half a mile from the foot of Edgehill; the King's forces descending the hill to meet them, and thereby abandoning one of the two advantages which they had at first,—the hill and the wind. The army of the Parliament was drawn up on a rising ground in this Vale of the Red Horse, many of the foot being a good space behind the horse when the battle began. The right wing of the Royalists was commanded by Prince Rupert, and May affirms that on this occasion the army of the Parliament would have undoubtedly been ruined, and an absolute victory gained on the King's side, if Prince Rupert and his pursuing troops had been more temperate in plundering, and had wheeled about to assist their distressed friends in other parts of the field. But Rupert followed the chase to Kineton, where the carriages of the Parliament army were, which they pillaged, using great cruelty to the unarmed waggoners and labouring men. Rupert, as being so nearly related to the King, had insisted on receiving no orders but from the King himself, though the command of the King's army had been given to the Earl of Lindsey, who thus had no control over the best part of his troops. Some part of the danger incurred by the army of the Parliament that day was caused by the treachery of Sir Faithful Fortescue, who, at the beginning of the fight, instead of charging the enemy fired his pistol on the ground, and with his troop went over to the King's army.

While Rupert was thus engaged in pursuit and plunder, the King's horse on his left wing were routed; and his centre gave way in spite of all the exertions of Lindsey, who, covered with wounds, fell into the enemy's hands and died that evening, while many other Royalist officers of distinction were either slain or taken prisoners. Among the slain was Sir Edmund Verney the King's standard-bearer. The royal standard was taken. Essex, to whom it had been brought, committed it to the custody of his secretary. Two Royalists, having assumed the uniform of their enemies, obtained it from the secretary and galloped off with it to their own army, for which one of them was knighted. Night put a stop to the battle, which began late in the afternoon, and therefore only lasted two or three hours. The Parliament army having obtained possession of the ground which their enemies had chosen to fight upon, remained there all night, and in the morning returned to a warmer place near Kineton, where they had quartered the night before; for they suffered from the cold and want of provisions.[1] The King's army had withdrawn to the top of the hill, where they made great fires all night.

[1] Ludlow says: "No man nor horse got any meat that night, and I had touched none since the Saturday before, neither could I find my servant who had my cloak, so that, having nothing to keep me warm but a suit of iron, I was obliged to walk about all night, which proved very cold by reason of a sharp frost" (i. 50). It may be inferred from this, and also from the fact mentioned in the same page, that, "having been dismounted, I could not without great difficulty recover on horseback again, being loaded with cuirassier arms, as the rest of the guard also were," that the general's lifeguard, to which Ludlow belonged, were armed *cap-à-pie*. But it is clear from the Order Books of the Council of State that the cuirassiers of the Parliamentary army were armed only with back and breasplates—or backs and breasts as they were then termed. (See Ludlow, i. 334, to the same effect.) Another circumstance mentioned by Aubrey shows that the cold was severe on the night after that battle of Edgehill. Aubrey says that Dr. William Harvey, the discoverer of the circulation of the blood, to whose care the Prince of Wales and the Duke of York, then twelve and ten years old, were committed during the fight, told him that "he withdrew with them under a hedge, and took out of his pocket a book to read, but he had not read very long before a bullet of a great gun grazed on the ground near him, which made him remove his station;" that Harvey also told him "that Sir [Col.] Adrian Scrope was dangerously wounded there, and left for dead amongst the dead men, stript; which happened to be the saving of his

About nine o'clock next morning the army of the Parliament drew out again and stood about three hours till the other army had quite left the hill, and then they withdrew into their quarter towards Kineton, and joined their other brigade, artillery, and ammunition, which, under the command of Colonels Hampden and Grantham had now come to Kineton. The King had drawn out his horse upon the further side of the hill, where he stayed till towards night, while his foot were retiring. A little before night his horse also withdrew. The army of the Parliament, having been refreshed by a supply of provisions brought in by the country people,[1] marched to Warwick; Essex thus suffering the King without interruption to pursue his intention of investing Banbury Castle, which surrendered without resistance, though garrisoned with 1000 men. This movement was contrary to the advice of Hampden. For, said he, had the army, instead of going to Warwick, marched toward Banbury, we should have found more victuals, and probably dispersed all the foot of the King's army, taken his cannon and carriages, and sent his horse further off: whereas now, because we did not follow them, though they quitted the field whereon they fought, and left their quarter before us, yet they began soon after to question who had the day. And Ludlow gives some strong reasons to the same effect. "Our army," he says, "was now refreshed and masters of the field; and having received such a considerable addition of strength, we hoped

---

life. It was cold, clear weather, and a frost that night, which staunched his bleeding; and about midnight, or some hours after his hurt, he awaked, and was fain to draw a dead body upon him for warmth sake."—Aubrey's Lives, vol. ii. p. 379.

[1] "That night," says Ludlow, "the country people brought in some provisions, but when I got meat I could scarce eat it, my jaws for want of use having almost lost their natural faculty" (i. 51).

that we should have pursued the enemy, who were marching off as fast as they could, leaving only some troops to face us upon the top of the hill; but instead of that, for what reason I know not, we marched to Warwick, of which the enemy having notice, sent out a party of horse under Prince Rupert, who on Tuesday night fell into the town of Kineton, where our sick and wounded soldiers lay, and after they had cruelly murdered many of them, returned to their army."[1] There are two men here that, according to the usages of warfare carried on by nations calling themselves in any degree Christian and civilised would have been marked out for punishment; Essex for a breach of his duty as general of the Parliament, and Rupert for barbarity worthy of the lowest savages. It is remarkable how this man afterwards contrived to escape the vengeance of Cromwell by land, and of Blake by sea.

"Howsoever it were," observes May, "true it is that the King no less than the Parliament pretended to be victorious in that battle; and so far ascribed the victory to his own side, that a prayer of thanksgiving to God was made at Oxford for it. There was also a thanksgiving on the Parliament side for the victory of that day. And it is certain that there were many marks of victory on both armies; colours and cannon were taken on both sides, without any great difference in the number of them. And though in speeches made afterwards by either party, and books printed, there is no consent at all concerning the number of men slain, but so great a discrepancy as it is almost a shame to insert into a history; yet surely, by the best account there were more slain on the King's side than on the other."[2] However that may be, and though the num-

[1] Ludlow's Memoirs, i. 52.
[2] May, Hist. of the Parlt., bk. iii. ch. i.; Parl. Hist., ii. 1495, *et seq.*; Rush., v. 33, *et seq.*

ber of the common soldiers (it was not till some years after that they were called private soldiers, when, according to Ludlow, they began to feel their importance, and would no longer be called common soldiers¹) could not be agreed upon, yet, adds May, "I have heard that the country-people thereabouts, by burying of the naked bodies, found the number to be about six thousand that fell on both sides, besides those which died afterwards of their wounds." It was remarked as singular, that on the same day of the same month the year before, namely the 23d of October 1641, the Irish massacre broke out.

Of what the country suffered from the licentiousness and want of discipline of the King's army, some idea may be formed from the statement Whitelock gives of his own case. His house was taken possession of by about 1000 horse under Sir John Byron and his brother, and though the soldiers were ordered by their commanders to abstain from insolence and plunder, they committed a series of outrages, for the least of which we shall see Cromwell would have hanged them had they been his soldiers on the nearest tree. "They carried their whores with them, consumed whatever they could find of meat or liquor, lighted their pipes with the choicest manuscripts, and even the title-deeds of his estates; littered their horses with sheaves of wheat; broke down his fences; cut his beds, and let out the feathers, that they might carry off the ticking, and left no sort of linen or household stuff. They took his horses, and, in a word, committed all the mischief and spoil that malice could provoke barbarous enemies to commit."²

[1] Ludlow says, writing of what followed the seizure of the King by Cornet Joyce, June 4, 1647, "Private soldiers, for they would no longer be called common soldiers."—Ludlow's Memoirs, i. 192, 2d edition. London, 1721.

[2] Whitelock, p. 63.

At the battle of Edgehill, the great cause of English liberty, says a contemporary [1] who watched the proceedings with an attentive and anxious eye, was tried but not decided. In fact, however, the event of the battle was favourable to the King, to whom it proved a kind of victory not to be at once defeated. For many of the nobility and gentry who had before remained neutral, in the hope that something might come to clear the doubt, and save them the danger of declaring themselves prematurely, now joined that side on which there seemed to them to be the least fears and the greatest hopes, which was the King's. For while on the Parliament's side nothing was promised but the free enjoyment of their native liberties, on the King's side they might look for honours, preferments, and estates of enemies; and on the other hand they reckoned, though not very wisely, as the event proved, that no such total ruin could be brought upon them by a victorious Parliament as from an incensed King and his followers eagerly looking out for the forfeited estates of the opposite party. These considerations do not evince a very extensive foresight or even a correct knowledge of what was going on in France at that very time, and, therefore, as an argument are open to the objections stated at this very time in one of the Parliament's declarations, that there were too many of the gentry of the kingdom who were content to submit themselves and their posterity to an arbitrary and unlimited power of government, so that they might for their own time partake of that power.

The considerations above mentioned may probably have had some weight also with the Parliament in inducing them to reopen their negotiations with the King. They

[1] May, Hist., bk. iii. ch. ii. p. 176. London, 1812.

petitioned Charles to take up his residence in London till the terms of a treaty were adjusted. The King appeared to listen to the overtures of the Parliament, but his real intentions soon manifested themselves. As soon as the Parliamentary Commissioners returned with the King's answer, that he was most willing to receive at Windsor such propositions of peace as the Parliament should send, and to treat with them, the King's artillery, with several troops of horse, closely followed by the King in person with his whole army, advanced towards London, and on the 12th of November, taking advantage of a dense November fog, fell unexpectedly upon Brentford, which was occupied by the regiment of Colonel Holles. Holles's men succeeded in stopping their march so long [1] at Brentford that the regiments of Hampden and Lord Brooke had time to come up. These three regiments, not without great loss, completely barred their passage during the greater part of the afternoon, and saved the artillery; and when Essex (warned of the danger by the noise of the firing, which was heard in the House of Lords, where he then was), with a considerable body of horse, arrived, he found that the Royalists had given over the attack, and were lying on the west side of Brentford. Charles, with his usual care of the royal person, kept himself safe at Hounslow, and there he lay that night. All that night

[1] I suppose John Libburne meant that he served as a volunteer in Holles's regiment, when he says at his trial, October 25th and 26th, 1649: "We were but about 700 men at Brentford that withstood the King's whole army in the field above five hours together, and fought it out to the very sword's point and to the butt-end of the musket, and thereby hindered the King from then possessing the Parliament's train of artillery, and by consequence the city of London, in which very act I was taken a prisoner."—State Trials, iv. 1271, 1272. Ludlow says that the King would certainly have surprised the Parliament's train of artillery "if two regiments of foot and a small party of horse that lay at Brentford had not, with unspeakable courage, opposed his passage and stopt the march of his army most part of the afternoon" (i. 53).

the city of London poured out men towards Brentford, and all the lords and gentlemen that belonged to the Parliament's army were there ready by Sunday morning, the 14th of November. The city trained bands marched forth with alacrity under the command of Major-General Skippon, one of the few old soldiers who, during the war, performed important services for the Parliament.[1] His rhetoric on this occasion was characteristic of the time, being to this effect: "Come, my boys, my brave boys, let us pray heartily and fight heartily; I will run the same fortunes and hazards with you. Remember, the cause is for God, and for the defence of yourselves, your wives, and children. Come, my honest, brave boys, pray heartily, and fight heartily, and God will bless us." The whole Parliamentary army was drawn out on Turnham Green, about a mile from Brentford, and consisted of 24,000 men, "stout, gallant, proper men," says Whitelock, "as well habited and armed as were ever seen in any army, and of as good courage to fight the enemy." This, however, is not altogether consistent with what Cromwell said about the inferiority of the Parliament's troops at the beginning of the war, and on such a point Cromwell will be admitted to have been a very much more competent judge than Whitelock.

By Essex's orders Hampden began to make a detour, with the intention of falling upon the King's rear, while the rest of the Parliament's army should attack him in front and turn his flanks. But soon after they had begun their march, Sir John Merick, Essex's major-general, galloped after them and told Hampden that the general had changed his mind, and ordered them back. About 3000 of the

[1] See Ludlow's Memoirs, i. 312, for an account of the Parliament's vote on Ludlow's motion of one thousand pounds a year to Skippon.

Parliamentary troops were quartered at Kingston. These, too, were removed from the King's rear and brought round by London Bridge to join the main body. These movements were all contrary to the opinion and advice of Hampden and most of the members of Parliament and gentlemen who were officers, who also advised that the army of the Parliament should advance and fall upon the King's forces. But the soldiers of fortune, the "old soldiers," who had prevented the King from being surrounded and his retreat cut off, and who love long campaigns as lawyers love long Chancery suits and physicians long diseases, were also against this too, and Essex adopted their opinions. While they were consulting, the King drew off his carriages and ordnance. Again the members of Parliament were for pursuing, but the old soldiers again carried it against them. It was afterwards admitted by the Royalists that they had not ammunition enough to have lasted a quarter of an hour. Charles returned to Oxford.[1]

In the beginning of 1643, the Parliament sent commissioners to the King at Oxford, and a negotiation was opened, which from the extreme discordance between the terms proposed by the respective parties might have been expected to be, as it was, fruitless. In the meantime, that is during the negotiation, hostilities continued, and the King's affairs began to wear a promising aspect. Though a cessation of arms was asked by the Parliament, and seemingly wished by the King, he, underhand, encouraged an address against it, being resolved against a peace that imported anything short of unconditional submission in his people.[2] Whitelock, who was one of the commis-

---

[1] May, Hist., bk. iii. c. ii.; Whitelock, pp. 65, 66; Rushworth, v. 56, *et seq.*; Parl. Hist., iii. 1-14.
[2] Clar. Life, i. 80, 157. The statements in Clarendon's History are here, as

sioners sent by the Parliament to treat with the King at Oxford, gives a description of what he witnessed of the cruelty of the Royalists towards their prisoners. Prince Rupert, with 4000 horse and foot had put the Earl of Stamford's regiment and other troops to the sword, and taken 1100 prisoners and 3000 stand of arms. The prisoners were stript almost naked in that cold season, tied together with cords, beaten, and driven along like dogs. When they arrived at Oxford, the King and lords, according to Whitelock, who was present, looked on them, and "too many smiled at their misery." One in particular, a noble-looking, handsome young man, the whiteness of whose skin is remarked by Whitelock, was placed almost naked, and covered with wounds, upon the bare back of a horse; but though the blood streamed in every direction from his body, he sat erect with an undaunted mien. As he approached the King, a woman exclaimed, "Ah, you traitorous rogue, you are well enough served." The young man having exerted himself to bestow on her the opprobrious epithet she deserved, instantly expired. "The beginning of such cruelty by Englishmen to their countrymen was afterwards," says Whitelock, "too much followed."[1]

The Parliament had prudently limited the powers of their commissioners by written articles, and had also limited the duration of the treaty to twenty days. Clarendon alleges that if the King's request to prolong the treaty had been granted, so that he could have consulted with the Queen, who had landed at Burlington Bay about the time the treaty began with many officers and a great quantity

elsewhere, in direct opposition to those in his Life, as they are generally to those in the Clarendon State Papers.

[1] Whitelock, p. 67.

of arms and ammunition, he would have been relieved from his engagement to her, not only not to conclude a peace, but not even to gratify any individual with office or honours without having first obtained her consent, and might have consented to measures which would probably have effected an accommodation. But the Queen was very far indeed from being disposed towards an accommodation, for she knew that she could not reduce England to the condition of France, except by the destruction of all the ancient constitutional franchises of England, and this, she was well aware, could only be done by force of arms, and by reducing the nobility and commons of England to unconditional submission, and rendering, as in France, the King and the State equivalent terms. I am grieved to say that by far her ablest coadjutor in this scheme was a man whose great abilities, hardihood, and daring, as well as the better part of his nature, which contained elements of generosity as well as heroism, would seem to have been bestowed for other ends. This man was James Graham, Earl and afterwards Marquis of Montrose.

It is remarked by May, speaking of those members of the Parliament who deserted it, that, besides the danger of invitation from a king, there is a class of men—men of great abilities, pride, and ambition—who are unusually apt to "take pet and grow angry" when any action of theirs has not received that honour which they expected; and that what such an anger may make proud and ambitious spirits do, even against their own country and the dictates of their conscience and reason, the world has been taught by many examples, some of high consequence and very remarkable, such as Coriolanus the Roman, and Julian the Spanish general.[1]

[1] May, Hist. of the Parl., bk. ii. ch. iv. p. 117. Maseres's edition. London,

Montrose seeing no hope for the exercise of those great military talents, which with the instinct of genius he felt that he possessed, in the service of the Covenanters, and having fully determined to offer his services to the royal cause, went directly to the Queen as soon as she landed at Burlington from Holland. Montrose's reasons for repairing to the Queen were twofold. He knew that her influence governed the King, and he had a scheme to propose to, or rather to discuss with, her (for it was not new to her, being in fact but a branch of the great Irish massacre of 1641, as that was a branch of the massacre of St. Bartholomew), in which he had good reason to expect her hearty concurrence. In order to render this perfectly intelligible, we must remember that this Queen, though a daughter of Henry IV., of whose frank and noble character she appears to have inherited not a trace, was also a daughter of the Medici; that her youth had been partly passed in that palace where Charles IX. and his mother, Catherine de Medici, had watched for the first pistol-shot that broke the stillness of that August night in 1572, and was the concerted signal at which Guise and his band of cut-throats, called King's guards, rushed out towards their appointed prey, while the tocsin of St. Germain l'Auxerrois called the Roman Catholic citizens to the massacre of the Protestants, most of them in their sleep, men, women, and little children; that that great crime had as yet been unavenged of God or man, and that therefore all the precepts of her education and all the associations of her youth had taught her to look on wholesale massacre as the approved royal highway to unbounded dominion, and all the blessings that came in its train. But Henrietta de

1812. May assumes as history the fabulous chronicle or romance of chivalry, in which Ilyan, lord of Ceuta and Tangiers, figures as the Count Don Julian.

Bourbon, though she might have hoped to be able to do as much for England as her relative Catherine de Medici had done for France, did not quite take into her calculations the character of the people whose liberties and ancient institutions she sought to destroy. From a land where the dominion of caste was established with a Hindu fixedness and torpor, that enabled a nobility worn out with luxury and idleness to domineer over all men who earned their bread by the labour of their hands or heads, she had come to a country where small freeholders and small farmers, where brewers, tailors, shoemakers, and such like "mean tradesmen" were to scatter and destroy the chivalry as well as the cut-throat kerne of this daughter of the Medici.

The scheme concerted with the Queen, and approved of by her husband, was that the Earl of Antrim, with whom Henrietta Maria had been in confidential communication for several years, should by high offers bribe Monro, the Scottish Lieutenant-General in Ireland, by whom the troops were really commanded, to declare for the King and bring over to England his army, lately increased to 10,000 men, while Antrim should raise a large body of the Catholics to invade Scotland and act in concert with Montrose; that the Macdonalds in the Isles, and the Gordons in the North of Scotland, should be suddenly raised, and under Montrose fall upon the Covenanters before they suspected danger, and then having secured Scotland, march in conjunction with the Irish to the South. Ormond was at the same time to conclude a cessation with the rebels, that the army under him might be brought across the Channel, and a fresh army raised from the insurgents. Whatever may have been Charles's defence in regard to the original insurrection in Ireland on the ground that no one could have predicted the frightful atrocities that marked it, after such experience of the unexampled cruelty of the Irish Catholics, what shall be said of a plan to introduce them into Britain, where, if successful, they must have been expected to act over again many of the scenes that had been exhibited in Ireland? When we reflect that he had declared in the most solemn manner, calling the Almighty to witness his sincerity, that his only object was to vindicate the laws against a faction; that he had with equal solemnity declared that he would never treat with the Irish rebels while he was treating with them at the very time, and that he depended solely upon the affection of his subjects in vindicating the rights of the Crown which involved their own, and never would call in foreign force, which he conceived would be fraught with the ruin of his dominions,[1] must we not conclude that the intentions if not the acts of this son of the Stuarts and the Guises, and of this daughter of the Medici, were fully on a level with the blackest crimes of the royal houses of Valois and Medici? If an army of native Irish had succeeded in taking London by storm, the "rebellious city," as it was called, we may fairly conclude from their doings in Ireland and Scotland that the fate of London would, under the tender mercies of Charles I. and Henrietta de Bourbon, have been similar to that of Paris under those of Charles IX. and Catherine de' Medici, and that the history of England would have contained its massacre of St. Bartholomew as well as that of France. Hamilton

[1] As Clarendon drew the papers in which the Almighty is so invoked, a comparison of them with some passages in his History (iii. 92-94)—in which he maintains that "princes are to be assisted and supported by one another, the function of kings being an order by itself"—will afford a view of his character.

objected to this scheme for its impracticability, and he so far prevailed over Montrose, whom he excelled in the arts of a courtier, that it was put off for the present. Part of it, however, was two years after carried into effect by Montrose, as I shall relate in its place.[1]

[1] Baillie's Letters and Journals (Edin. 1841), ii. 73, 74. Appendix to Carte's Ormunde, pp. 3, 4, *et seq.* Carte's Letters, i. 19, 20. Wishart's Memoirs of Montrose, p. 32, *et seq.*, and Appendix, p. 422, *et seq.* Burnet's Memoirs of the Dukes of Hamilton, p. 212, *et seq.* Burnet's History, i. 74. In the Oxford edition (1833) of Burnet's History, the editor gives the following note to the passage respecting the encouragement given by the Queen to the plot of the Irish insurrection :—" Mr. Brodie, in his History of the British Empire during this era, whilst he endeavours to establish the truth of almost all the charges brought by the old Republicans against King Charles I., remarks on this passage of Burnet, that he cannot distinguish between the King and Queen, considering their dark correspondence and joint plots."

(291)

CHAPTER XI.

*SIEGE OF READING—WALLER'S PLOT—BATTLES OF STRATTON—
—LANSDOWN—ROUNDWAY DOWN—DEATH OF SIR BEVILL
GRENVILLE—OF SIDNEY GODOLPHIN—OF HAMPDEN—TIME
AT WHICH THE AFFAIRS OF THE PARLIAMENT WERE AT
THE LOWEST—FIRST BATTLE OF NEWBURY—DEATH OF
LORD FALKLAND—SOLEMN LEAGUE AND COVENANT—
DEATH OF PYM—CHARACTER OF THE YOUNGER HOTHAM.*

THE commissioners of the Parliament having finally returned to London upon the 17th of April 1643, Essex immediately advanced with an army of about 16,000 foot and 3000 horse to besiege Reading, which was held by a garrison of 3000 of the King's forces, with twenty pieces of ordnance."[1] According to May, Essex was loth to storm the town for fear of destroying so many innocent people who remained in it, "which compassion of his was well approved of by the Parliament." Therefore it was surrendered upon composition within sixteen days by the Deputy-Governor, Colonel Fielding—the Governor, Sir Arthur Aston, being wounded and unable to perform the office. The town being infected, caused a great mortality in the army of the Parliament. The soldiers, moreover, were discontented, because, though their pay was much in arrear, they were not suffered to plunder. For the Parliament had promised the soldiers twelve shillings a man besides their pay to induce them to forbear plundering. But neither of these promises was then performed, money

[1] May, Hist. of the Parl., pp. 180, 181. Maseres' edition. London, 1812.

beginning already to be wanting, and the great magazine of treasure in Guildhall being quite consumed. As the promises were, however, manifestly made in good faith, the fact here related sets the humanity of the Parliament of England in strong contrast with the inhumanity of the foreigners who ruled on the opposite side, namely, King Charles, who had not a drop of English, nor, as I think, of Scottish blood in his body; his German nephew, and his French-Italian queen. While they stayed there expecting money, the sickness and mortality daily increased, and many of the soldiers disbanded and went away. "Then," says May, "began a tide of misfortune to flow in upon the Parliament, and their strength almost in every place to decrease at one time; for during the time of these six months, since the battle of Keynton (Edgehill) until this present distress of the Lord General's army which was about the beginning of May, the war had gone on with great fury and heat almost through every part of England."[1] The words of Mrs. Hutchinson are to the same effect as those of May. "The King," she says, "had sent forth commissioners of array, and the Parliament had given out commissioners for their militia, and sent off their members into all counties to put them in execution," so that "every county had the civil war, more or less, within itself."[2]

On the 12th of May a plot was discovered at Bristol to betray that city to the King's troops, and two of the conspirators were hanged. Not long after Bristol was surrendered to Prince Rupert by Colonel Nathaniel Fiennes, second son of Viscount Say, in a manner which brought upon him a sentence of death on a charge of cowardice;

[1] May, Hist. of the Parl., p. 182. Maseres' edition. London, 1812.
[2] Memoirs of Colonel Hutchinson, p. 116.

but he received a pardon. In the course of the same month another plot of a higher and more dangerous nature was discovered in London. Waller the poet, a member of the House of Commons, who had been active on the popular side, with Tomkyns, his brother-in-law, Challoner,[1] and a few others, had undertaken to seize the persons of the leading members of the House of Commons, and to deliver up London to Charles, who had sent secretly a commission of array by a daughter of the Earl of Suffolk, the Lady Aubigny, whose husband, the Lord Aubigny, had fallen at Edgehill.[2] A servant of Tomkyns having overheard the conversation of the conspirators, carried the information to Pym, and Waller and the rest were apprehended, examined by Pym and other members of Parliament, tried, and all condemned. None, however, were executed but Tomkyns and Challoner, who were both hanged at their own doors,—Tomkyns in Holborn, Challoner in Cornhill. Alexander Hampden, another relative of Waller's, was kept in prison till he died. Some others had their estates confiscated, and were long kept in prison. Waller was kept in prison in the Tower; but about a year after, upon payment of a fine of £10,000, was pardoned and permitted to travel abroad. May says that the only reason he could ever hear

[1] I have not been able to discover whether this Challoner was any relation of Thomas Challoner, member for Richmond, and also a member of the Council of State of the Commonwealth. See a description of him by Aubrey, Lives, ii. 281.

[2] It is doubtful whether Waller's plot had any connection with another plot detected about the same time—a project of a Royalist London merchant, Sir Nicholas Crispe, to raise an armed force in the city, for which purpose he had obtained a commission of array from the King. It is to be observed that the Lord Aubigny here mentioned was not an English peer. His son, Charles Stuart, who is described as the son and heir of George, Lord Aubigny in France, brother of James, Duke of Richmond, was created Baron Stuart of Newbury and Earl of Litchfield, 10th December 1645. Sir Harris Nicolas's " Synopsis of the Peerage," art. " Litchfield."

given why Waller, being the principal agent in that conspiracy, escaped with life when Tomkyns and Challoner, who had been drawn in by him, were both executed, was that Waller had been so free in his confessions at the first, without which the plot could not have been clearly detected, that Pym and others of those who conducted the examinations of the witnesses had engaged their promise to do whatever they could to save his life. "He seemed also," adds May, "much smitten in conscience, and desired the comfort of godly ministers, being extremely penitent for that foul offence; and afterwards in his speech to the House, when he came to be put out of it, much bewailed his offence, thanking God that so mischievous and bloody a conspiracy had been discovered before it could take effect."[1]

According to Whitelock, Waller was tried and condemned by a council of war, but was reprieved by Essex. He lay in prison a year, and was then set at liberty on an understanding that he should leave the country. A fine of £10,000 was imposed upon him. But it is said that he expended three times that sum besides in bribes, and that he was obliged to sell estates to the value of £10,000 per annum on this occasion. It is probable that the celebrity of Waller as a poet has invested with more importance than really belongs to it the affair which has received the name of Waller's Plot, for it does not seem likely that any enterprise of a person of so pusillanimous a spirit as Waller and of so weak a mind—for a man may write such verses and make such speeches as Waller's and still be of but a very limited intelligence—could be formidable to such a cause as that of the Long Parliament. But Waller has had several biographers who have dilated on this plot, and among them Johnson, in his " Lives of the

[1] May's Hist. of the Parl., bk. iii. ch. ii. p. 186. London, 1812.

Poets," has not only dilated on this plot, but has taken an opportunity of venting his own Jacobitism by calling Hampden, whom some call the patriot, "the zealot of rebellion," and by calling the Long Parliament "the rebellious conventicle." When one sees this in a man of Johnson's admitted ability, it seems idle to reason at all on politics. "According to Johnson," says Lord Macaulay, "Charles II. and James II. were two of the best Kings that ever reigned. Laud was a prodigy of parts and learning. Hampden deserved no more honourable name than that of 'the zealot of rebellion.' Even the ship-money, condemned not less decidedly by Falkland and Clarendon than by the bitterest Roundheads, Johnson would not pronounce to have been an unconstitutional impost."[1]

In the same month of May it was resolved by the Lords and Commons to make a new great seal to supply the place of that which had been carried away from the Parliament to the King.[2] About the same time the House of Commons impeached the Queen of high treason, on the grounds that she had pawned the crown jewels in Holland, that she had raised the rebellion in Ireland, that she had endeavoured to raise a party in Scotland against the Parliament, that she had gone at the head of a Popish army in England. The impeachment stuck for many months in the House of Lords, but was afterwards passed there also.[3]

In the month of February of the same year (1642-43), while a body of the Parliament troops were engaged in the siege of Litchfield Close, their commander, the Lord Brooke, as he looked out of a window, received a shot in

[1] Lord Macaulay's Essay on Samuel Johnson. The work referred to is the article "Samuel Johnson" in Macaulay's Miscellaneous Writings, p. 311.
[2] May, Hist. of the Parl., bk. iii. ch. ii. p. 188. London, 1812.
[3] Ibid., p. 191.

the head and died immediately—"a man," says May, "as much lamented by the Parliament as any that ever fell on that side, and as much honoured for his piety, valour, and fidelity.[1] After his death Sir John Gell succeeded to his command, and about the beginning of March took the Close with very little loss of blood. They had their mines ready prepared to blow up the Close. The besieged for this reason asked for quarter, which they obtained; for the soldiers of the Parliament "thought it not honourable, being in cold blood, to revenge their general's death by putting them to the sword." About the middle of that month of March Sir John Gell, with fifteen hundred horse and foot, encountered the Earl of Northampton with about twelve hundred horse at Salt Heath, about four miles from Stafford, and Sir William Brereton coming in to his assistance during the fight, which at first went against him, obtained a victory.[2] In this affair, which was hotly disputed, the combatants "fighting pell-mell for a long time," the Earl of Northampton and many of his officers were slain. "Thus," says the historian of the Parliament, "it fell out that these two peers, the Earl of Northampton and the Lord Brooke, who first of all the nobility at the breaking out of this civil distraction, had personally contested in one county about the Parliament's ordinance for the militia and the King's commission of array, within a small distance both of place and time ended their days by this unhappy war."[3]

[1] May's Hist. of the Parl., bk. iii. ch. ii. p. 210. London, 1812.

[2] Mrs. Hutchinson, who gives a very unfavourable portrait of Sir John Gell, says, "This man kept the journalists in pension, so that whatever was done in the neighbouring counties against the enemy was attributed to him; and thus he hath indirectly purchased himself a name in story which he never merited." Memoirs of Colonel Hutchinson, p. 128. Bohn's edition. London, 1854.

[3] May, Hist. of the Parl., bk. iii. ch. ii. p. 211. London, 1812.

The Parliament, in the middle of winter, when Lancashire was in the greatest distraction, had sent down Sir John Seton, a Scottish knight, "an experienced and stout commander," as Major-General of the forces in that shire. Seton marched from Manchester about the beginning of February, with about ten companies and about two thousand clubmen, to take Preston, which, though well fortified and very stoutly defended, was so furiously assaulted by the Parliament's forces, that it was taken after two hours of very hard fighting, with small loss on the side of the Parliament, though on the other side many fell. Two hundred prisoners were taken, of whom many were gentlemen of good rank. Shortly after, Lancaster was taken by a detachment sent from Preston. Wigan also was taken, with many prisoners and great store of arms, by Sir John Seton.[1]

But though in these affairs the Parliament was successful, in other parts the advantage was on the side of the King. Sir William Waller, who commanded under Essex a detachment of the army of the Parliament, had taken Winchester, Chichester, Tewksbury, Chepstow, Monmouth, and obtained other advantages over the enemy, making rapid marches and sudden attacks; but he afterwards declined rather than rose in reputation.

The Earl of Stamford, in command of a body of the Parliament's troops, had taken up his position on a hill at Stratton, on the borders of Cornwall, and had despatched his lieutenant-general, Sir George Chudleigh, into Cornwall with 600 horse. The absence of Sir George Chudleigh was taken advantage of by his son, Major Chudleigh, to betray the army to which he belonged. According to a previous arrangement, fully disclosed by letters which

[1] May's Hist. of the Parl., bk. iii. ch. ii. pp. 211, 212. London, 1812.

were afterwards intercepted, Sir Ralph Hopton, who commanded a body of troops for the King, according to the Royalist writers, not half so numerous as those of the Parliament, which amounted, according to the same authority, to near 7000, attacked Stamford's army; and Chudleigh in the heat of action going over to the enemy with a party, and charging the Parliamentary troops, Stamford sustained a defeat. The Royalists charged up the hill in four divisions led by the principal gentry of the county, one division being commanded by Lord Mohun and Sir Ralph Hopton, another by Sir Bevill Grenville and Sir John Berkeley, a third by Slanning and Trevannion, a fourth by Basset and Godolphin. For this service Hopton was created Lord Hopton of Stratton.[1]

Hopton having been reinforced by part of the troops under Prince Maurice and the Marquis of Hertford, Waller was sent against him, and a battle was fought between them at Lansdown near Bath, with great loss on both sides, but without a decisive issue.[2] Among the killed on the side of the Royalists was the gallant Sir Bevill Grenville, one of the best of those English gentlemen who held that to fight under the King's standard was the only course which could render them worthy of "those ancestors of theirs who had so many of them, in several ages, sacrificed their lives for their country."[3] I fear the gallant cavalier is in error when he thus speaks of so many ancestors of those who fought for the Stuarts having sacrificed their lives for their country. Was it for their country that they sacrificed their lives, for instance,

---

[1] Rush., v. 271, 272. Clar., iii. 268, *et seq.*
[2] Rush., v. 284. Clar., iii. 277, *et seq.*
[3] An expression in a letter of Sir Bevill Grenville's, published by Lord Nugent in his "Memorials of Hampden," ii. 193. 1st ed.

when, at the battle of Northampton, on that 10th of July 1460, "at two of the clock afternoon, the Earls of March and Warwick let cry thorow the field that no man should lay hand upon the King, nor on the common people, but on the lords, knights, and esquires?"[1] If those lords, knights, and esquires died for their country, their so dying did not, as the result proved, much benefit their country. On the contrary it enabled that Earl of March, first to become King Edward IV., then to introduce torture into England, and to transform the English King into an Asiatic sultan. If they were well-meaning men, Sir Bevill Grenville and his associates would seem to have laboured under some strange delusions respecting England and its history. But if any of those gentlemen had ancestors whose seals were affixed to Magna Charta, or who had fought under Simon de Montfort, as the ancestor of one here named did, Ralph Basset[2] of Drayton, slain at Eve-

[1] Stow, p. 409.
[2] This companion in arms of Simon de Montfort was great-grandson of Richard Basset of Weldon, Chief Justiciary of England under Richard I., of a seal of whom attached to a deed Sir Simonds D'Ewes says (Life, ii. 75), "This armorial seal being above five hundred years old, and the oldest by at least seventy years that I ever saw, may well compare with, if not excel, in respect of the antiquity thereof, the seals of arms of Montmorency itself, which are accounted by some the first gentlemen of France and of Christendom itself." There were at one time in England six barons by tenure of this name and family. The last person who held the office and bore the title of *Capitalis Justitiarius Angliæ* was Philip Basset; and the first who held the office of *Capitalis Justitiarius ad placita coram rege tenenda*, *i.e.*, as Chief-Justice of the King's Bench, was Robert de Bruis, appointed in the fifty-second year of Henry III. (Dugd. Orig., 38). Sir Edward Coke indulged his vanity in giving the same title, Chief-Justice of England, to himself, and the Grand Justiciary, the *Capitalis Justitiarius Angliæ*, which was commented on by Lord Chancellor Ellesmere in his address to Sir Henry Montague, Coke's successor, upon his being sworn in Chief-Justice in these words:—"Instead of containing himself within the words of the writ to be the Chief-Justice as the King called him, *ad placita corum nobis tenenda*." The absurdity of Coke's confounding the Chief-Justiciary of England with the Chief-Justice of the King's Bench, who ranks below the Lord Chancellor, will be seen from the fact that

sham, when the founder of the English Commons' House of Parliament "with all his peerage fell,"—those ancestors of theirs marched and fought under a very different standard from the royal standard, and were men as fit to be proud of as any ancestors the Stuart Royalists, whether they style themselves Cavaliers or Jacobites, could boast of.

Not long before the Royalist side had lost another gallant and accomplished man, Sidney Godolphin, a friend of Grenville's,[1] of Lord Falkland's, and of a greater man than either, Thomas Hobbes, who dedicates his "Leviathan" to Francis Godolphin of Godolphin, out of regard to his brother's memory. "Your most worthy brother," begins the dedication, "Mr. Sidney Godolphin, when he lived, was pleased to think my studies something, and otherwise to oblige me, as you know, with real testimonies of his good opinion, great in themselves, and the greater for the worthiness of his person." Sidney Godolphin's portrait afforded, from the striking contrasts between his mental and bodily qualities, and between his love of books and of solitude and aversion to bodily labour and inconvenience, and a daring spirit, a subject for Lord Clarendon's pencil, of a nature analogous to that afforded him by Lord Falkland, who, according to Clarendon, used to say merrily that he thought it was a great ingredient in his friendship for Mr. Godolphin that he was pleased to be found in the

the Chief Justiciary was, by virtue of his office, regent of the kingdom during the King's absence, and at those times writs ran in his name and were tested by him (Madox's History of the Exchequer, p. 16). One of the most eminent men who held this high office was Ranulph de Glanville, who is usually regarded as the author of the *Tractatus de Legibus et Consuetudinibus Angliæ*, the oldest book extant on English law (Madox, p. 35; Beames's "Glanville").

[1] In one of the letters of Sir Bevill Grenville, published by Mr. Forster in his "Life of Cromwell" (i. 105), the death of Sidney Godolphin, in an obscure skirmish, is mentioned as a loss "that is unvalluable."

company of a man of a smaller body than himself, or "in his company where he was the properer man." For of Sidney Godolphin Clarendon says, "There was never so great a mind and spirit entertained in so little room; so large an understanding and so unrestrained a fancy in so very small a body."[1] Though Sidney Godolphin was a member of the Long Parliament, and though, in the opinion of Clarendon and Hobbes, two men likely to have been competent judges in such a matter, he was a most accomplished man, he was a silent member—at least, as far as I know, there is no record of any speech of his—and has left no memorial of his name but the eulogy of Hobbes and Clarendon.

Waller having refreshed his men by two days' rest at Bath, marched towards Devizes, a town in Wiltshire, to which Hopton had retired, and to which Waller laid siege. Prince Maurice and the Marquis of Hertford had returned to Oxford, but the Earl of Carnarvon had been despatched to the assistance of Hopton with upwards of 2000 horse, and by the remissness of Essex, not to say more, for a jealousy had arisen between him and Waller, had been allowed to approach within two or three miles of Waller's camp without interruption. Waller determined to attack this body of cavalry before they could act in concert with the besieged, and he immediately drew out his army on Roundway Down, about a mile and a-half to the

[1] I will quote here Hobbes's character of Sidney Godolphin, as it is, I believe, little known. "I have known," says Hobbes, "clearness of judgment and largeness of fancy, strength of reason and graceful elocution, a courage for the war and a fear for the laws, all eminently in one man; and that was my noble 'and honoured friend Mr. Sidney Godolphin, who, hating no man, nor hated of any, was unfortunately slain in the beginning of the late civil war, in the public quarrel, by an undiscerned and an undiscerning hand."—Leviathan, p. 390. London, folio. Printed for Andrew Crooke, at the Green Dragon in St. Paul's Churchyard. 1651.

north of Devizes. Waller's horse, under Sir Arthur Haselrig, were on their first attack put to a disorderly retreat, and, having joined the reserve, were on a second charge totally routed. The infantry fought better; but being attacked on one side by Wilmot's cavalry, and on the other side by Hopton sallying from the town, they were also in a short time defeated. Many prisoners and four pieces of ordnance, with a great quantity of small arms, fell into the hands of the Royalists. Waller, whose reputation, which was previously high, sank considerably, loudly complained of Essex, and with much appearance of justice, for having allowed Carnarvon and Wilmot to pass him.[1]

After the siege of Reading, Essex remained long in that neighbourhood in a state of inactivity; but being at length roused by the murmurs on every side, he advanced towards Oxford, where the King and his Court then were, and the siege of which Hampden and those who were most earnest in the cause recommended should be immediately undertaken. Essex then fixed his headquarters at Thame, in Buckinghamshire, in order to protect that county; but the body of his forces lay scattered at some distance in different directions. About this time Colonel Urry, or Hurry, a soldier of fortune and a colonel of horse in the service of the Parliament, deserted to the King. Clarendon attempts to justify him by saying that he had stated and published his discontents long before; that he had delivered up his commission to the Earl of Essex, and being then pressed to promise that he would not serve the King, that he positively refused to give any such engagement.[2] This man went to Oxford, and having been graciously received by the King, he informed Prince

[1] Rush., v. 285; Clar., iii. 287, *et seq.;* Whitelocke, p. 70.
[2] Clar., iii. 394.

Skirmish at Chalgrove.

Rupert where the Parliamentary horse lay, and how loose they were in their quarters, and showed how, by a sudden attack upon the scattered troops, much execution might be done. He offered to prove his fidelity to the King by going as a volunteer with a good party against the enemy. The Prince having assigned a strong force for the service, they beat up the quarters of a regiment of the Parliament's horse, and killed or took most of the officers and soldiers.

Upon his return to Oxford, Urry proposed to the Prince to attack the quarters near Thame; for Urry, having passed through those quarters when he came to Oxford, was well acquainted with the position which the troops occupied. The Prince was so well satisfied with what had been already done, that he resolved to conduct this enterprise in person. They left Oxford in the evening of Saturday, the 17th of June 1643, and marched beyond all the quarters as far as Wycombe. They then fell in at the further end of that town towards London, where no guards were stationed, as no enemy was expected from that quarter. A regiment of horse and one of foot were quartered there; these were cut off or taken prisoners. Thence they marched back to another quarter, not two miles distant from the general's own quarters. The men there being lodged with the same want of precaution as at Wycombe, not expecting any enemy from that direction, met with the same fate.

The sun was now rising, and the Prince thought it time to retire to Oxford, and gave orders accordingly to march with all convenient speed till they should come to a bridge, which was yet two miles distant, where he had stationed a guard to favour their retreat. But the alarm had by this time spread through the Parliamentary army, and those troops being hastily collected which were nearest to the spot, were directed by the general to follow the Prince, and retard his progress till he should come up himself with the foot and other troops. Hampden, ever foremost in any dangerous service, and eager on this occasion to avenge the loss and disgrace which his party had just sustained, joined the troops of horse which were first ready, as a volunteer (he himself being a colonel of foot), and eagerly urged them forward in pursuit of the enemy.

Accordingly, when Rupert's troops had almost passed a plain called Chalgrove Field, from which a lane led to the bridge already alluded to, the enemy's horse were discovered marching after them with speed. As they might easily overtake his party in the lane, and so throw it into great disorder, the Prince resolved to wait and receive them upon the open field, though his horses were all tired, and the sun had become very strong, it being about eight o'clock in the morning of the 18th of June; a day·which was destined to be a disastrous one to two[1] far greater soldiers than John Hampden. The Prince then directed that the guard of the prisoners should make what haste they could to the bridge, but that all the rest should return, for some had already entered the lane. The enemy advanced with more haste, says Clarendon, and with less order than they should have done. Clarendon also states that it was confessed by the prisoners who were taken that day, that when the Prince made a stand, all the officers were of opinion to stay till the main body came up, and that Hampden alone persuaded and prevailed with them to advance.[2] The Parliamentary horse then charged,

---

[1] Frederic II. of Prussia at the battle of Kolin, and Napoleon Bonaparte at that of Waterloo.
[2] Clar., iii. 396.

being led on by many of their best officers; but the principal of these falling, the rest began to waver, and in a short time were broken and pursued till they came near the Earl of Essex's body. The Prince, with his troops, then hastened his retreat, passed the lane, and reached the bridge before any of Essex's forces came up, and about noon entered Oxford.

One of the prisoners taken in the action said, "that he was confident Mr. Hampden was hurt, for he saw him ride off the field before the action was done, which he never used to do, with his head hanging down, and resting his hands upon the neck of his horse," from which he concluded he was hurt. His conclusion was but too correct. Hampden was hit in the shoulder with two carbine-balls, which broke the bone and entered his body. He succeeded, though faint from pain and loss of blood, in reaching home, where, after nearly six days of great suffering, he died on the 24th of June. He was buried in the parish church of Great Hampden.[1]

This point of time may be noticed as that at which the affairs of the Parliament were at the lowest ebb. Towards the end of July 1643 they had no forces at all to keep the field, their main armies being quite ruined, and in appearance no hope left but to keep for a short time—for unless their fortune changed they could not hope to keep them long—those forts and towns which they still possessed. "Thus," says May, "seemed the Parliament to be quite sunk beyond any hope of recovery, and was so believed

---

[1] Clar., iii. 390–399. 8vo edition. Oxford, 1807. Lord Nugent's Memorials of Hampden, ii. 435, 436. Sir Philip Warwick's Memoirs, p. 239. Sir Philip Warwick says (p. 241), "I found the King would have sent him over any chirurgeon of his, if any had been wanting; for he looked upon his interest, if he could gain his affection, as a powerful means of begetting a right understanding betwixt him and his two Houses."

by many men. The King was possessed of all the western counties from the farthest part of Cornwall, and from thence northward as far as the borders of Scotland. His armies were full and flourishing, free to march whither they pleased, and enough to be divided for several exploits."[1]

In this state of affairs, which was apparently owing to the appointment of peers to stations of supreme command for which they were totally unqualified, some Lords and many of the Commons deserted the Parliament and fled to Oxford. A majority of the Lords which remained desired peace, while Essex himself, one of the most signal examples of incapacity, or lukewarmness in the cause for which he fought (for in his march to the relief of Gloucester and in the battle of Newbury he showed considerable military talent, as on all occasions he displayed personal courage), recommended it. But the Commons rejected the Lords' propositions for peace, notwithstanding the presentation of a petition for peace by 2000 or 3000 women, and a tumult at Westminster, in which a cry was raised, "Peace, peace; give us those traitors that are against peace, that we may tear them in pieces; give us that dog Pym!"[2] This mob, whether excited by the Royalists, as some writers suppose, or not, cannot be considered as by any means proving that there

---

[1] May, Hist., pp. 212, 213. London, 1812. May adds, "What the King's party conceived then of the other side was expressed in many writings; one of which, in the nature of a jeering epigram, was made at Oxford, and is, I think, worthy to be here inserted on account of the strong expressions it contains of the low condition of the Parliament at that time." This epigram, which is dated July 20, 1643, concludes with the assertion that there is nothing left for the King (styled by the Oxford epigrammatist "Britannicus Cæsar") to subdue but "νεομαινομένου preces Gregis," the prayers of the revolutionary herd or rabble.

[2] Echard's History of England, bk. ii. ch. iii. p. 429. Fol. 1718.

was at that time in the city of London a large and influential party favourable to the King. In the course of the preceding spring an entrenchment had been made, which encompassed not only the city of London but the whole of the suburbs on every side, containing about twelve miles in circuit. This great work was carried on with such vigour, that the people went out every day by thousands to dig,—all professions, trades, and occupations taking their turns; and not only inferior tradesmen, but gentlemen of the best quality, knights, and even ladies, for the encouragement of others, resorted daily to the works, not as spectators, but as workers, carrying themselves spades, mattocks, and other tools for digging, so that "it became a pleasing sight in London to see them going out in such order and numbers, with drums beating before them."[1]

The only place of importance in the west which still held out for the Parliament was the city of Gloucester. The King marched thither and summoned it to surrender, but the Governor, Colonel Massey, heartily and nobly seconded by the magistrates and inhabitants, defended it with singular skill and valour. Essex marched to its relief at the head of an army of 14,000 men, composed of the city regiments and auxiliaries, and some of the regiments of the old army reunited. At the same time another army was raising for Waller, and the Earl of Manchester undertook to raise one in the associated counties over which he presided, to act with the troops under

[1] May, Hist., p. 214. May adds, "But fruitless in probability had that labour proved, and not timely enough to save London, if the King had marched thither instead of laying siege to Gloucester." This remark would seem to have been made from May's having given a wrong date for the making of those entrenchments, namely, August 1643, instead of February to June 1643.—Somers's Tracts, iv. 538.

Colonel Cromwell, of whom I shall have to speak presently. On the 5th of September Essex drew up his army in sight of Gloucester. The King's force immediately raised the siege, and Essex with his army entered Gloucester on the 8th, and lodged there two nights, "much extolling the skilful valour and indefatigable industry of Colonel Massey, and praising the patient constancy of the city."[1] Having furnished Gloucester with ammunition, money, and other necessaries, and hearing that a body of the King's army was in Cirencester, and had then laid in a large supply of provisions for their army, he marched thither, surprised two regiments of horse belonging to Sir Nicholas Crispe and Colonel Spencer, and took forty load of provisions, of which his army stood much in need, six standards, all the officers except the two colonels, who were absent, above 300 soldiers and 400 horses."[2] From Cirencester Essex proceeded by short marches, and on Tuesday, the 19th of September, marched from Hungerford towards Newbury. When he came within two miles of that town he discovered the King's army stationed upon a hill. The Royal army was strongly posted, and intercepted the march of Essex. An action was therefore unavoidable, and Essex prepared for it on the following morning.

On the 20th of September the battle commenced at eight o'clock in the morning, and was fought with great and steady valour on both sides till darkness separated the combatants and left the victory undecided. "All were Englishmen," says Whitelocke, "and pity it is that such courage should be spent in the blood of each other."[3] The King's horse, though successful at some points against

[1] May, Hist., p. 222. [2] Ibid., p. 223.
[3] Whitelocke, p. 73.

Essex's horse, could make no impression upon his infantry, who received them with a continued fire and an impregnable rampart of pikes. The London trained bands are mentioned by the best authorities as having particularly distinguished themselves. May states that "the two trained bands of London, though they were often charged by the horse and foot, stood to it with undaunted resolution,"[1] and even Clarendon bears testimony to the same effect. "The London trained bands and auxiliary regiments," he says (of whose inexperience of danger or any kind of service beyond the easy practice of the artillery garden men had till then too cheap an estimation), "behaved themselves to wonder, and were, in truth, the preservation of that army that day. For they stood as a bulwark and rampire to defend the rest; and when their wings of horse were scattered and dispersed, kept their ground so steadily that, though Prince Rupert himself led up the choice horse to charge them, and endured their storm of small shot, he could make no impression upon their stand of pikes, but was forced to wheel about,—of so sovereign benefit and use is that readiness and dexterity in the use of their arms which hath been so much neglected."[2] This statement is fully supported by other Royalist writers,[3] who represent the militia of London, though drawn but a few days before from their ordinary occupations, yet having learned all military exercises, as equalling on this occasion what could be expected from the most veteran troops. Essex ex-

[1] May, Hist., p. 224.
[2] Clar., Hist., iv. 235, 236. Oxford, 1826.
[3] Hobbes, while he admits that these London troops "were very hardly to be driven out of the field," accounts for it in a strange way, saying that they would have been "fearful enough of death and wounds approaching visibly in glistering swords, but for *want of judgment* scarce thought of such death as comes invisibly in a bullet."—Behemoth, p. 188. London, 1682.

pected a renewal of the action next day, and made preparations for it, but the King drew off his army, and Essex pursued his march by Reading to London. The King's loss in this battle and the previous skirmishes was estimated at 2000, and said to be four times that of Essex.[1]

In the battle of Newbury three of the nobility fell on the King's side, the Earl of Carnarvon, Lord Spencer, lately created Earl of Sunderland, who thus fell a victim to the "grinning honour," which, as he wrote to his wife, and not approbation of his cause, made him stay with the King, and Viscount Falkland, then Secretary of State. The tempting offers of the Court, backed by the artful persuasions of Hyde, had determined Lord Falkland to desert to the King, for which he was denounced as a traitor by the Parliament and excepted from pardon. He used every effort to reconcile the contending parties. It is probable that his failure in this, and the sanction given by him in his official capacity to the most solemn declarations, which he must have known to be destitute of truth, produced that settled melancholy which for some time before his death had replaced his natural cheerfulness, deprived him of sleep, made him neglect his dress and personal appearance, and would shortly, he said, break his heart. In the morning of that day he called for a clean shirt, and being asked the reason of it, answered that if he was slain in battle they should not find his body in foul linen. Being dissuaded by his friends from going into battle as not being a military officer, he said he was weary of the times and foresaw much misery to his country, but believed he should be out of it ere night. "His death," says Whitelocke, "was much lamented by all that knew him or heard of him, being a gentleman of great parts, ingenuity,

[1] Rush., v. 293. May, Hist., p. 228.

and honour, courteous and just to all, and a passionate promoter of all endeavours of peace betwixt the King and Parliament."[1] He was in his thirty-fourth year.[2]

On the 5th of July of this year the Commons—having then just received information that the Earl[3] of Newcastle had entirely routed the Lord Fairfax's forces at Atherton Moor near Bradford—at a conference with the Lords, earnestly pressed them to nominate a committee of their House to go forthwith into Scotland, and to desire the Scots nation to send aid into England "against the Papists and others, now in arms to destroy the Protestant religion and the liberty of the kingdom."[4]

The Commissioners of the English Parliament embarked on their voyage to Scotland on the 20th of July 1643, and arrived at Leith on the 7th of August. They found the leading Presbyterians in Scotland willing to run every risk and to make every exertion with the view of destroying the hierarchy of the Church of England, and introducing into that kingdom a form of church government on the Presbyterian model. The English Commissioners were ready to join with this scheme so far as concerned the destruction of Prelacy; but they knew that there existed a great difference of opinion in the English Parliament on the point of substituting the Presbyterian system in its place. The Independents were utterly opposed to the introduction of any national church government whatever, and were particularly averse to Presbyterianism, the clergy of that denomination having in their opinion shown a disposition to be as tyrannical and intolerant as the prelates had been.

---

[1] Whitelocke, p. 73.   [2] Clar., Hist., iv. 257.
[3] The compilers of the new Parliamentary History call him Marquis, but he was not created Marquis of Newcastle till 27th October 1643.
[4] Parl. Hist., iii. 144.

Under these circumstances, the English Commissioners, with a dexterity which has been attributed to the astute Sir Henry Vane,[1] the younger one of their number, conducted the negotiation in such a manner that the Scottish Convention believed, or at least imagined, that the Presbyterian system would be made as powerful and absolute in England as it was in Scotland, while in fact they bound the English Parliament to nothing specific on the subject.

The new edition of the "Solemn League and Covenant," which was taken by both Houses of the English Parliament on the 25th of September with much solemnity,[2] contained the following clause, from which it is by some writers supposed that the Scots inferred that the system of Presbyterianism was undoubtedly to be forthwith adopted by the English Parliament:—"That we shall sincerely, really, and constantly, through the grace of God, endeavour, in our several places and callings, the preservation of the Reformed religion in the Church of Scotland, in doctrine, worship, discipline, and government, according to the Word of God,[3] and the example of the best Reformed Churches; and we shall endeavour to bring the Churches of God, in the three kingdoms, to the nearest conjunction and uniformity in religion, confession of faith,

---

[1] Baillie says, "When we met, there appeared four gentlemen,—Sir William Armine, Sir Hary Vaine younger, one of the gravest and ablest of that nation; Mr. Hatcher, and Mr. Darley, with two ministers, Mr. Marshall and Mr. Nye. They presented to us a paper introductory, drawn by Master Marshall, a notable man, and Sir Hary, the drawers of all their writes."—Baillie's Letters and Journals, ii., 89. Laing's ed. There was another commissioner, John, Earl of Rutland.—Parl. Hist., iii. 151.

[2] Parl. Hist., iii. 173, 174.

[3] The words in the first clause of the Instrument as agreed to by the English Parliament, "according to the Word of God," were inserted by Vane, and enabled the English Parliament to deny that they had sworn to adopt the Presbyterian form of church government.

form of church government, directory for worship and catechising; that we, and our posterity after us, may as brethren live in faith and love, and the Lord may delight to dwell in the midst of us."[1] According to the "Explications" which the Assembly of Divines at Westminter on being consulted by the Commons advised should be subjoined to the Covenant, by the clause in the first article of the Covenant, "according to the Word of God," they understood, "so far as we do, or shall, in our consciences, conceive the same to be according to the will of God."[2] We may add as characteristic of the spirit of the time, that the sixth clause binds the subscribers not to give themselves "*to a detestable indifferency or neutrality* in this cause."[3]

The reader may judge how far all this bound the English Parliament to make Presbyterianism the form of religious worship throughout England. There is certainly an ambiguity, perhaps, as Sir Walter Scott says, a "studied ambiguity,"[4] in the wording of the clause; but that the Scots were completely imposed on by it, as was afterwards asserted, there is good reason to deny. Baillie, one of the Scottish Commissioners, writing from London towards the end of this year (1643), says: "The Independents being most able men, and of great credit, fearing no less than banishment from their native country if Presbyteries were erected, are watchful that no conclusion be taken for their prejudice. It was my advice, which Mr. Henderson presently applauded, and gave me thanks for it, to eschew a public rupture with the Independents, till we were more able for them. As yet a Presbytrie to this people is

[1] Parl. Hist., iii. 170.
[2] Ibid., p. 172.   [3] Ibid., p. 171.
[4] History of Scotland in "Tales of a Grandfather," i. 428.

conceived to be a strange monster. It was our good therefore to go on hand in hand so far as we did agree, against the common enemy, hoping that in our differences, when we behooved to come to them, God would give us light; in the meantime, we would assay to agree upon the directory of worship, wherein we expect no small help from these men to abolish the great idol of England, the Service-Book."[1] The conclusion of the sentence in Baillie, "and to erect in all the parts of worship a full conformity to Scotland in all things worthy to be spoken of," does indeed show that the Scottish Presbyterians were by no means disposed to stop there, but what precedes and has already been quoted, as well as subsequent passages, show they were fully aware that they had small chance of making Presbyterians of the Independents.

The first and second clauses of the Solemn League and Covenant contain the cream of the matter, which was to enable the Scotch nobility to keep the church lands they had got, namely those of Scotland; and to get in addition a part of the church lands of England.

It is a strange omission on the part of the compilers of the new Parliamentary History that they should take no notice of the death of John Hampden. It is also strange that Essex, in a letter to the Speaker of the House of Lords, dated "Thame, June 30, 1643," should take no notice of Hampden's death, which had taken place there six days before.[2] This omission would seem to have some significance in relation to the zeal or ability, or both, of those who then led the Parliament, as well as of those who then commanded the Parliamentary forces: unless, indeed, they may have been of the opinion expressed

[1] Baillie's Letters and Journals, note by Laing, ii. 117.
[2] Parl. Hist., iii. 139, 140.

in Sir Philip Warwick's Memoirs, that notwithstanding Hampden's undisputed ability and courage, as well as popular influence, "he had greater interest to raise the men than aptitude to range or fight them."[1] We have no satisfactory evidence to prove these words of Sir Philip Warwick untrue. The facts of the case, as well as the statement of Cromwell, rather go to show that Hampden, with all his unquestioned practical talent, as well as activity and courage, had not found out where the real difficulty, and, consequently, the true remedy, lay.

It is further remarkable, that while the death of Hampden is thus passed over in silence, that of Pym, which took place a few months after, namely on the 8th of December of the same year (1643),[2] is thus noticed in the Parliamentary History:—" Dec. 11. Some orders made by the House of Commons this day give us occasion to mention the death of Mr. Pym, one of the most active members that ever sat in that House. The respect showed to his memory is without a precedent in the whole course of this history. For we find in the Journals, 'That a committee was appointed to consider of the estate of Mr. Pym, deceased, and to offer what they think fit to be done in consideration of it to the House; likewise to take care to prepare a monument for him, at the charge of the Commonwealth.' It was also ordered that the body of Mr. Pym be interred in Westminster Abbey, without any charge for breaking open the ground there, and that the Speaker, with the whole House, do accompany his body to the interment."[3]

[1] Sir Philip Warwick's Memoirs, p. 240.
[2] Rushworth, v. 376.
[3] Parl. Hist., iii. 186, 187. Baillie writes : "On Wednesday Mr. Pym was carried from his house to Westminster, on the shoulders, as the fashion is " [he means in England ; in Scotland the fashion was to carry the coffin on

It is affirmed by Lord Clarendon and others, and repeated by Anthony à Wood, that Pym died, in great torment, of the loathsome disease called *morbus pediculosus*. The mentioning such a report as disparaging to an individual is a signal proof of the superstition of that age, since, as the continuator of the "Athenæ Oxonienses" justly remarks, even had it been the case, it would have inflicted no stigma on his memory, seeing it was a visitation to which, under Providence, the best as well as the vilest of mankind are subject. There exists, however, very conclusive evidence on this point in a document attested by seven physicians, two surgeons, and an apothecary, which sets forth that the disease of which he died was an imposthume in the bowels. Ludlow also relates in his Memoirs that Pym's body was for several days exposed to public view in Derby House before it was interred, in confutation of the report above mentioned.[1] And Rushworth mentions that his dead body was viewed by many hundreds of people, adding, "the true natural cause of his death seeming to be the great pains he took, joined with a competent old age [he was about sixty], and at best but an infirm constitution."[2]

From the words used by the compilers of the Parliamentary History, "It appears that Pym died greatly in debt, though possessed of the place of Lieutenant of the Ordnance,"[3] the inference would be that Pym was a man

poles, the ends of which rested in the hands of the bearers], "of the chief men in the Lower House, all the House going in procession before him, and before them the Assembly of Divines. Marshall had a most eloquent and pertinent funeral sermon, which we would not hear, for funeral sermons we must have away, with the rest. The Parliament has ordered to pay his debt, and to build him, in the chapel of Henry VII., a stately monument."—Baillie's Letters and Journals, ii. 118, by Laing.

[1] Ludlow's Memoirs, i. 80. 2d edition. London, 1721.
[2] Rushworth, v. 376. [3] Parl. Hist., iii. 187.

of very improvident, if not prodigal, habits. But the fact is that he was only appointed Lieutenant of the Ordnance in November 1643, and he died on the 8th of December of the same year. The assertions made respecting Pym's public spirit and disinterestedness would hardly have been ventured in the sermon preached before the Parliament, at his funeral, had they been altogether unsupported by facts. He is there represented as " knowing neither brother, kinsman, nor friend, superior nor inferior, when they stood in the way to hinder his pursuit of the public good." And it is mentioned that he would say, " Such a one is my entire friend, to whom I am much obliged, but I must not pay my private debts out of the public stock ; " and that when his friends frequently put him in mind of his children, and pressed upon his consideration that although he regarded not himself, yet he ought to provide that it might be well with them, his usual answer was : " If it were well with the public, his family was well enough." [1]

Under these circumstances we find that on the 13th of January 1643, the Commons referred it to the committee before mentioned, "to consider of some other way for a recompense to the posterity of Mr. Pym, and payment of those debts he had contracted for the service of the Commonwealth, than they had yet thought on ; and to use all diligence to find out some fit return answerable to the memory and merit of so great a man." And, accordingly, afterwards, the whole House undertook to pay the debts of Mr. Pym, not exceeding £10,000.[2]

The contrast between this public funeral and these Parliamentary honours and rewards voted to Pym, and

---

[1] Stephen Marshall's Sermon, preached before the Parliament at the funeral of Mr. Pym, p. 28. 4to, 1644. King's Pamphlets, Brit. Mus.
[2] Parl. Hist., iii. 187.

the comparative obscurity of Hampden's obsequies, is suggestive of much food for grave reflection. It is the old story, often told in so many successive ages, of the contest between Ajax and Ulysses for the arms of Achilles, in which the man of many and eloquent words carried off the prize from the man of brave and great deeds, but comparatively few and rude words:

> "Et, quid facundia posset,
> Re patuit, fortisque viri tulit arma disertus."

When a body of men meet together for the purpose of talking, it is to be expected that the best, or, which is more to the point here, the most agreeable talker, should appear to them an infinitely greater and more important personage than the man of words comparatively few and ungraced by the charm of eloquence; even though the man of few words may have done for their cause what none else have done; nay more, even though the orator may have been indebted to the other man's judgment for much of his success.[1] To the consideration of this view of this matter we may have to return hereafter, inasmuch as it may possibly be found to contain one of the most apparently forcible grounds of defence for men like Cromwell acting as they have been too apt to do, namely, turning fiercely round upon the men of fine words and showing them by unmistakable signs that they are but

---

[1] Clarendon says of Pym: "Besides his exact knowledge of the forms and orders of the House of Commons, he had a very comely and grave way of puffing himself, with great volubility of words, natural and proper. He understood likewise the temper and affections of the kingdom as well as any man, and had observed the errors and mistakes in government. . . . At the first opening of the Long Parliament, though he was much governed in private designing by Mr. Hampden and Mr. St. John, yet he seemed of all men to have the greatest influence upon the House of Commons, and was at that time and for some months after, the most popular man and the most able to do hurt that hath lived in any time."—Clarendon, Hist., iv. 437. Oxford, 1826.

men of words after all, and by no means entitled to carry off all the profit as well as all the honour of whatever is done. There needs, indeed, the unswerving devotedness to one great purpose of public duty, the almost more than human self-abnegation of a Washington, to withstand the temptation to engrave on such men's minds and memories as with red-hot steel the truth that mankind are not delivered from the fangs of their oppressors by speeches, however long and fine, made either in parliaments, in congresses, or anywhere else. But the after and mature judgment of mankind and history, which ought to be its true and impartial record and interpreter, does indeed in time redress the wrong. And in this case we see that it has been already redressed, for the name of Hampden is familiar to thousands who never heard of Pym or his eloquence.

While the fortune of the Parliament was at so low an ebb in the south, it was only saved from sinking to the same level in the north by the extraordinary energy of some individual officers. Upon the news of Newcastle's intended approach to Nottingham, which seemed very unlikely to be able to offer an effective resistance, Colonel Hutchinson was sent up to inform the Parliament of their condition,[1] and he procured an order for Colonel Cromwell, Colonel Hubbard, Lord Grey, and Sir John Gell, to unite their forces at Nottingham, whither they came in the Whitsun holidays, 1643. At the same time there also came to Nottingham the younger Hotham, son of Sir John Hotham, the governor of Hull, with some troops out of Yorkshire. Young Hotham at that time was carrying on a secret treaty with the Queen, and every day received and sent trumpets of which he would give no account. At

[1] Mrs. Hutchinson's Memoirs of Colonel Hutchinson, p. 151.

this time Nottingham was more distressed by its friends than by its enemies; for Hotham's and Gell's men not only lay upon free quarters, as all the rest did, but made a great havoc and plunder of friend and foe alike. When the committee, as being better acquainted with the country, offered Hotham to assign him quarters for his men, he would tell them he was no stranger to any English ground. And when Colonel Hutchinson applied to Hotham for restitution of the property of some of the inhabitants which his soldiers had taken, Hotham replied, "he fought for liberty, and expected it in all things." He had, says Mrs. Hutchinson,[1] "a great deal of wicked wit, and would make sport with the miseries of the poor country; and having treason in his heart, licensed his soldiers, which were the scum of mankind,[2] to all the villanies in the country that might make their party odious." But Hotham had on this occasion a man to deal with who was very unlikely to understand rude jesting, or to receive insults with impunity. Among the Parliamentary officers who at this

[1] Memoirs of Colonel Hutchinson, pp. 151, 152.
[2] Cromwell no doubt had such fellows in his mind when he afterwards gave his well-known description of the character of the Parliamentary troops at the beginning of the war. The character of the younger Hotham here portrayed by Mrs. Hutchinson agrees well with an anecdote respecting him given by Mr. Forster from Sir Simonds D'Ewes' MS. Journal in the Harl. MSS. (Brit. Mus.), 163, f. 474, a. "Some coming in and refusing to pay, whilst the aforesaid petition was reading, divers called out to them to pay, and so interrupted the clerk's assistant, who was reading it. Mr. John Hotham stood up and said that the time appointed for men to come yesterday by the order was eight, and that the chimes for that hour went just as he came into the house. But the Speaker telling him that prayers being past, he must pay, and he still refusing, it was put to the question, ruled affirmatively, and ordered accordingly. Whereupon he took his shilling, and threw it down upon the ground: upon which some called him to the bar, others that he should withdraw; and the Speaker, standing up, did sharply reprove him for that action, as being a contempt to the House. Which caused him, as I conceive, a little after, to withdraw out of the House, though he returned again this forenoon."—Arrest of the Five Members. By John Forster. London, 1860, p. 249.

time were at Nottingham, was, as has been said, Colonel Cromwell, who, though then only known as an active and enterprising colonel of horse, was a dangerous man for Hotham to try his insolence on. Colonel Cromwell, who, as well as Colonel Hutchinson, had received great provocations from Hotham, became, like Hutchinson, exasperated at the country's injuries, and the idle waste of such a considerable force, five or six thousand men, through the incapacity of the chief commander, Lord Grey, and the disobedience and irregularities of the others. So these two consulted together to seek a remedy, and despatched a post to London to inform the Parliament of Hotham's conduct, and the strong presumptions they had of his treachery, and the ill management of their forces. The messenger soon returned with a commitment of Hotham, who, however, escaped from his guard on their march to London. The town of Hull was thereby put into great hazard. But the Hothams were soon after surprised, sent up prisoners to London, and after some time executed.[1] The preservation of Hull proved fortunate for Lord Fairfax, who, after several successful actions in the north, had been defeated at Atherton Moor by the Earl of Newcastle, and pursued into Hull, where he was soon besieged.

Thus the result of the first year's military operations was on the whole favourable to the King in the north as well as in the south. For at Atherton Moor, as well as at Stratton and Roundway Down, the troops of the Parliament had been incontestably defeated; while though in two battles, Edgehill and Newbury, they had certainly not been beaten, in neither had they gained a decisive victory. The Parliament had also nearly lost the only place of

[1] Mrs. Hutchinson's Memoirs of Colonel Hutchinson, pp. 150-153. Bohn's edition. London, 1854.

strength they retained in the north, Hull, through the treachery of the Hothams. But the plot having been discovered, the Hothams were seized and sent prisoners to London; and Hull, thus preserved to the Parliament, afforded shelter to Lord Fairfax after his defeat at Atherton Moor by the Earl of Newcastle, who besieged him there, after taking Gainsborough. Sir Philip Warwick relates a jest of the Earl of Newcastle on the occasion of his going to see the Earl at the siege of Hull, where his men being very badly entrenched, he said to Sir Philip, who remarked it, "You hear us often called the Popish army, but you see we trust not in our *good works*."

END OF VOL. I.

www.ingramcontent.com/pod-product-compliance
Lightning Source LLC
Chambersburg PA
CBHW030003240426
43672CB00007B/811